FRATER

JON ELLIS
HUGO PETRUS

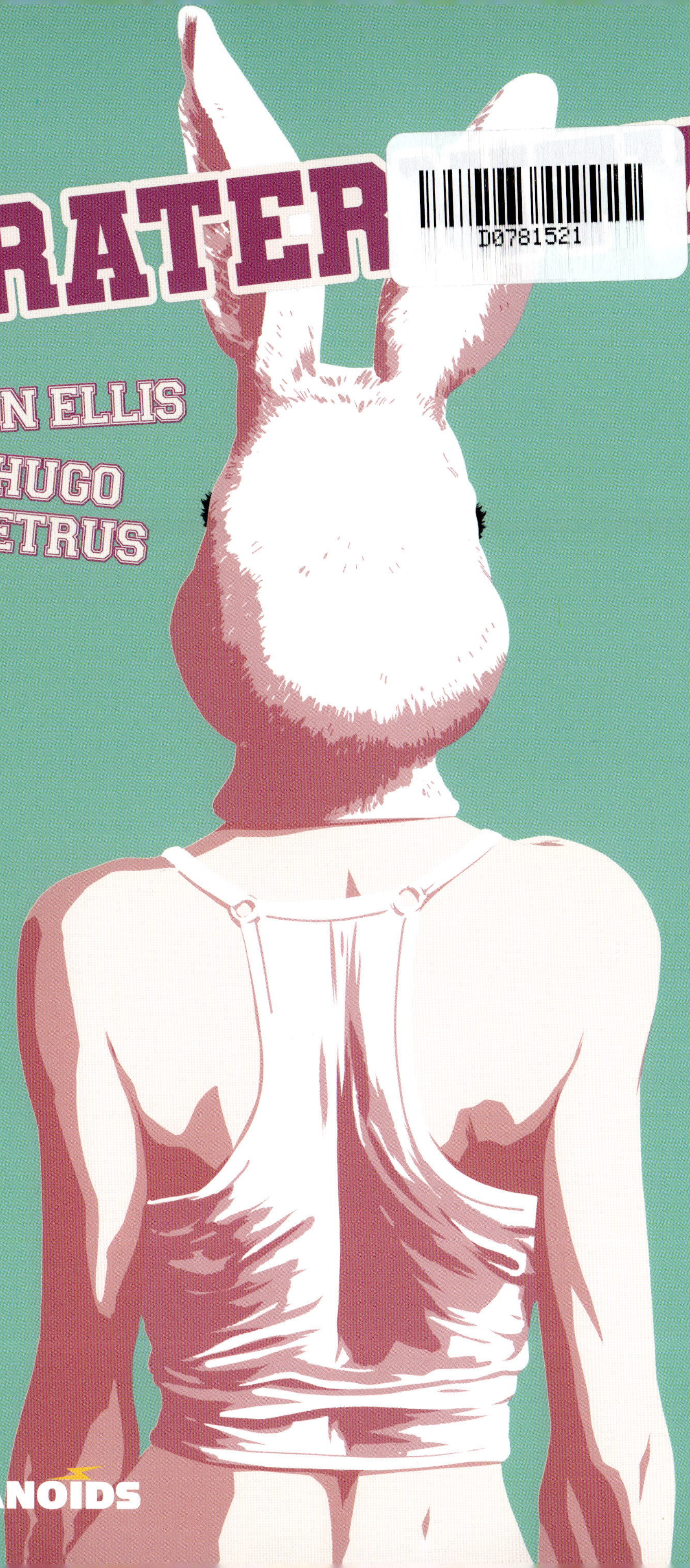

HUMANOIDS

JON ELLIS
WRITER

HUGO PETRUS
ARTIST

LEE LOUGHRIDGE
COLORIST

AND WORLD DESIGN
(DC HOPKINS)
LETTERER

JAKE THOMAS & ROB LEVIN
EDITORS

SANDY TANAKA
DESIGNER

JERRY FRISSEN
SENIOR ART DIRECTOR

MARK WAID
PUBLISHER

Rights and Licensing - licensing@humanoids.com

Press and Social Media - pr@humanoids.com

FRATERNITY. First Printing. This book is a publication of Humanoids, Inc. 8033 Sunset Blvd. #628, Los Angeles, CA 90046. Copyright Humanoids, Inc., Los Angeles (USA). All rights reserved. Humanoids® and the Humanoids logo are registered trademarks of Humanoids, Inc. in the U.S. and other countries.

Library of Congress Control Number: 2021945378

FRATERNITY 101: AN INTRODUCTION BY TIM SEELEY

I have this brother.

We're only two years and some change apart, so we spent various points in our youth at the same school. We never had that relationship where I didn't want my "lame kid brother" around or whatever. We got along fine. We both liked to draw. We were obsessed with *He-Man* and *Thundercats*. We traded comics and superhero cards. Eventually we had a kind of merged friend group, even. We worked together at Burger King, covering for each other's smoke breaks or smuggling chicken tenders. But we had different lives. We did our own things.

When I was in college my brother got into a car accident. I was out with my girlfriend at the time and heard ambulance sirens. I worried for a second that it was him. But I thought it couldn't be. I'd know. In my gut. And then the phone call from my mom. Steve is alive. His girlfriend was killed. He's hurting bad. And not just physically.

And, I dunno...something changed in me. Before that, we'd been friends, but y'know, I was cool with him having his own life. But after that... Jesus...I kind of tear up now, typing at my computer, 25 years later. We went to different colleges, but we talked on the phone a lot. We visited. Got drunk at each other's basement parties. I probably kinda bugged him, even. I guess I just really felt like I had to BE THERE, because I knew how close I'd been to losing him.

Reading FRATERNITY made me think of that. And yeah, it's a horror comic about devil worshipping frat boys, featuring exploding people and squished frogs, but it's also about those moments when you realize how much someone means to you...how hard it'd be for you to go on without them.

So, by all means, enjoy the gore and the boobs and the insanely beautiful linework of Hugo Petrus. But feel free to let your mind linger back to the hard moments of loss, and the ties that make us family, whether there's blood involved or not.

**It's in the title: Fraternity. It's about brotherhood.
It's about brothers.**

Chicago, Il
March 9, 2022

CHAPTER ONE
WELCOME WEEK

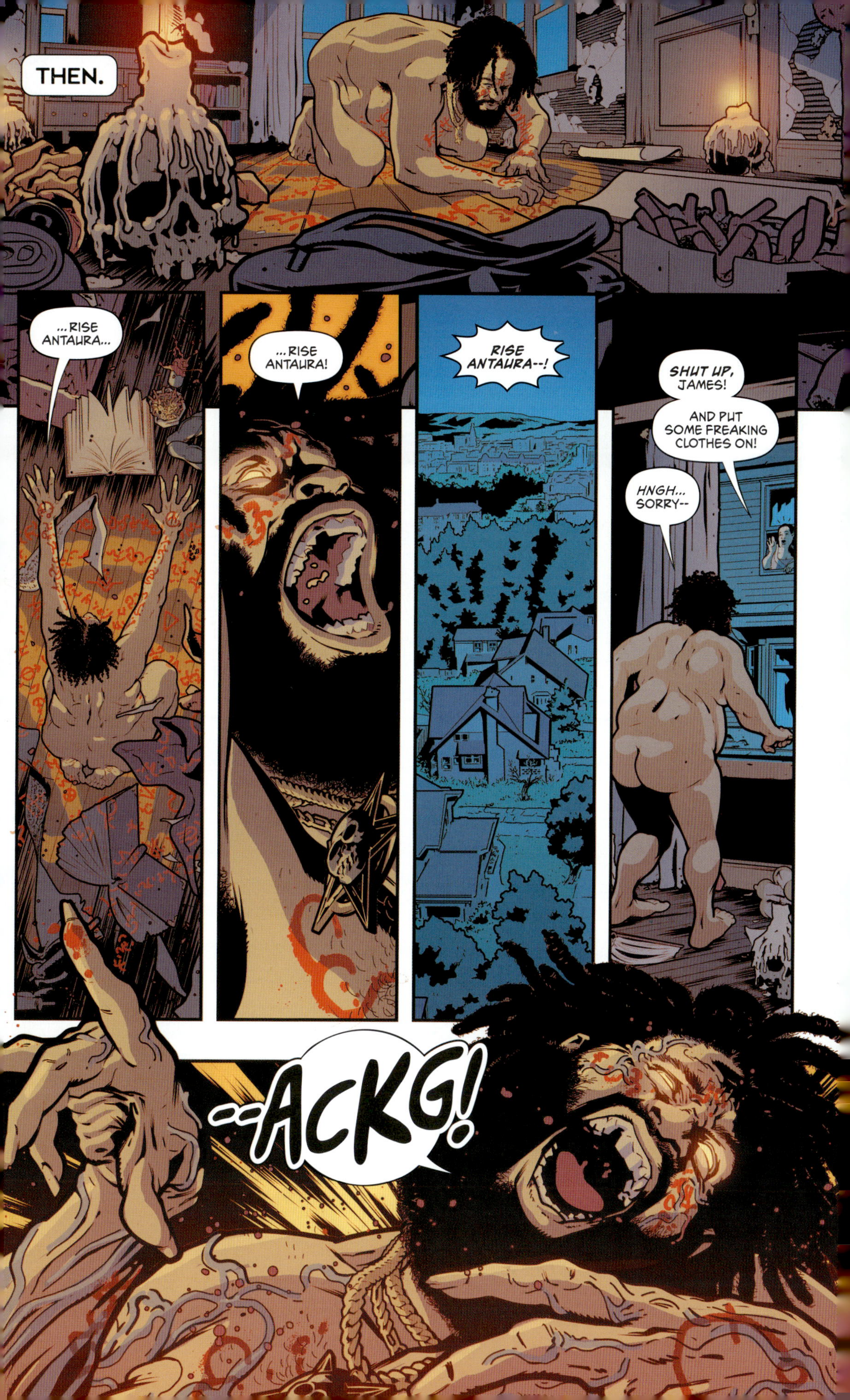
THEN.
...RISE ANTAURA...
...RISE ANTAURA!
RISE ANTAURA--!
SHUT UP, JAMES!
AND PUT SOME FREAKING CLOTHES ON!
HNGH... SORRY--
--ACKG!

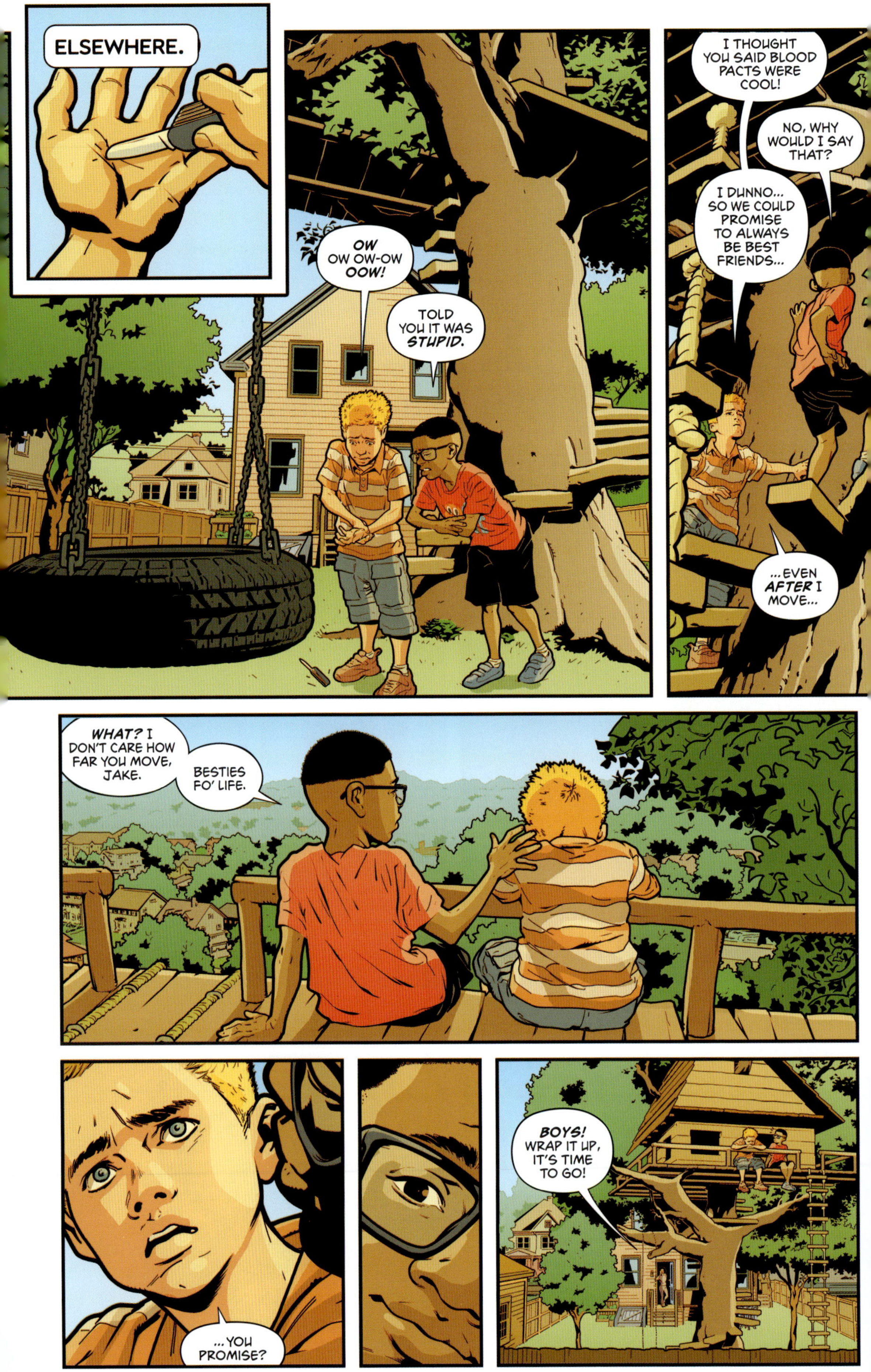
ELSEWHERE.
OW OW OW-OW OOW!
TOLD YOU IT WAS STUPID.
I THOUGHT YOU SAID BLOOD PACTS WERE COOL!
NO, WHY WOULD I SAY THAT?
I DUNNO... SO WE COULD PROMISE TO ALWAYS BE BEST FRIENDS...
...EVEN AFTER I MOVE...
WHAT? I DON'T CARE HOW FAR YOU MOVE, JAKE.
BESTIES FO' LIFE.
...YOU PROMISE?
BOYS! WRAP IT UP, IT'S TIME TO GO!

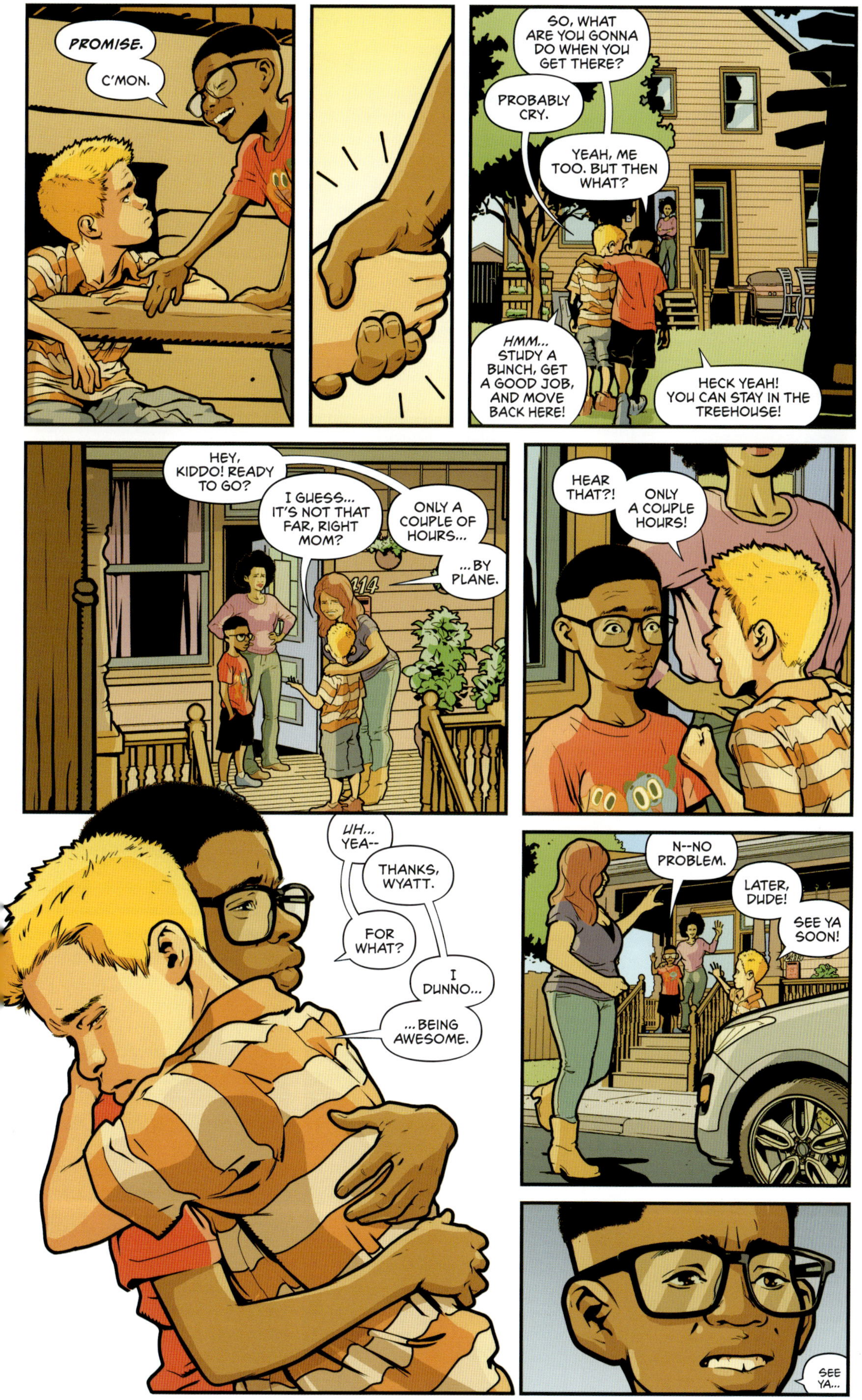
PROMISE.
C'MON.
SO, WHAT ARE YOU GONNA DO WHEN YOU GET THERE?
PROBABLY CRY.
YEAH, ME TOO. BUT THEN WHAT?
HMM... STUDY A BUNCH, GET A GOOD JOB, AND MOVE BACK HERE!
HECK YEAH! YOU CAN STAY IN THE TREEHOUSE!
HEY, KIDDO! READY TO GO?
I GUESS... IT'S NOT THAT FAR, RIGHT MOM?
ONLY A COUPLE OF HOURS...
...BY PLANE.
HEAR THAT?!
ONLY A COUPLE HOURS!
UH... YEA--
THANKS, WYATT.
FOR WHAT?
I DUNNO...
...BEING AWESOME.
N--NO PROBLEM.
LATER, DUDE!
SEE YA SOON!
SEE YA...

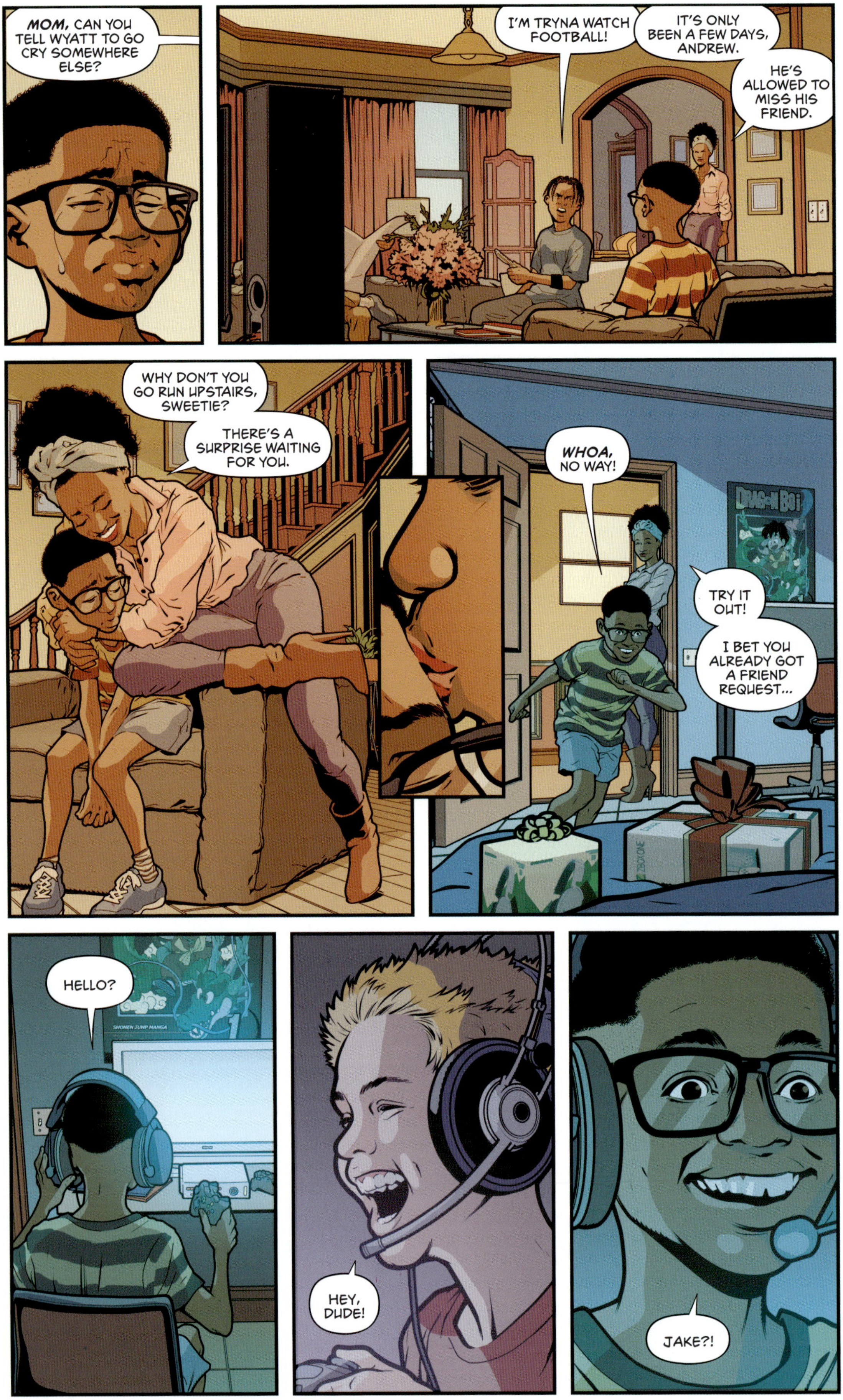
MOM, CAN YOU TELL WYATT TO GO CRY SOMEWHERE ELSE?
I'M TRYNA WATCH FOOTBALL!
IT'S ONLY BEEN A FEW DAYS, ANDREW.
HE'S ALLOWED TO MISS HIS FRIEND.
WHY DON'T YOU GO RUN UPSTAIRS, SWEETIE?
THERE'S A SURPRISE WAITING FOR YOU.
WHOA, NO WAY!
TRY IT OUT!
I BET YOU ALREADY GOT A FRIEND REQUEST...
HELLO?
HEY, DUDE!
JAKE?!

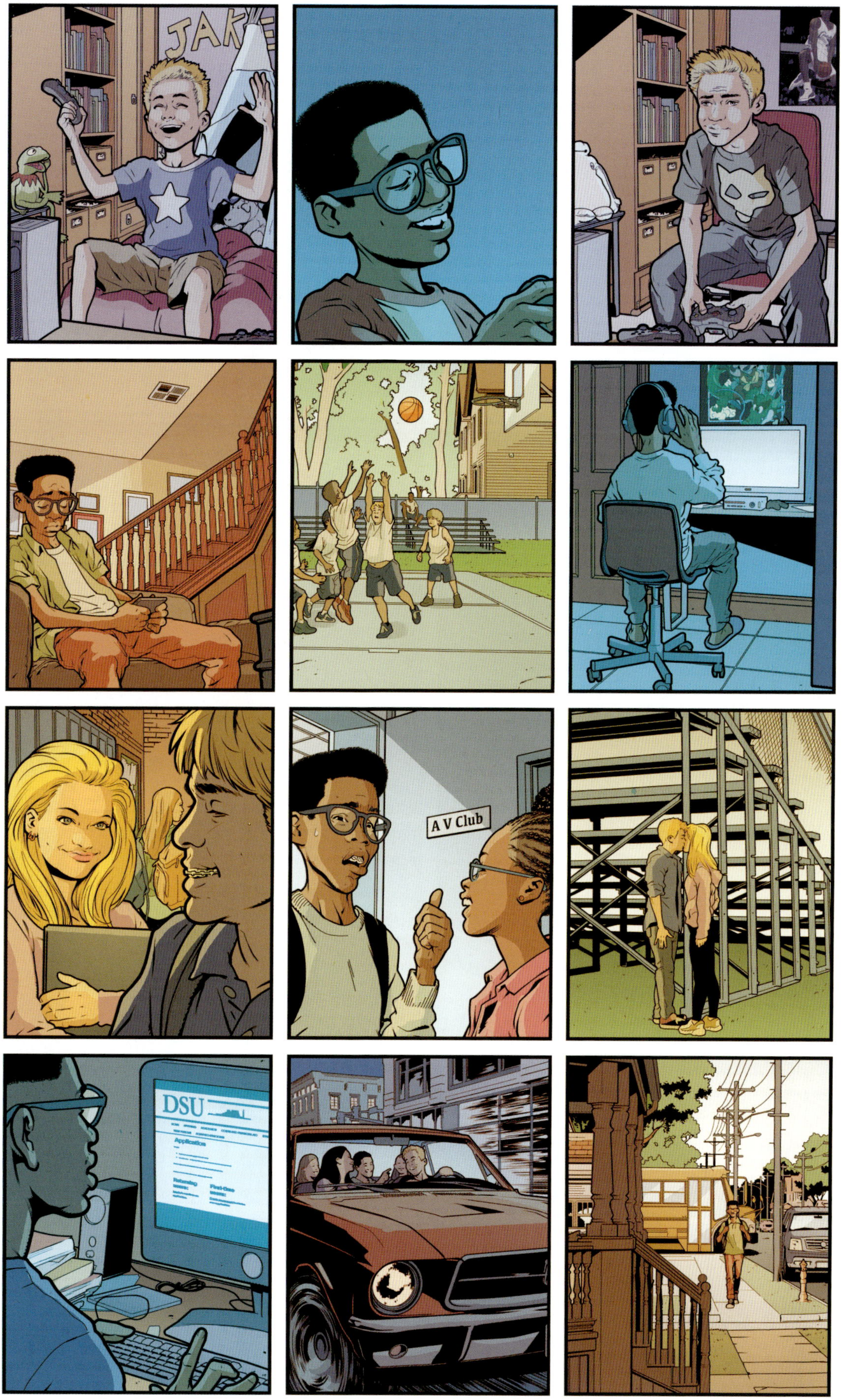
A V Club
DSU
Application

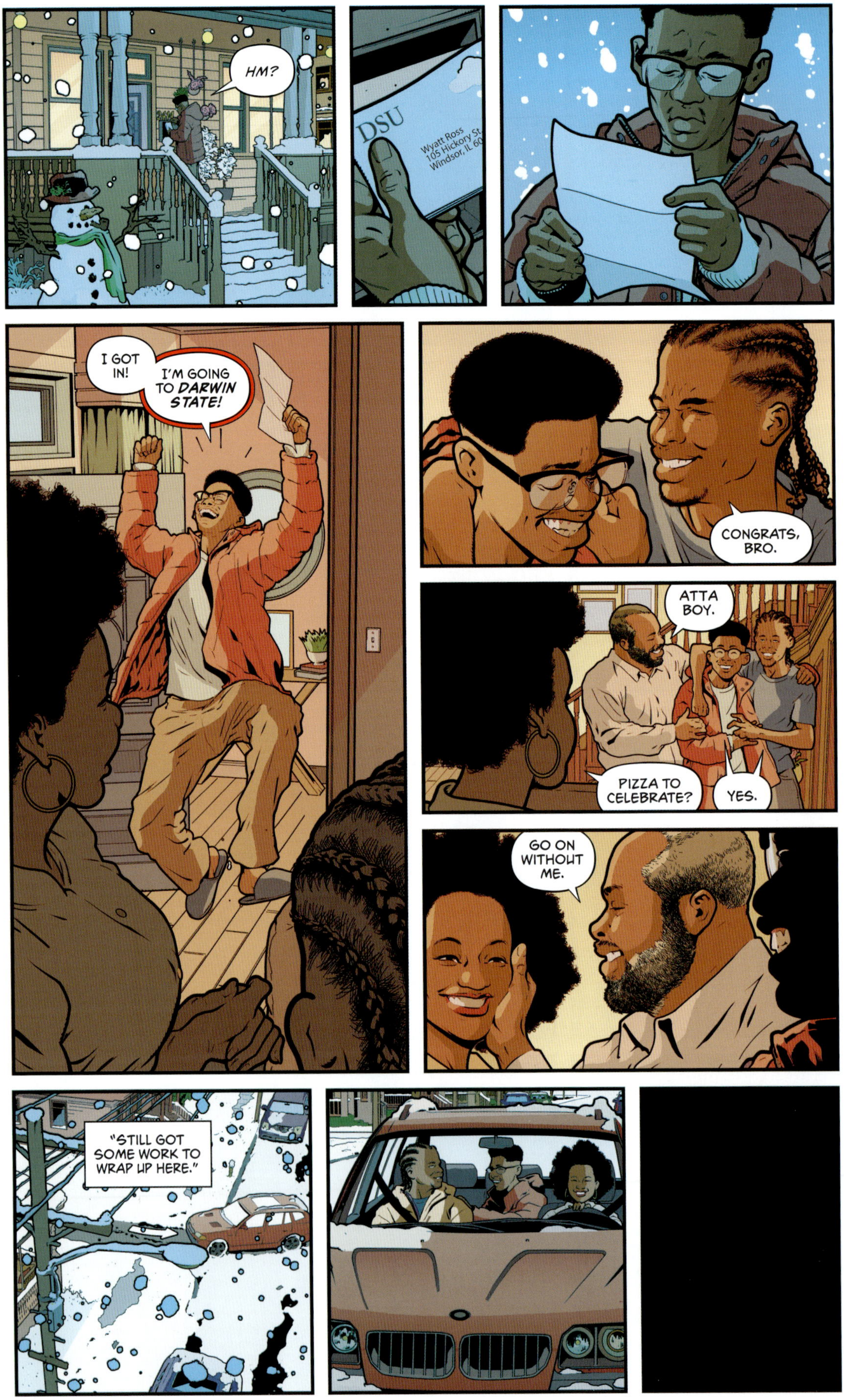
HM?
DSU
Wyatt Ross
105 Hickory St.
I GOT IN!
I'M GOING TO DARWIN STATE!
CONGRATS, BRO.
ATTA BOY.
PIZZA TO CELEBRATE?
YES.
GO ON WITHOUT ME.
"STILL GOT SOME WORK TO WRAP UP HERE."

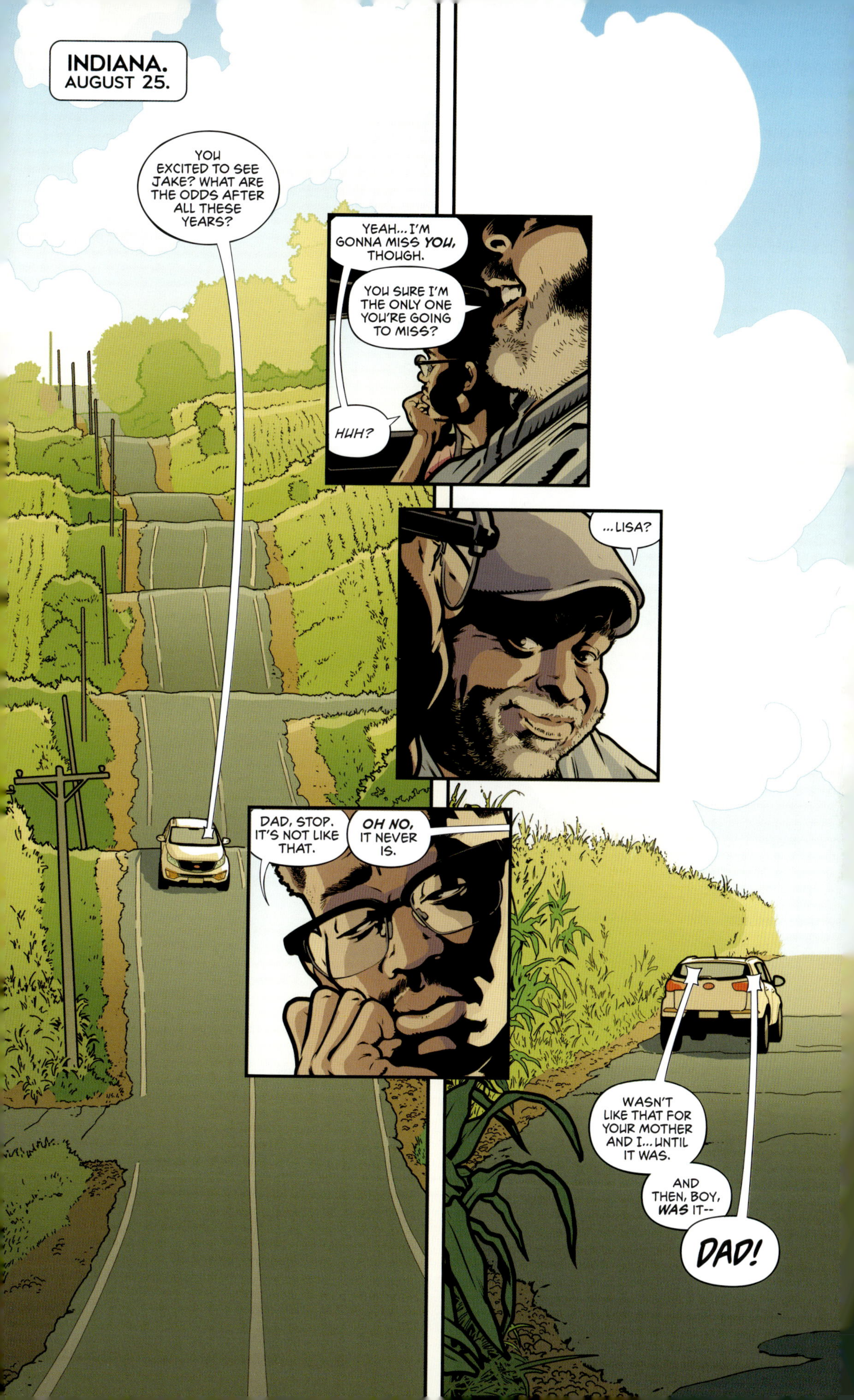

INDIANA.
AUGUST 25.
YOU EXCITED TO SEE JAKE? WHAT ARE THE ODDS AFTER ALL THESE YEARS?
YEAH... I'M GONNA MISS *YOU,* THOUGH.
YOU SURE I'M THE ONLY ONE YOU'RE GOING TO MISS?
HUH?
...LISA?
DAD, STOP. IT'S NOT LIKE THAT.
OH NO, IT NEVER IS.
WASN'T LIKE THAT FOR YOUR MOTHER AND I... UNTIL IT WAS.
AND THEN, BOY, *WAS* IT--
DAD!

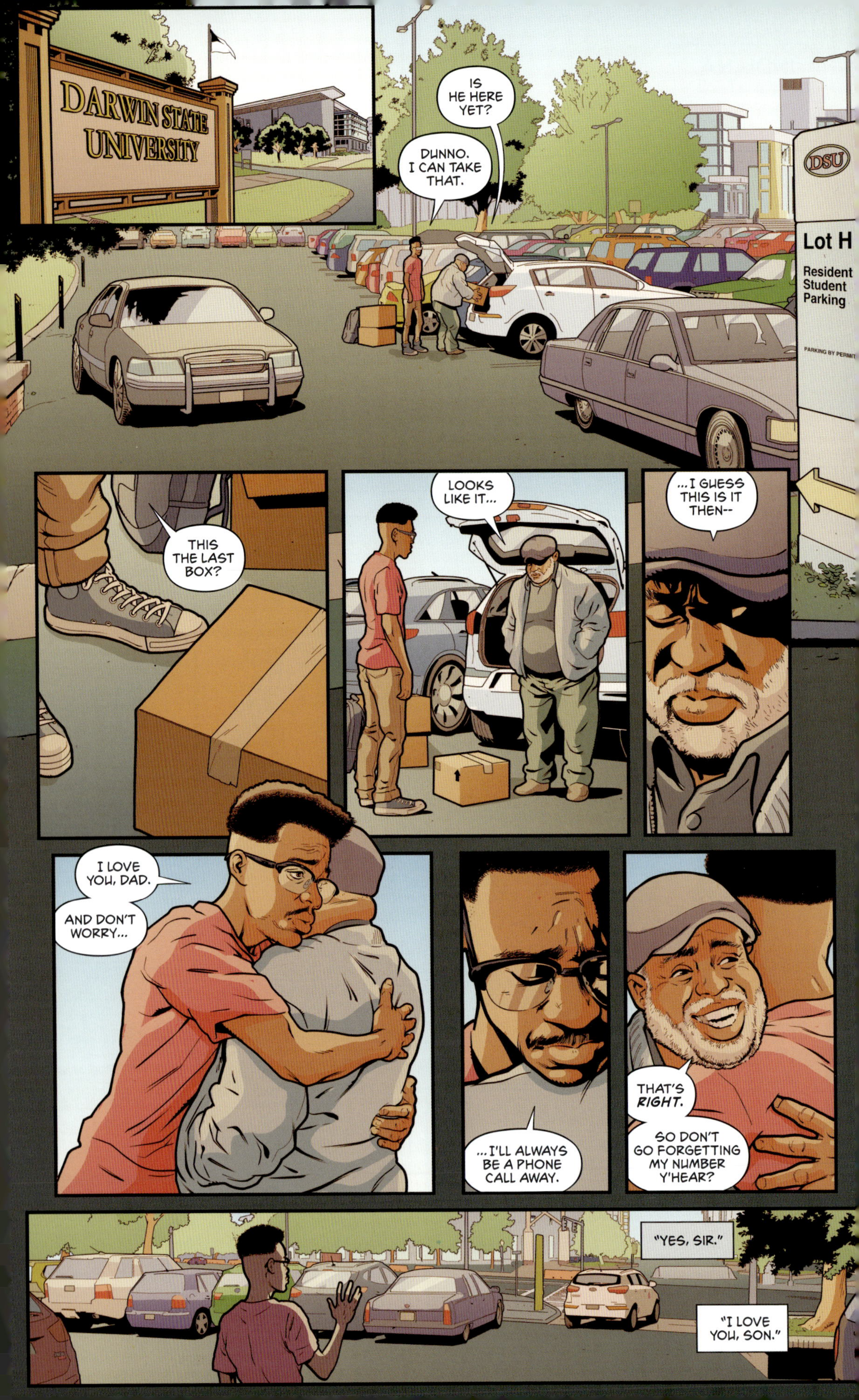
DARWIN STATE UNIVERSITY
IS HE HERE YET?
DUNNO. I CAN TAKE THAT.
DSU
Lot H
Resident Student Parking
PARKING BY PERMIT
THIS THE LAST BOX?
LOOKS LIKE IT...
...I GUESS THIS IS IT THEN--
I LOVE YOU, DAD.
AND DON'T WORRY...
...I'LL ALWAYS BE A PHONE CALL AWAY.
THAT'S *RIGHT.*
SO DON'T GO FORGETTING MY NUMBER Y'HEAR?
"YES, SIR."
"I LOVE YOU, SON."

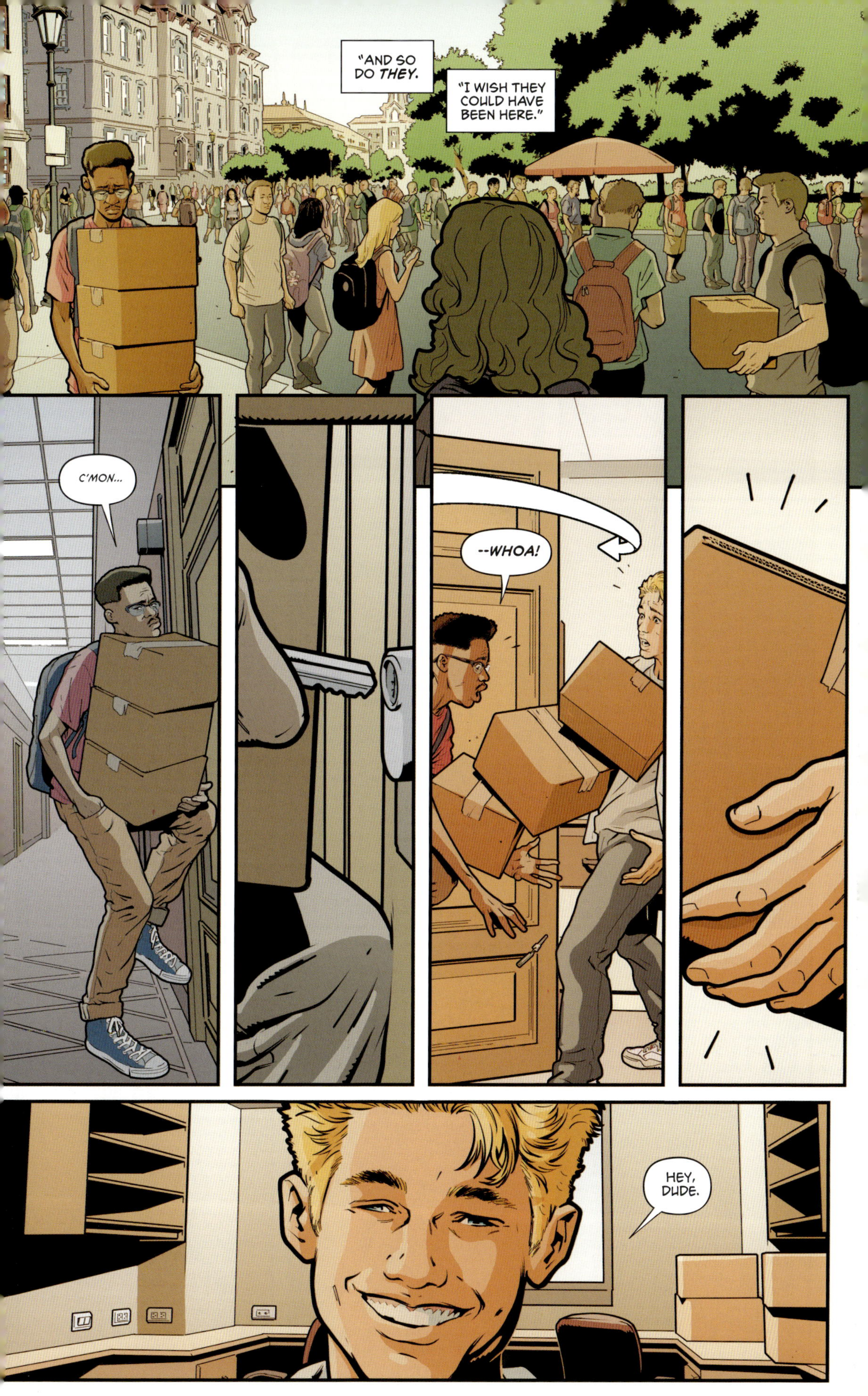
"AND SO DO *THEY*.
"I WISH THEY COULD HAVE BEEN HERE."
C'MON...
--WHOA!
HEY, DUDE.

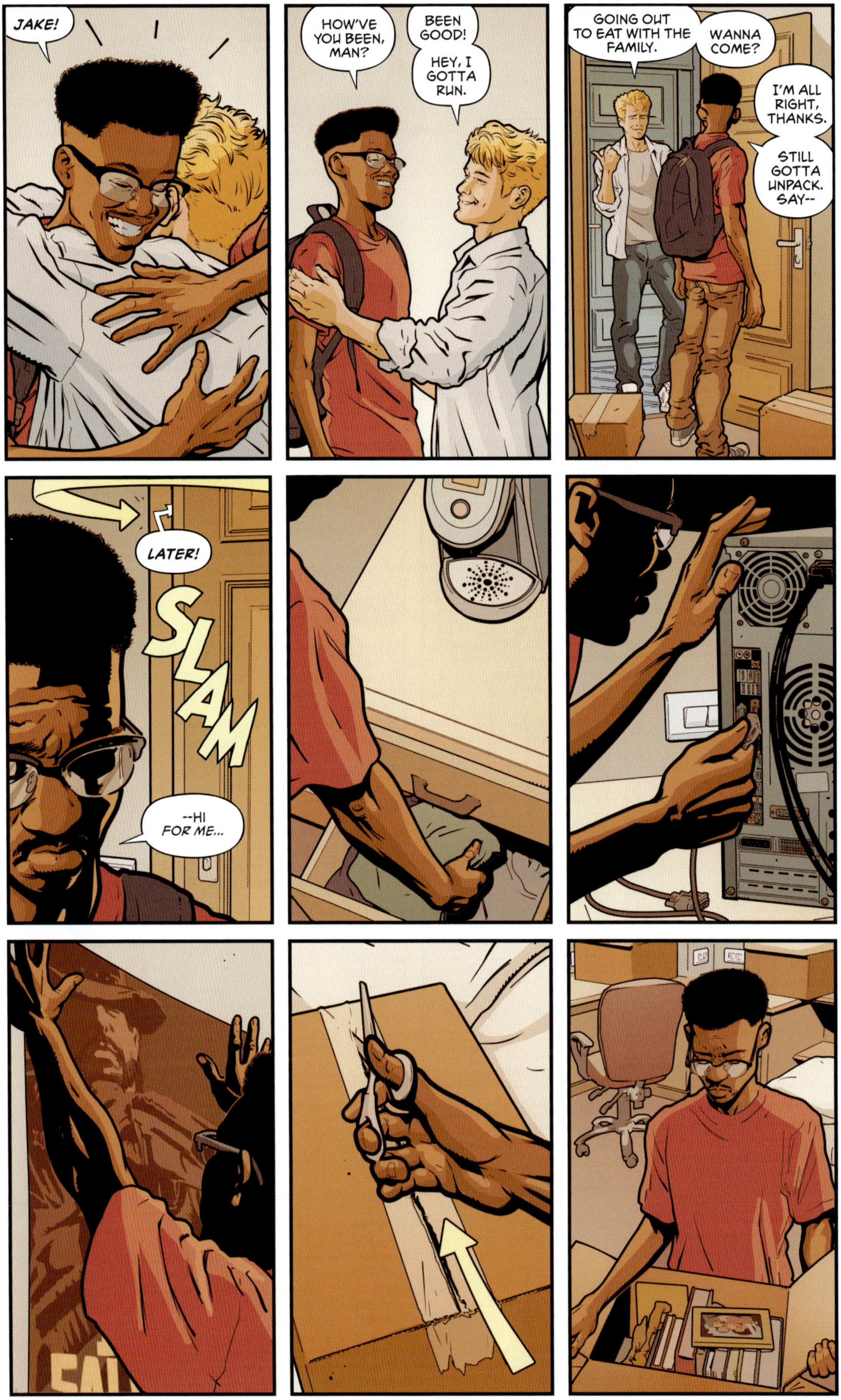
JAKE!
HOW'VE YOU BEEN, MAN?
BEEN GOOD!
HEY, I GOTTA RUN.
GOING OUT TO EAT WITH THE FAMILY.
WANNA COME?
I'M ALL RIGHT, THANKS.
STILL GOTTA UNPACK. SAY--
LATER!
SLAM
--HI FOR ME...

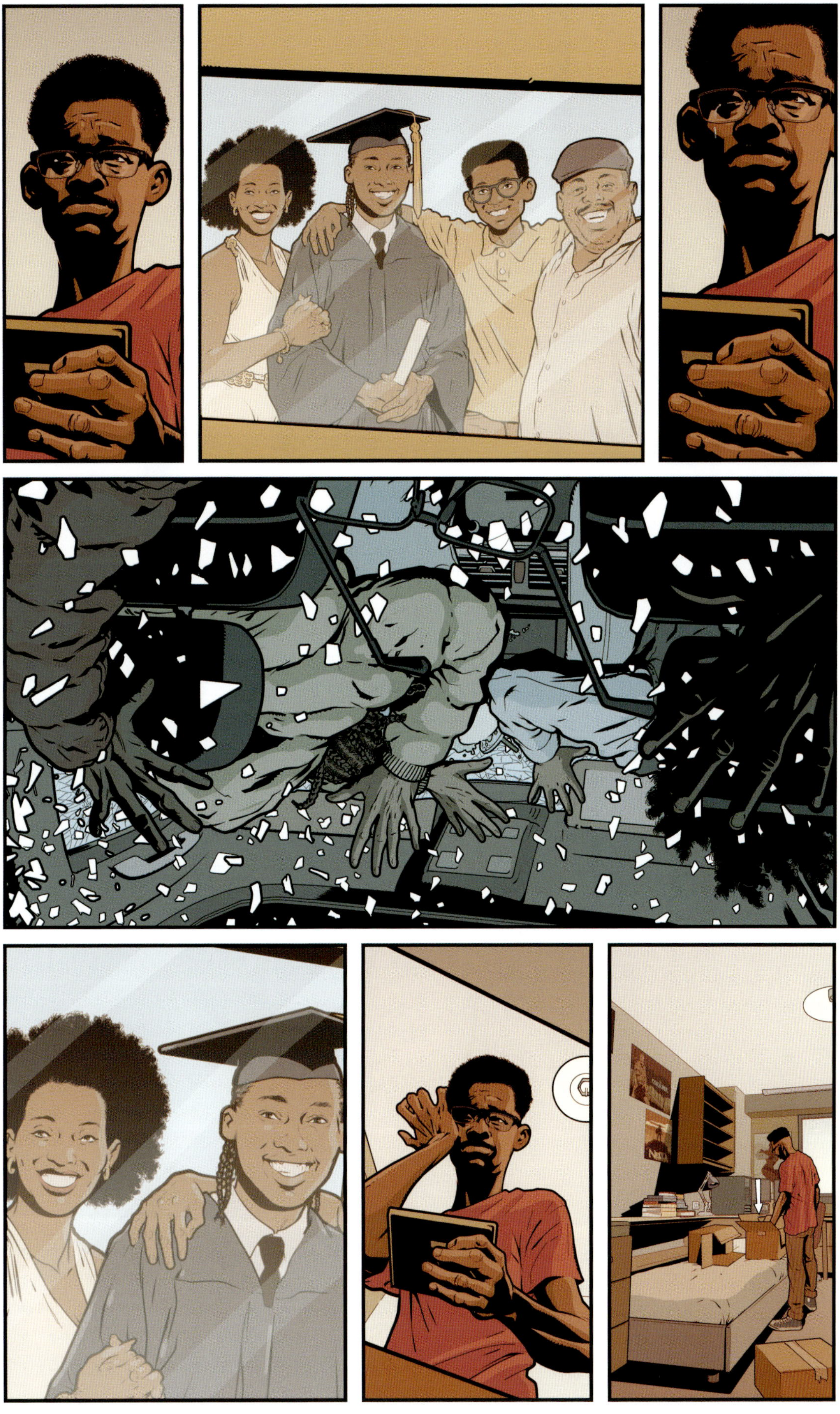

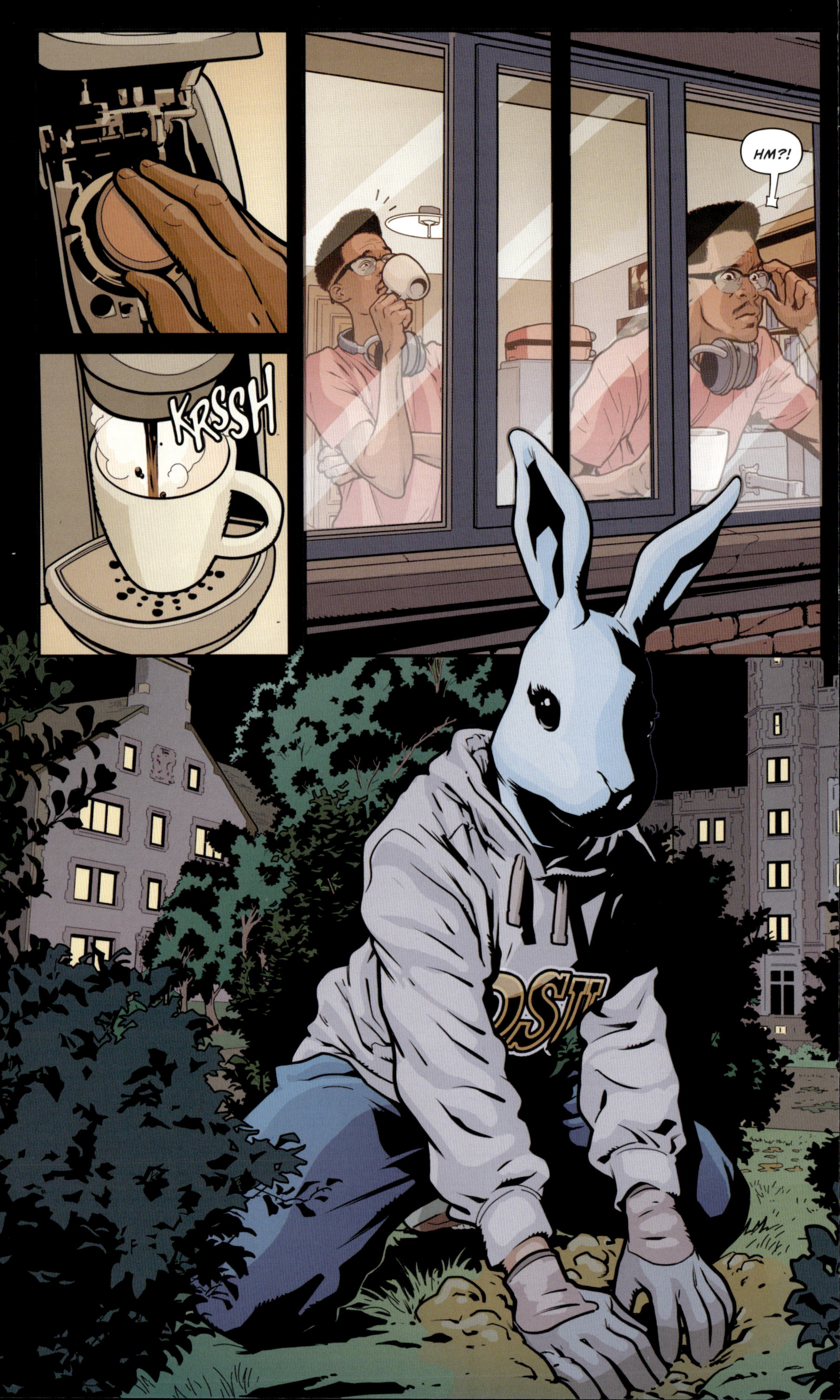
KRSSH
HM?!

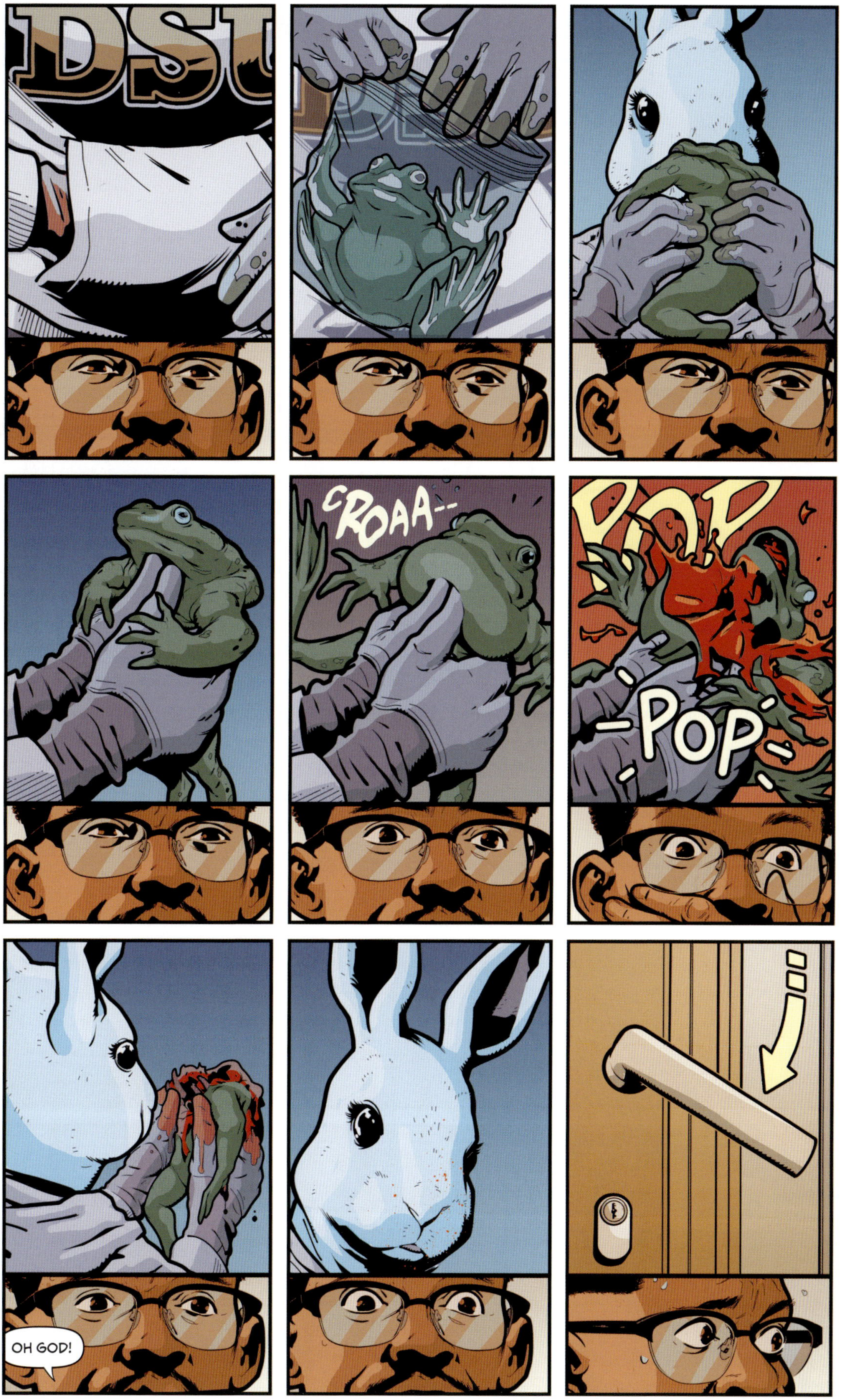
CROAA--
POP
POP
OH GOD!

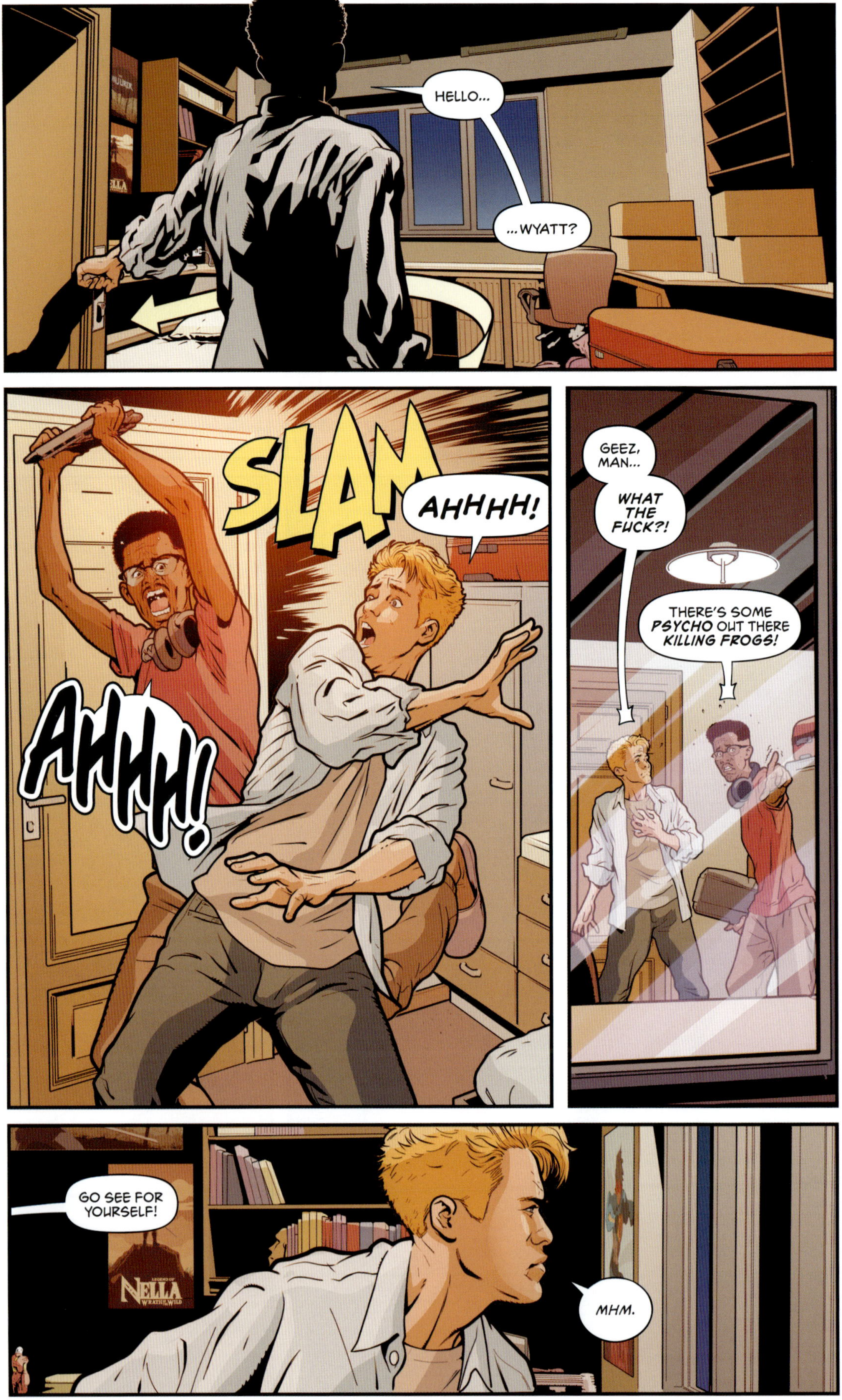
HELLO...
...WYATT?
SLAM
AHHHH!
AHHH!
GEEZ, MAN...
WHAT THE FUCK?!
THERE'S SOME PSYCHO OUT THERE KILLING FROGS!
GO SEE FOR YOURSELF!
MHM.

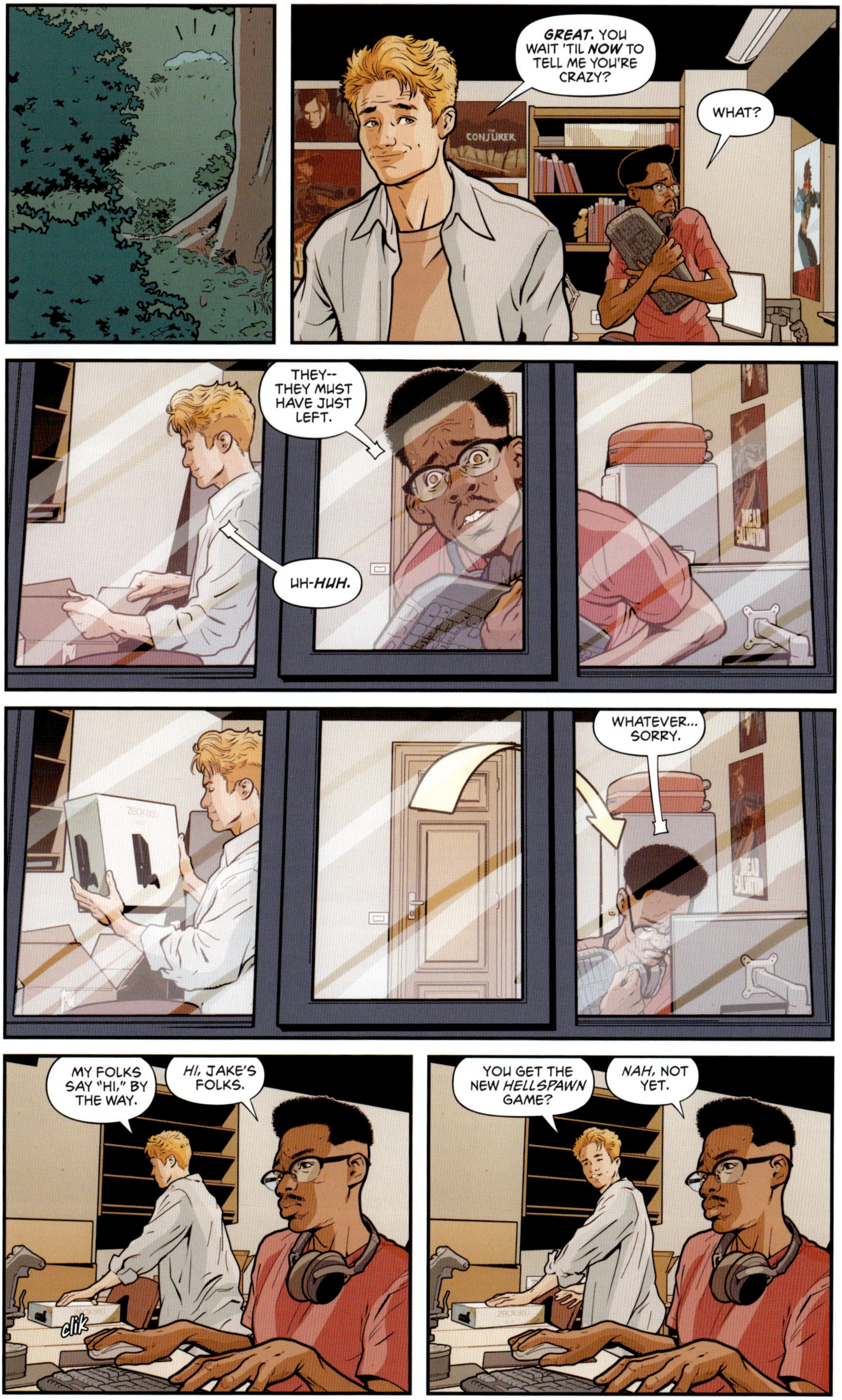
GREAT. YOU WAIT 'TIL NOW TO TELL ME YOU'RE CRAZY?
WHAT?
THE CONJURER
THEY-- THEY MUST HAVE JUST LEFT.
UH-HUH.
DREAD SALVATION
WHATEVER... SORRY.
MY FOLKS SAY "HI," BY THE WAY.
HI, JAKE'S FOLKS.
clik
YOU GET THE NEW HELLSPAWN GAME?
NAH, NOT YET.

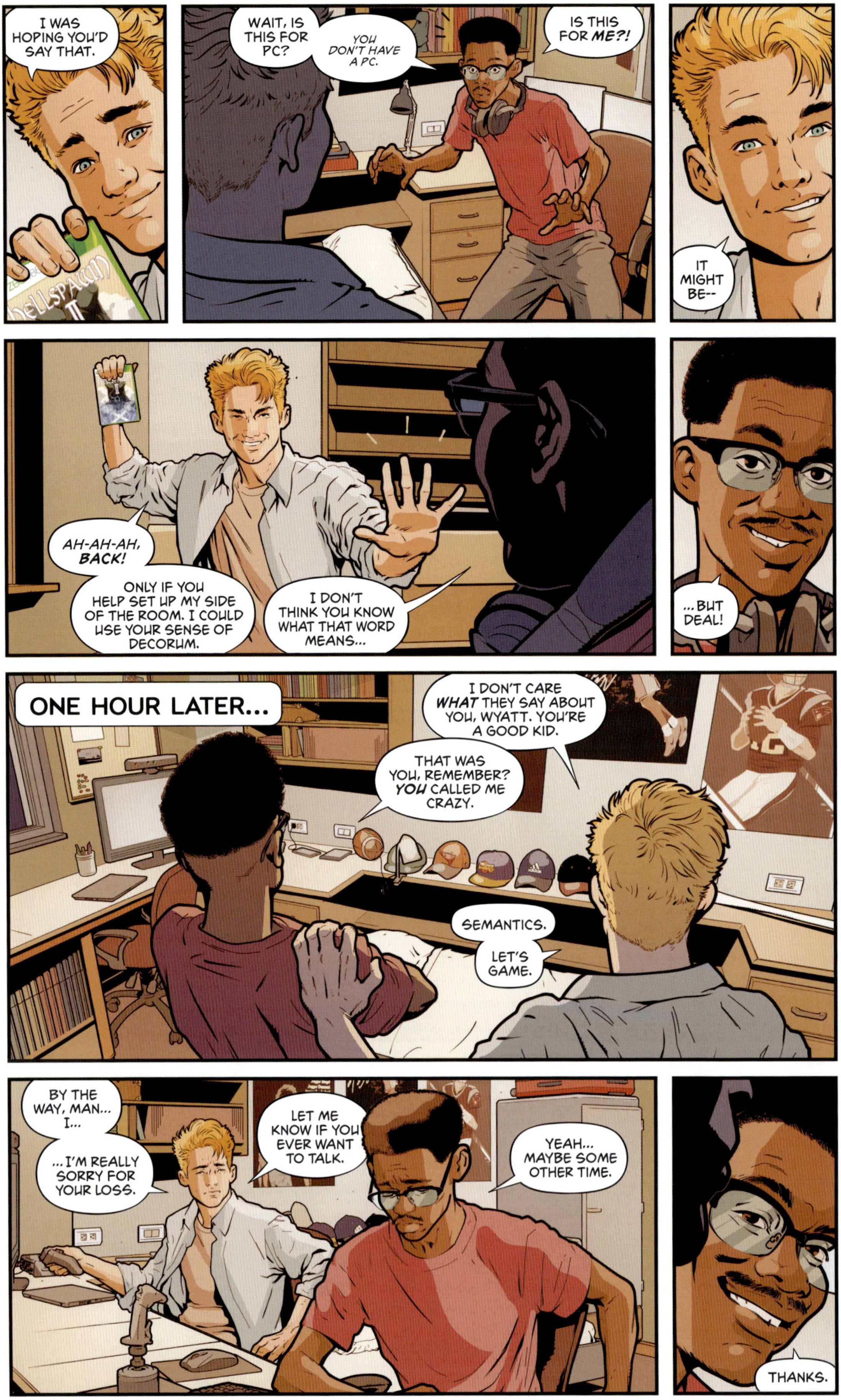
I WAS HOPING YOU'D SAY THAT.
HELLSPAWN II
WAIT, IS THIS FOR PC?
YOU DON'T HAVE A PC.
IS THIS FOR ME?!
IT MIGHT BE--
AH-AH-AH, BACK!
ONLY IF YOU HELP SET UP MY SIDE OF THE ROOM. I COULD USE YOUR SENSE OF DECORUM.
I DON'T THINK YOU KNOW WHAT THAT WORD MEANS...
...BUT DEAL!
ONE HOUR LATER...
I DON'T CARE WHAT THEY SAY ABOUT YOU, WYATT. YOU'RE A GOOD KID.
THAT WAS YOU, REMEMBER? YOU CALLED ME CRAZY.
SEMANTICS.
LET'S GAME.
BY THE WAY, MAN... I...
...I'M REALLY SORRY FOR YOUR LOSS.
LET ME KNOW IF YOU EVER WANT TO TALK.
YEAH... MAYBE SOME OTHER TIME.
THANKS.

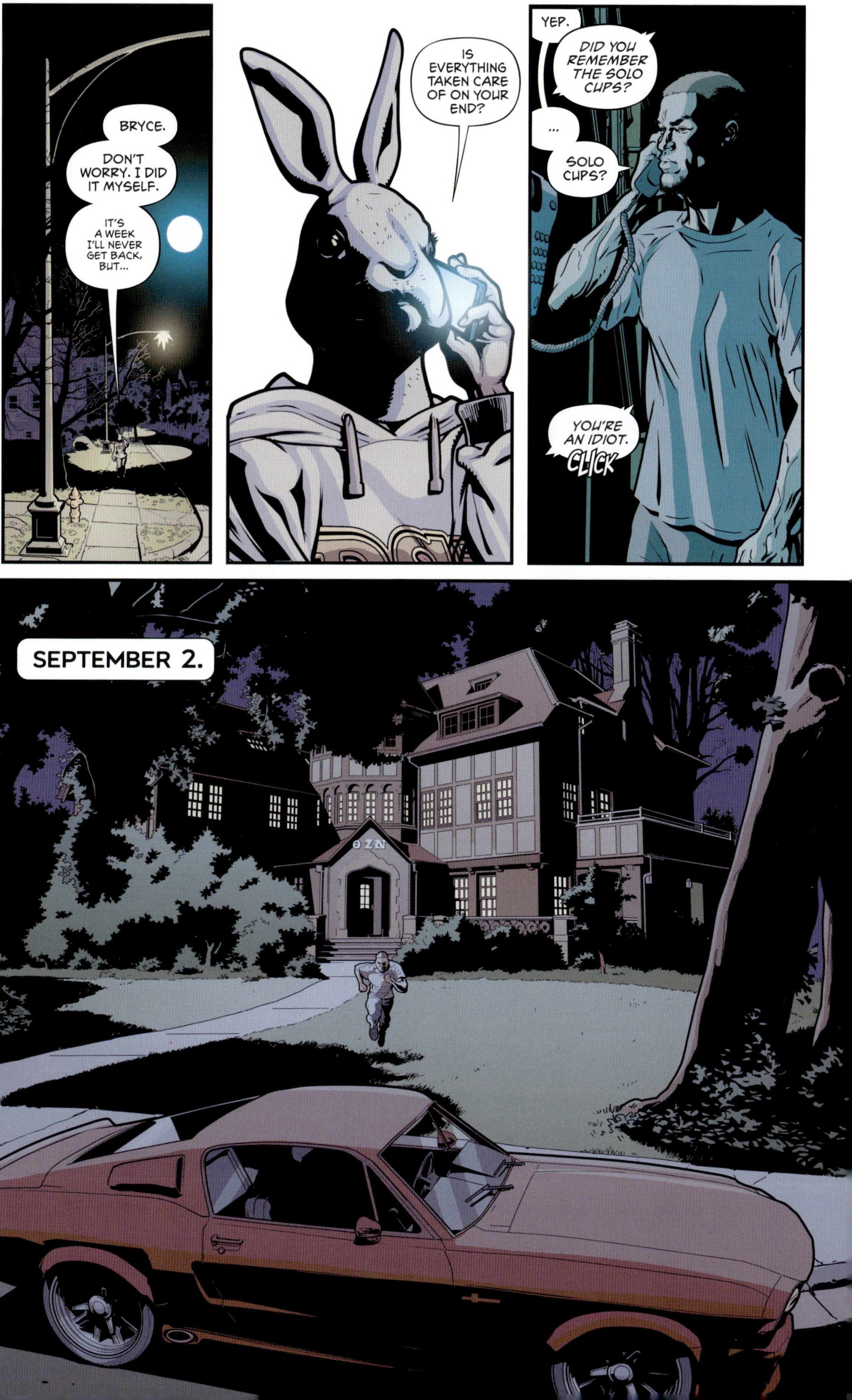
BRYCE.
DON'T WORRY. I DID IT MYSELF.
IT'S A WEEK I'LL NEVER GET BACK, BUT...
IS EVERYTHING TAKEN CARE OF ON YOUR END?
YEP.
DID YOU REMEMBER THE SOLO CUPS?
...
SOLO CUPS?
YOU'RE AN IDIOT.
CLICK
SEPTEMBER 2.

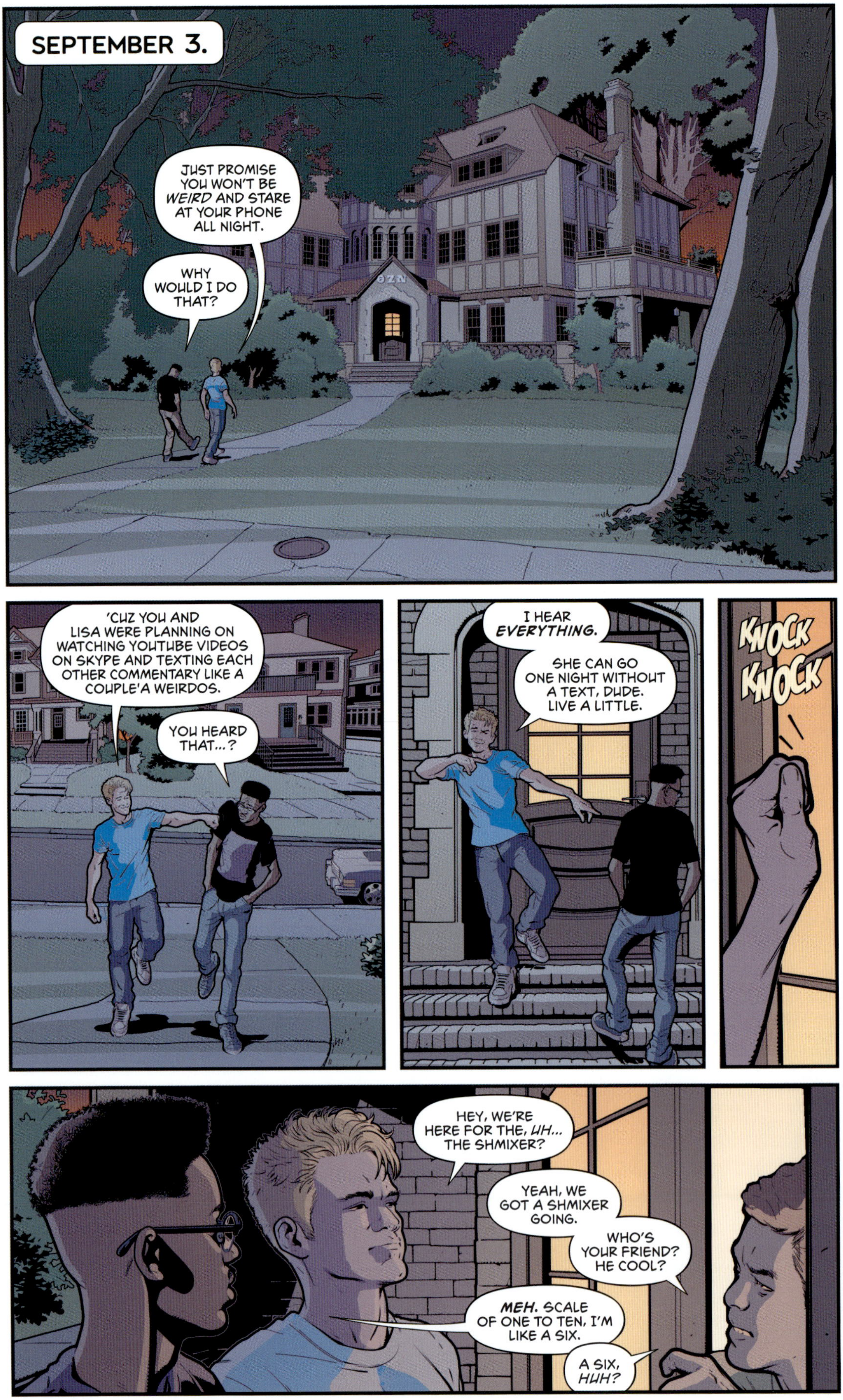
SEPTEMBER 3.
JUST PROMISE YOU WON'T BE WEIRD AND STARE AT YOUR PHONE ALL NIGHT.
WHY WOULD I DO THAT?
'CUZ YOU AND LISA WERE PLANNING ON WATCHING YOUTUBE VIDEOS ON SKYPE AND TEXTING EACH OTHER COMMENTARY LIKE A COUPLE'A WEIRDOS.
YOU HEARD THAT...?
I HEAR EVERYTHING.
SHE CAN GO ONE NIGHT WITHOUT A TEXT, DUDE. LIVE A LITTLE.
KNOCK KNOCK
HEY, WE'RE HERE FOR THE, UH... THE SHMIXER?
YEAH, WE GOT A SHMIXER GOING.
WHO'S YOUR FRIEND? HE COOL?
MEH. SCALE OF ONE TO TEN, I'M LIKE A SIX.
A SIX, HUH?

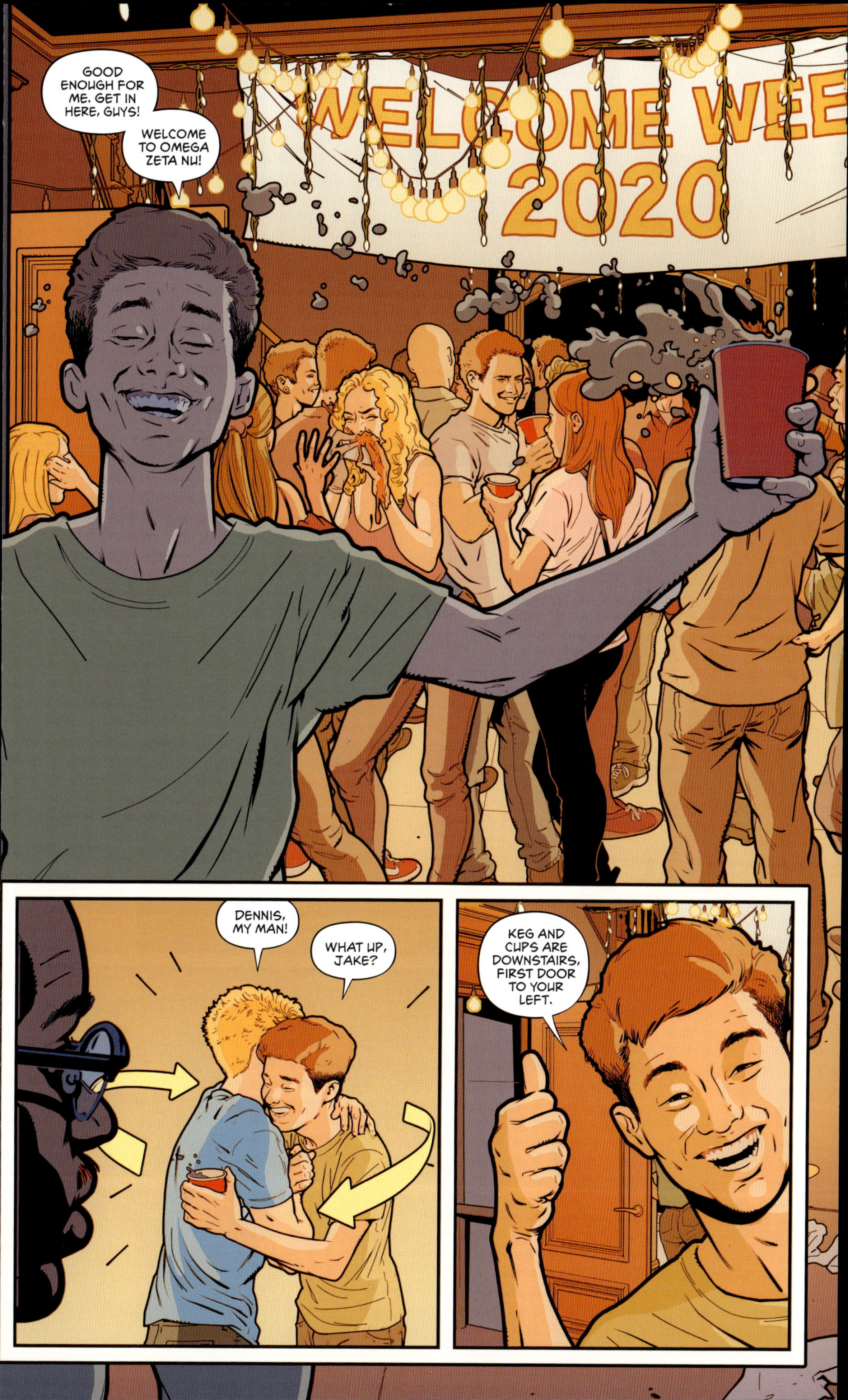
GOOD ENOUGH FOR ME. GET IN HERE, GUYS!
WELCOME TO OMEGA ZETA NU!
WELCOME WEE
2020
DENNIS, MY MAN!
WHAT UP, JAKE?
KEG AND CUPS ARE DOWNSTAIRS, FIRST DOOR TO YOUR LEFT.

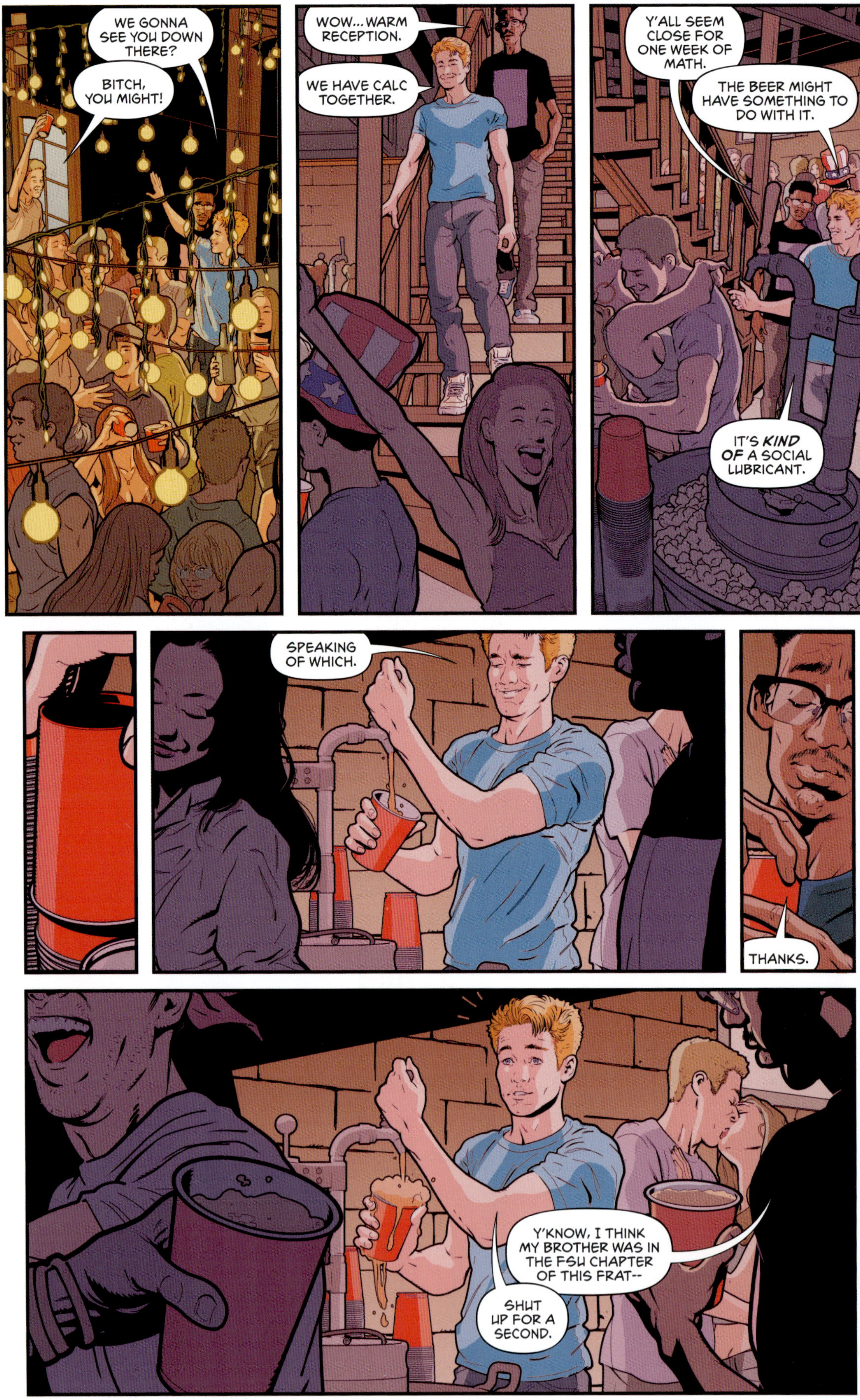

WE GONNA SEE YOU DOWN THERE?
BITCH, YOU MIGHT!
WOW... WARM RECEPTION.
WE HAVE CALC TOGETHER.
Y'ALL SEEM CLOSE FOR ONE WEEK OF MATH.
THE BEER MIGHT HAVE SOMETHING TO DO WITH IT.
IT'S *KIND OF* A SOCIAL LUBRICANT.
SPEAKING OF WHICH.
THANKS.
Y'KNOW, I THINK MY BROTHER WAS IN THE FSU CHAPTER OF THIS FRAT--
SHUT UP FOR A SECOND.

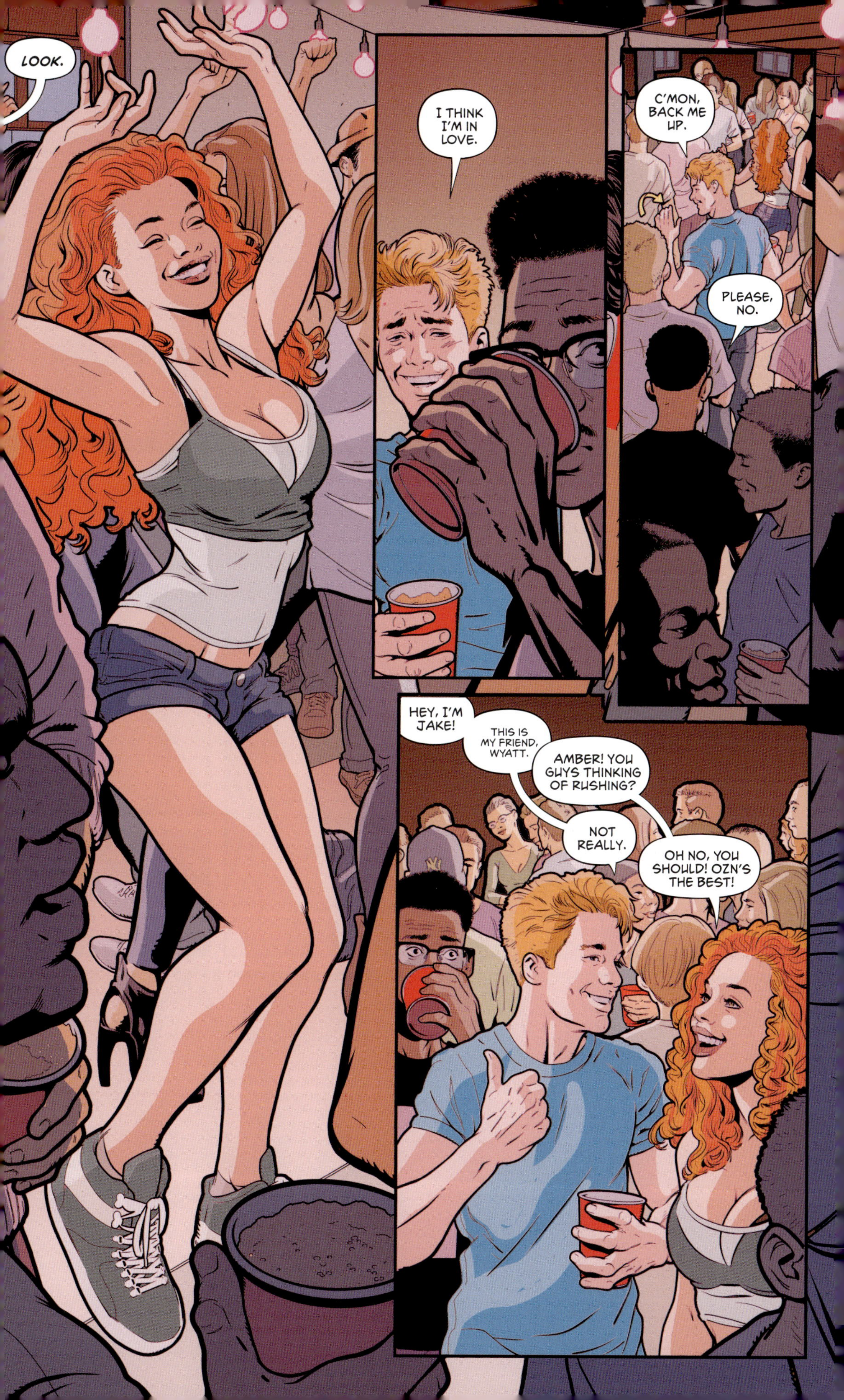
LOOK.
I THINK I'M IN LOVE.
C'MON, BACK ME UP.
PLEASE, NO.
HEY, I'M JAKE!
THIS IS MY FRIEND, WYATT.
AMBER! YOU GUYS THINKING OF RUSHING?
NOT REALLY.
OH NO, YOU SHOULD! OZN'S THE BEST!

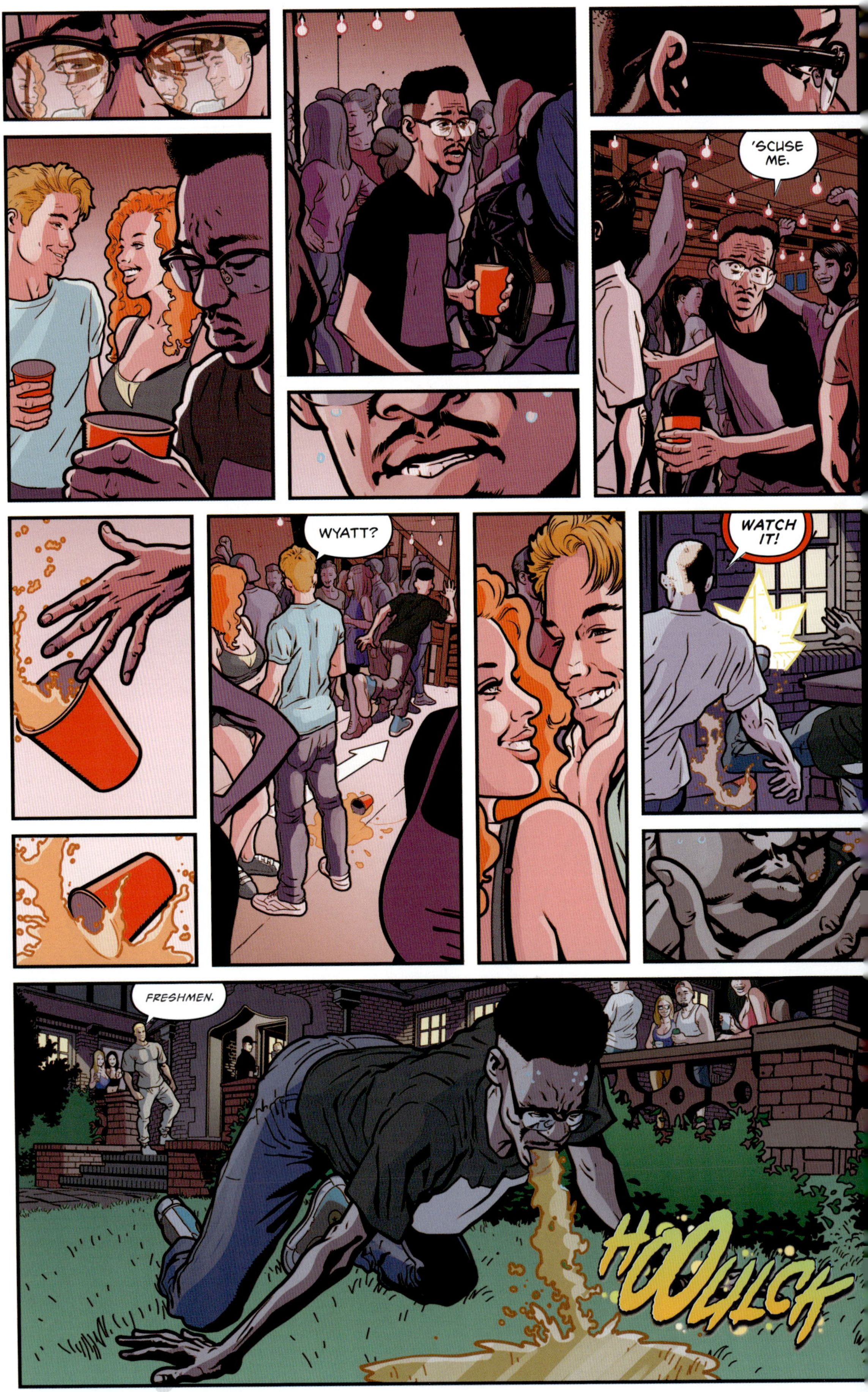
'SCUSE ME.
WYATT?
WATCH IT!
FRESHMEN.
HOOULCH

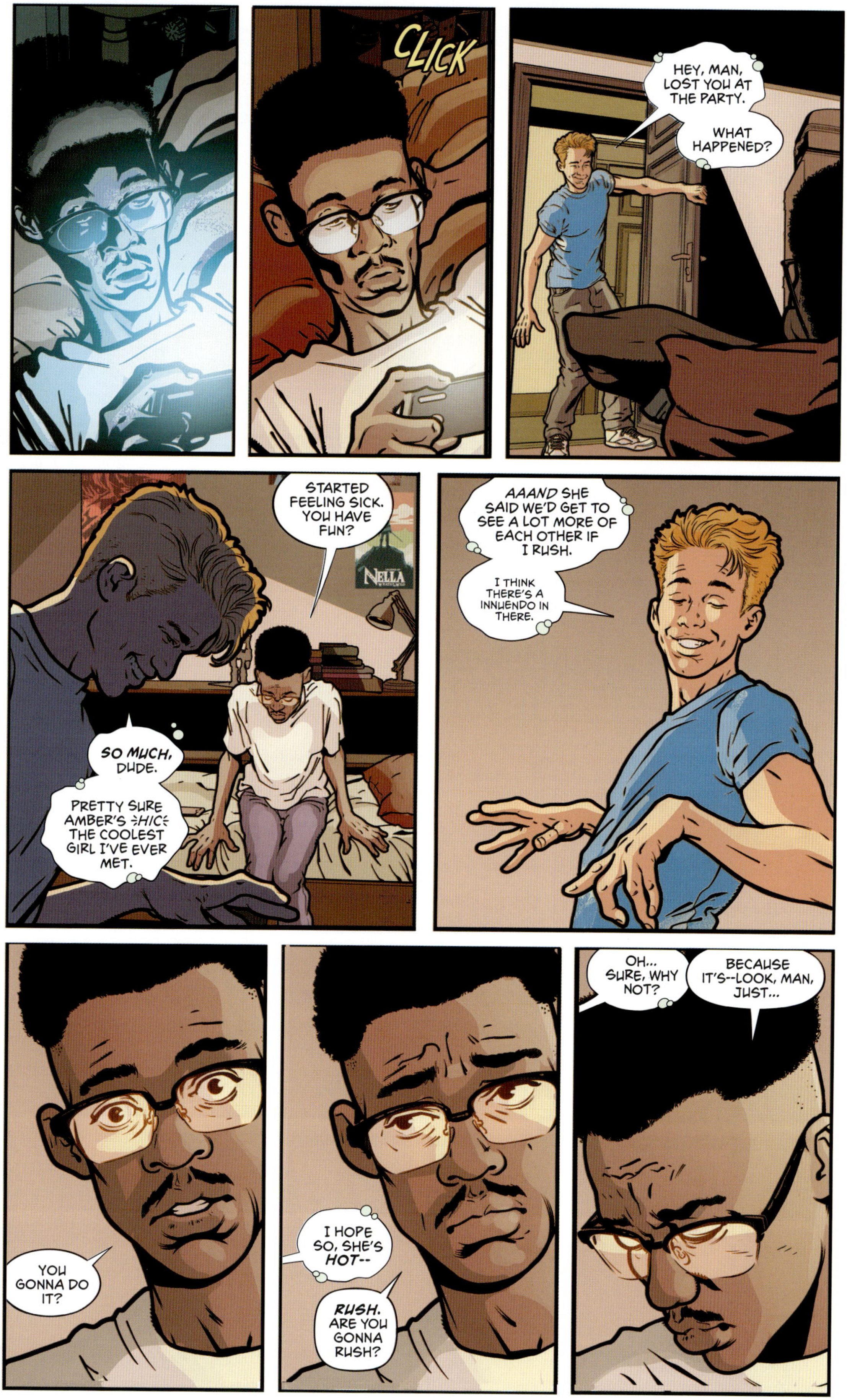
CLICK
HEY, MAN, LOST YOU AT THE PARTY.
WHAT HAPPENED?
STARTED FEELING SICK. YOU HAVE FUN?
SO MUCH, DUDE.
PRETTY SURE AMBER'S *HIC* THE COOLEST GIRL I'VE EVER MET.
NELLA
AAAND SHE SAID WE'D GET TO SEE A LOT MORE OF EACH OTHER IF I RUSH.
I THINK THERE'S A INNUENDO IN THERE.
YOU GONNA DO IT?
I HOPE SO, SHE'S HOT--
RUSH. ARE YOU GONNA RUSH?
OH... SURE, WHY NOT?
BECAUSE IT'S--LOOK, MAN, JUST...

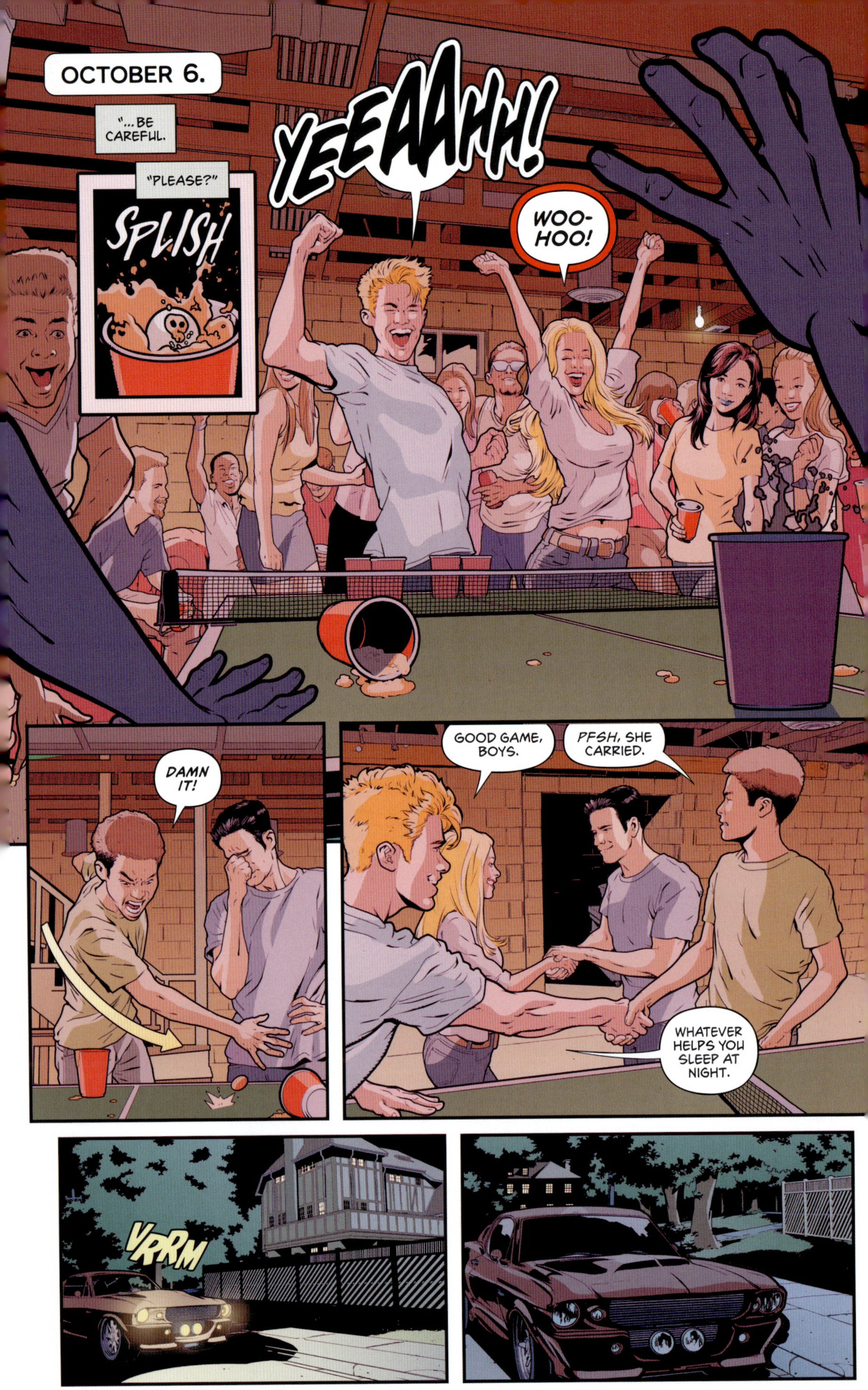
OCTOBER 6.
"...BE CAREFUL.
"PLEASE?"
SPLISH
YEEAAHH!
WOO-HOO!
DAMN IT!
GOOD GAME, BOYS.
PFSH, SHE CARRIED.
WHATEVER HELPS YOU SLEEP AT NIGHT.
VRRM

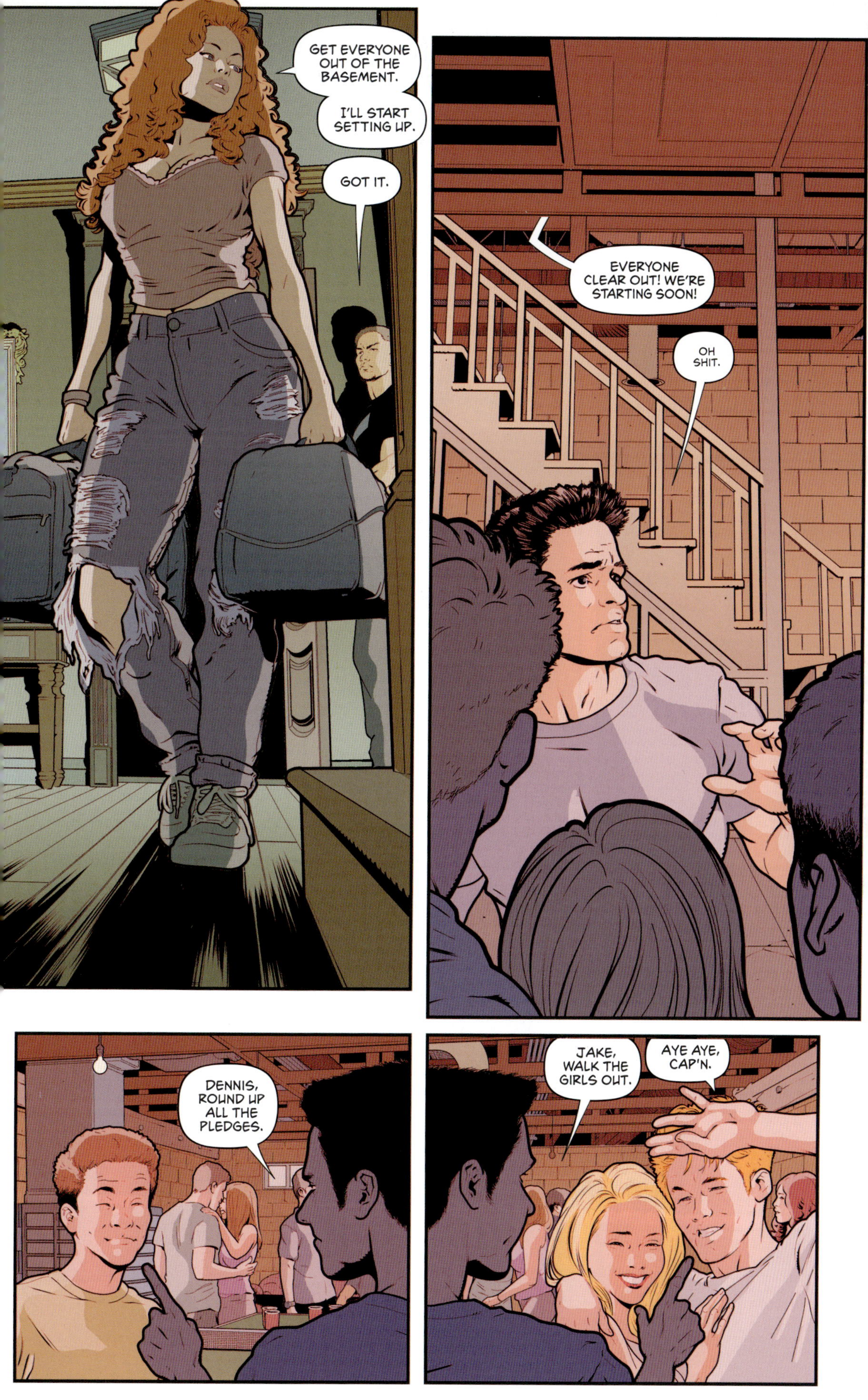
GET EVERYONE OUT OF THE BASEMENT.
I'LL START SETTING UP.
GOT IT.
EVERYONE CLEAR OUT! WE'RE STARTING SOON!
OH SHIT.
DENNIS, ROUND UP ALL THE PLEDGES.
JAKE, WALK THE GIRLS OUT.
AYE AYE, CAP'N.

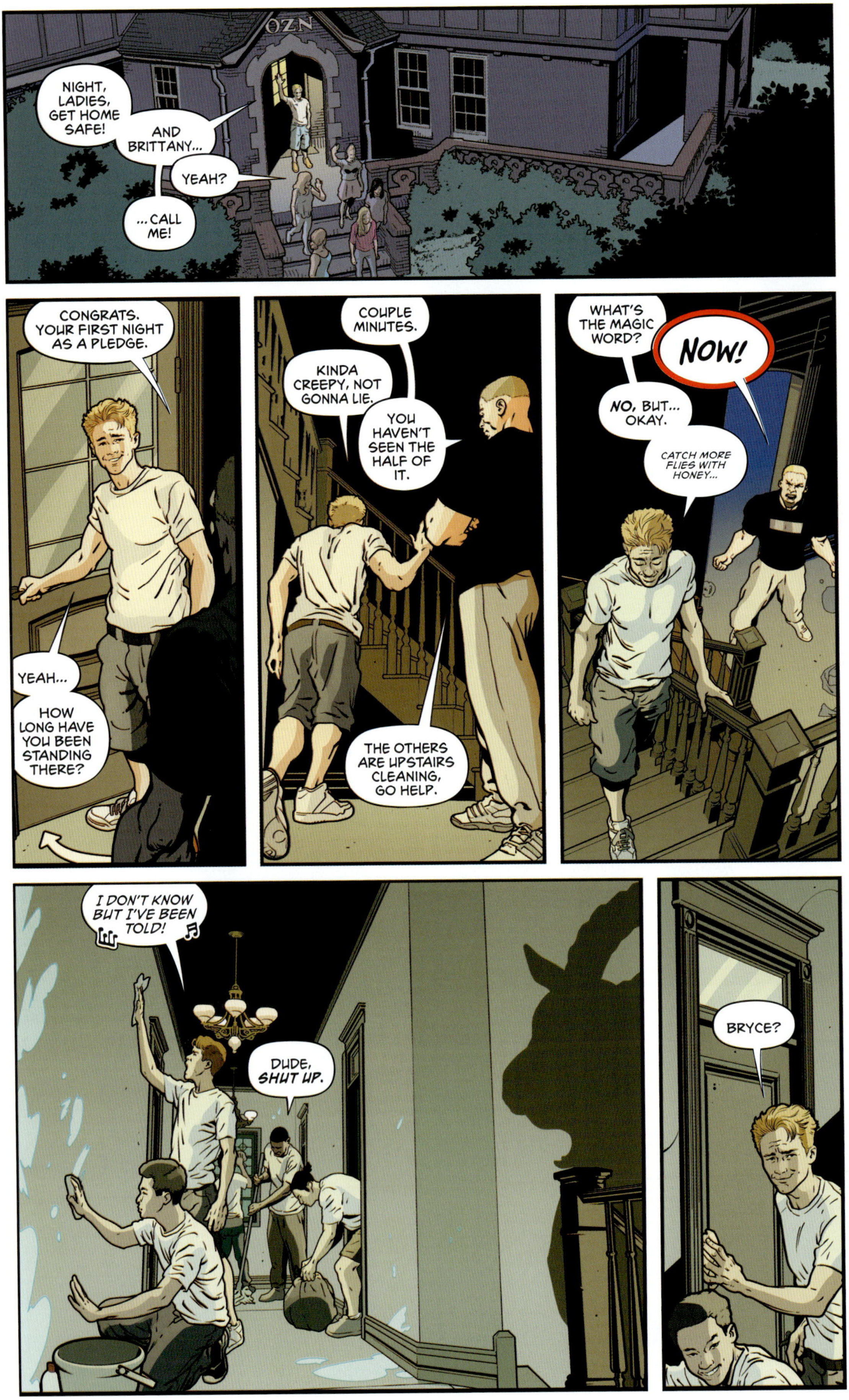
OZN
NIGHT, LADIES, GET HOME SAFE!
AND BRITTANY...
YEAH?
...CALL ME!
CONGRATS. YOUR FIRST NIGHT AS A PLEDGE.
YEAH...
HOW LONG HAVE YOU BEEN STANDING THERE?
COUPLE MINUTES.
KINDA CREEPY, NOT GONNA LIE.
YOU HAVEN'T SEEN THE HALF OF IT.
THE OTHERS ARE UPSTAIRS CLEANING. GO HELP.
WHAT'S THE MAGIC WORD?
NOW!
NO, BUT... OKAY.
CATCH MORE FLIES WITH HONEY...
I DON'T KNOW BUT I'VE BEEN TOLD!
DUDE, SHUT UP.
BRYCE?

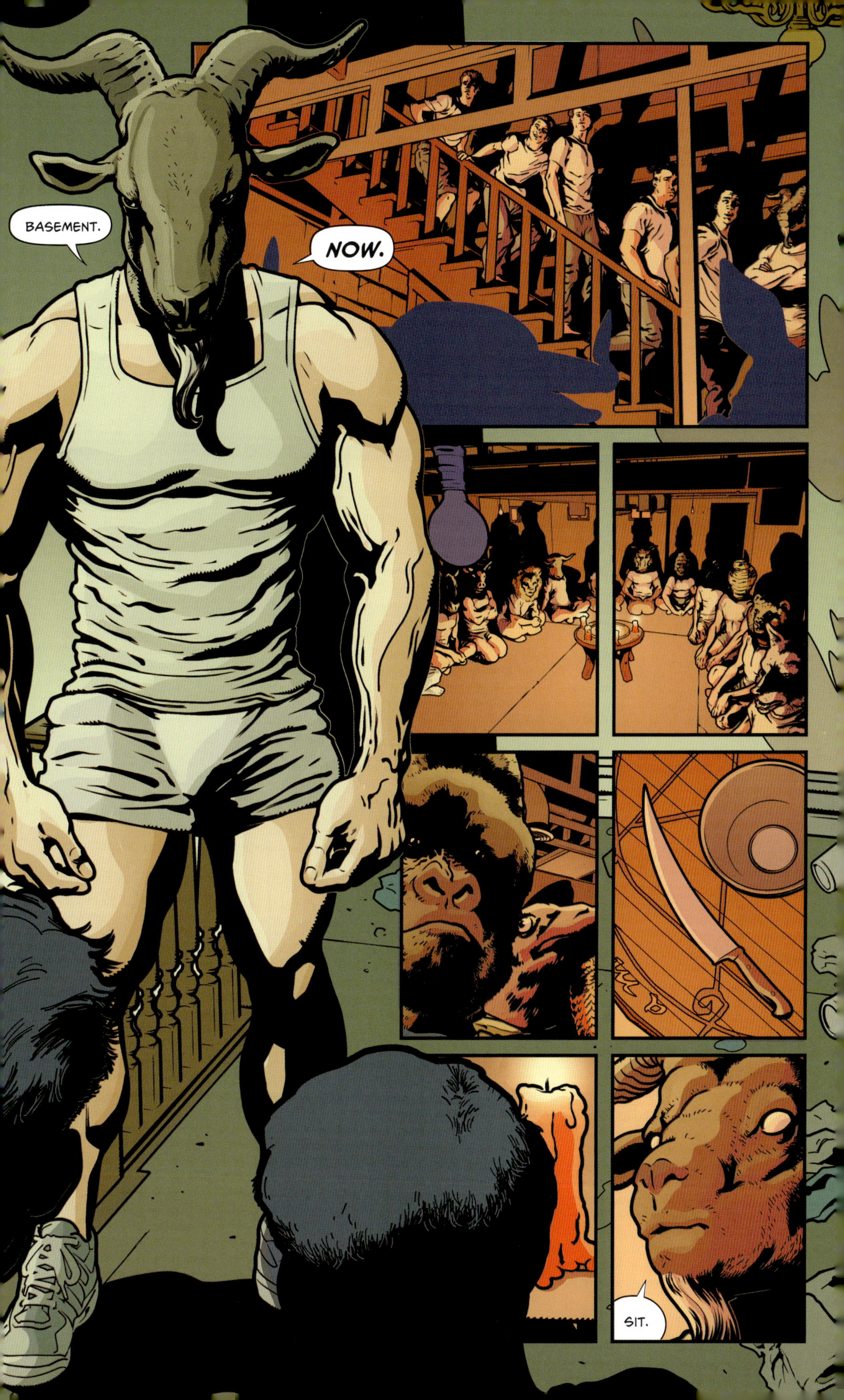
BASEMENT.
NOW.
SIT.

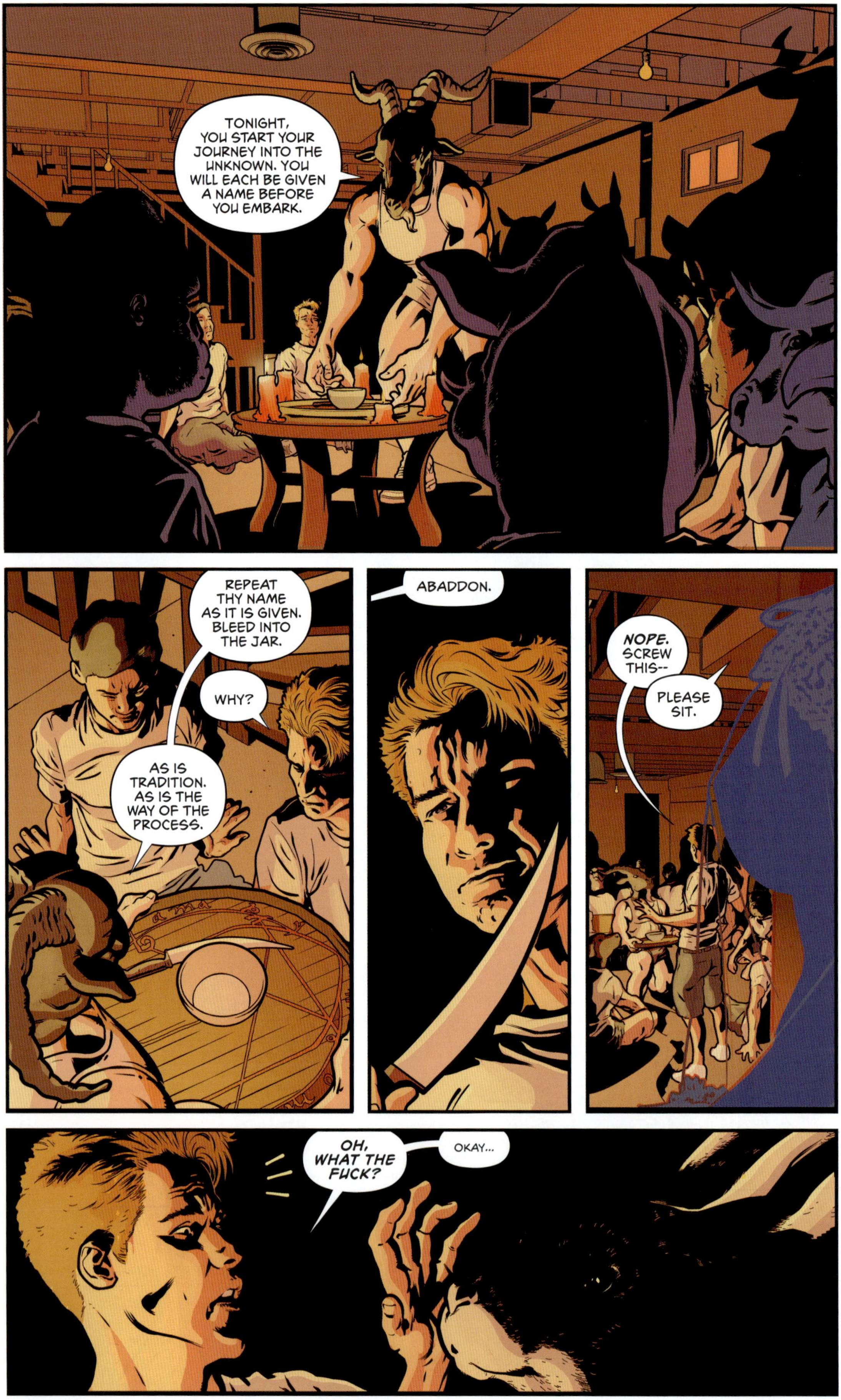
TONIGHT, YOU START YOUR JOURNEY INTO THE UNKNOWN. YOU WILL EACH BE GIVEN A NAME BEFORE YOU EMBARK.
REPEAT THY NAME AS IT IS GIVEN. BLEED INTO THE JAR.
WHY?
AS IS TRADITION. AS IS THE WAY OF THE PROCESS.
ABADDON.
NOPE. SCREW THIS--
PLEASE SIT.
OH, WHAT THE FUCK?
OKAY...

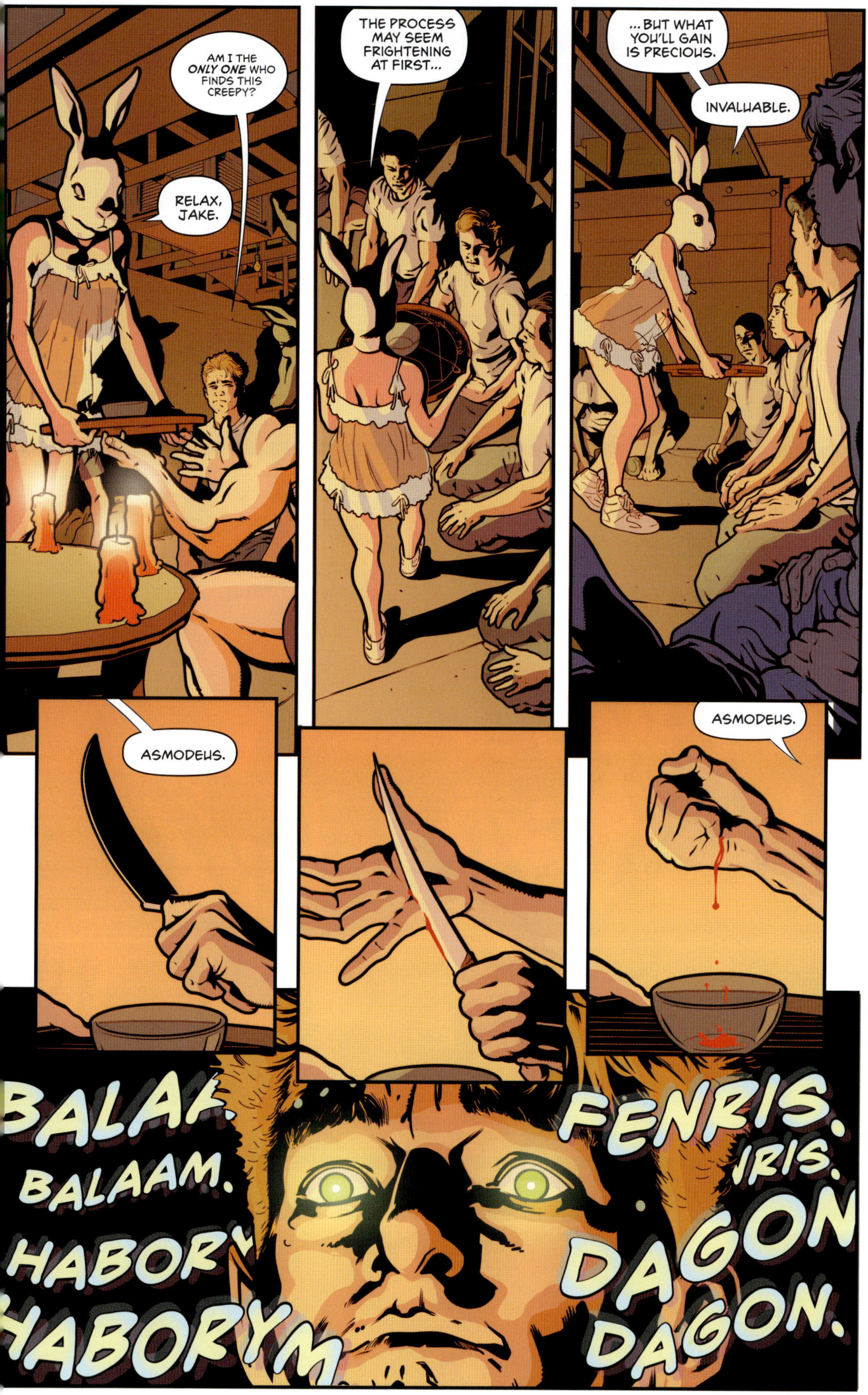
AM I THE *ONLY ONE* WHO FINDS THIS CREEPY?
RELAX, JAKE.
THE PROCESS MAY SEEM FRIGHTENING AT FIRST...
...BUT WHAT YOU'LL GAIN IS PRECIOUS.
INVALUABLE.
ASMODEUS.
ASMODEUS.
BALAAM.
HABORYM
FENRIS.
DAGON.
DAGON.

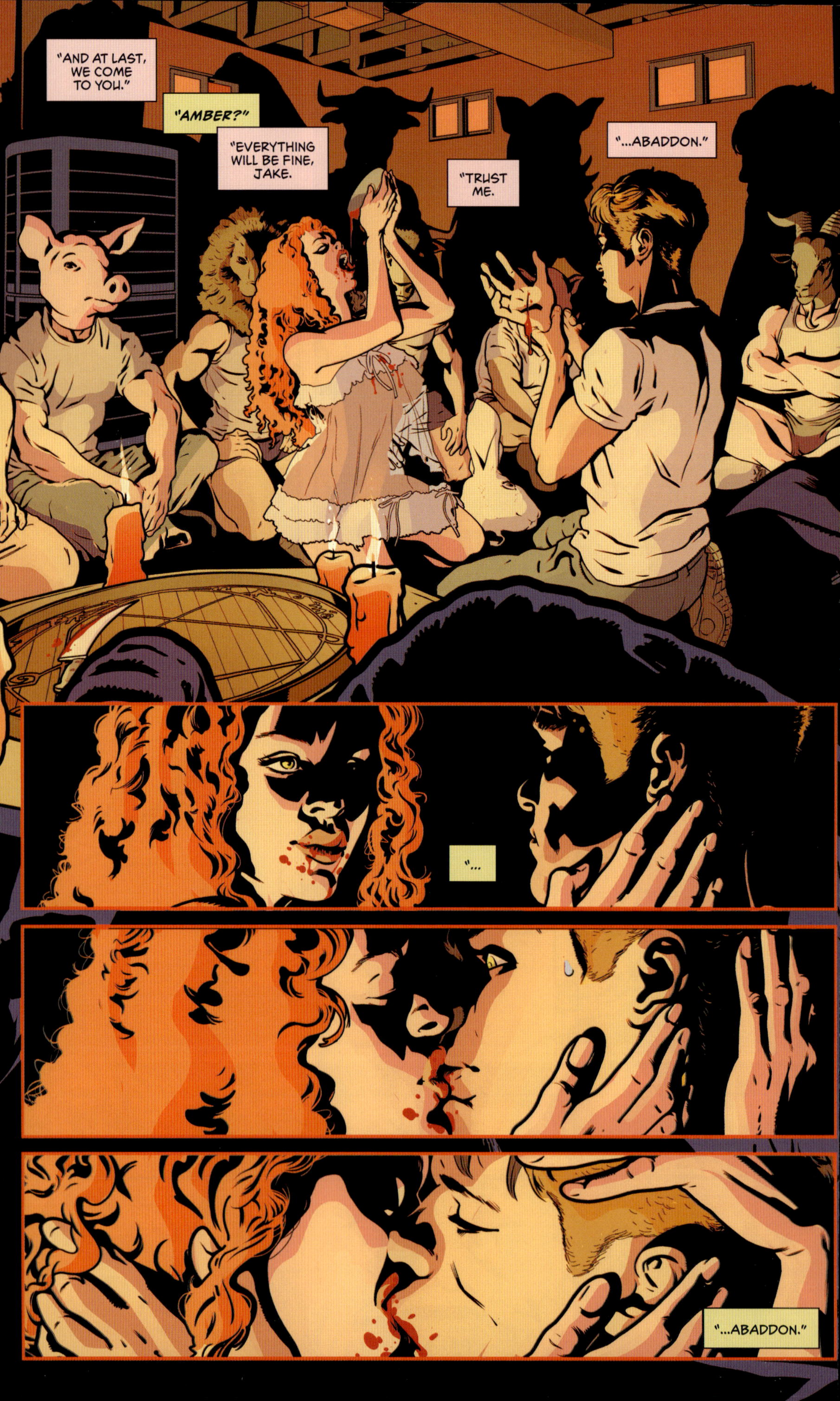
"AND AT LAST, WE COME TO YOU."
"AMBER?"
"EVERYTHING WILL BE FINE, JAKE.
"TRUST ME.
"...ABADDON."
"...
"...ABADDON."

CHAPTER TWO

DAYS GONE BY

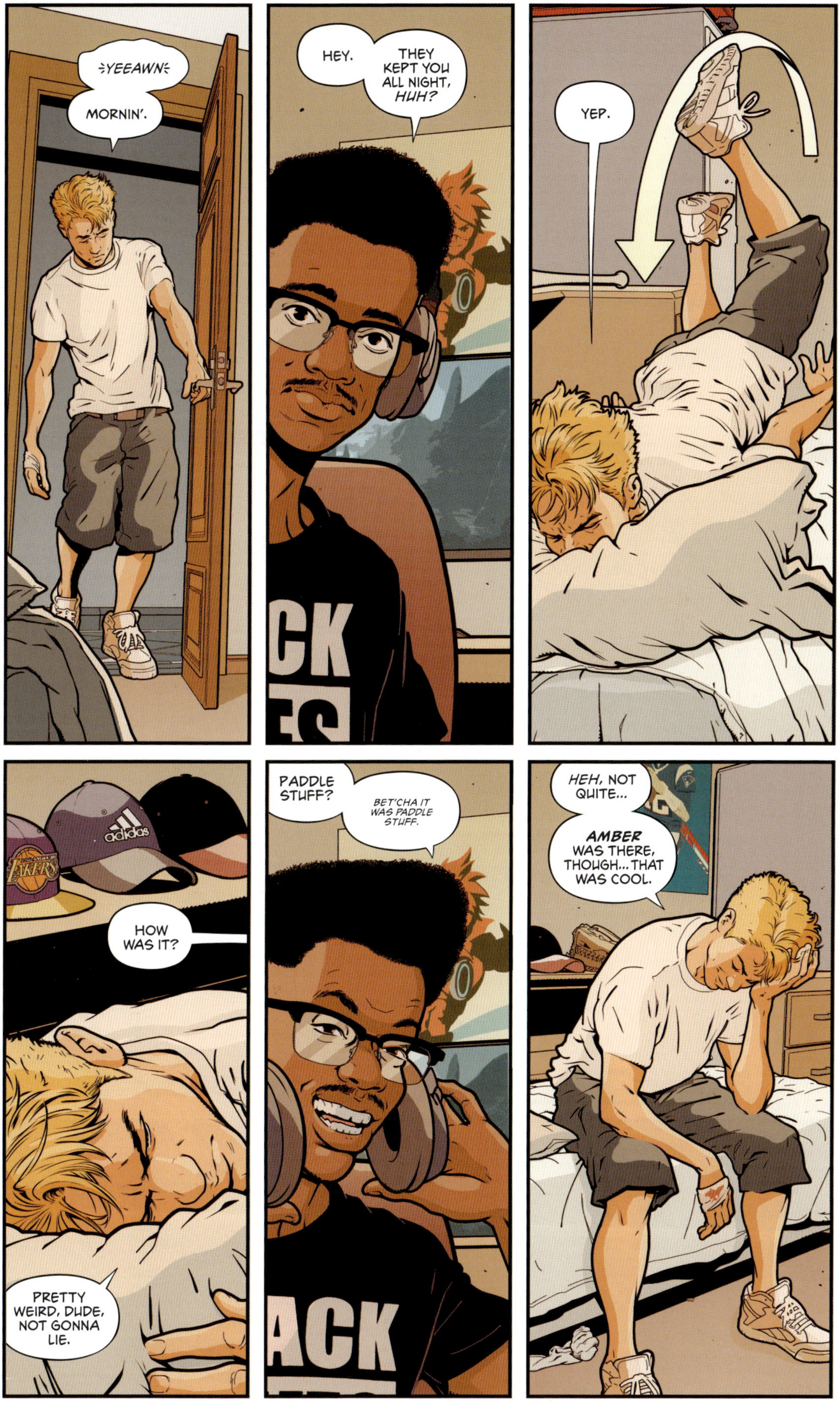

≑YEEAWN≑
MORNIN'.
HEY.
THEY KEPT YOU ALL NIGHT, *HUH?*
YEP.
HOW WAS IT?
PRETTY WEIRD, DUDE, NOT GONNA LIE.
PADDLE STUFF?
BET'CHA IT WAS PADDLE STUFF.
HEH, NOT QUITE...
AMBER WAS THERE, THOUGH... THAT WAS COOL.

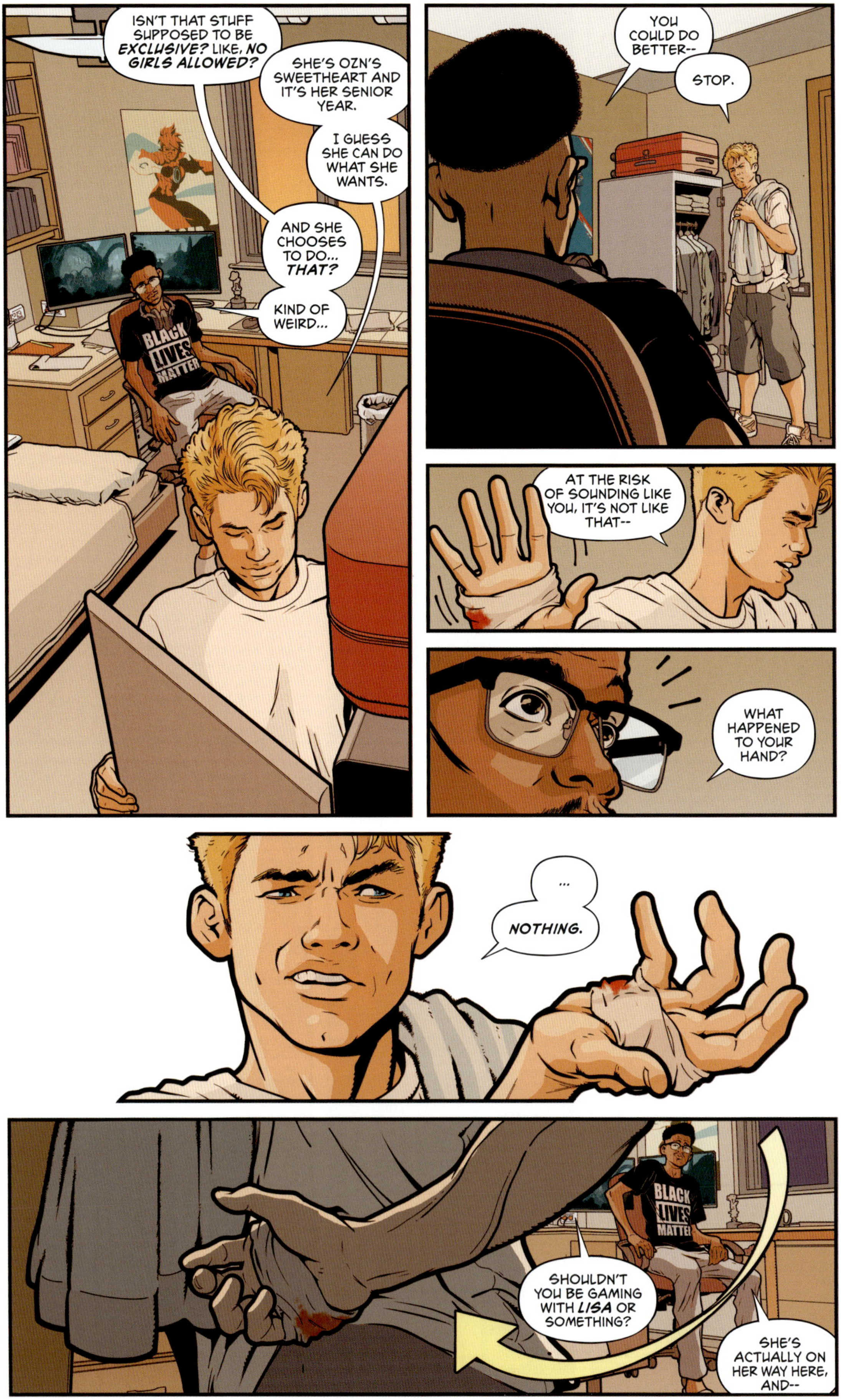
ISN'T THAT STUFF SUPPOSED TO BE *EXCLUSIVE?* LIKE, *NO GIRLS ALLOWED?*
SHE'S OZN'S SWEETHEART AND IT'S HER SENIOR YEAR.
I GUESS SHE CAN DO WHAT SHE WANTS.
AND SHE CHOOSES TO DO... *THAT?*
KIND OF WEIRD...
YOU COULD DO BETTER--
STOP.
AT THE RISK OF SOUNDING LIKE YOU, IT'S NOT LIKE THAT--
WHAT HAPPENED TO YOUR HAND?
...
NOTHING.
SHOULDN'T YOU BE GAMING WITH *LISA* OR SOMETHING?
SHE'S ACTUALLY ON HER WAY HERE, AND--

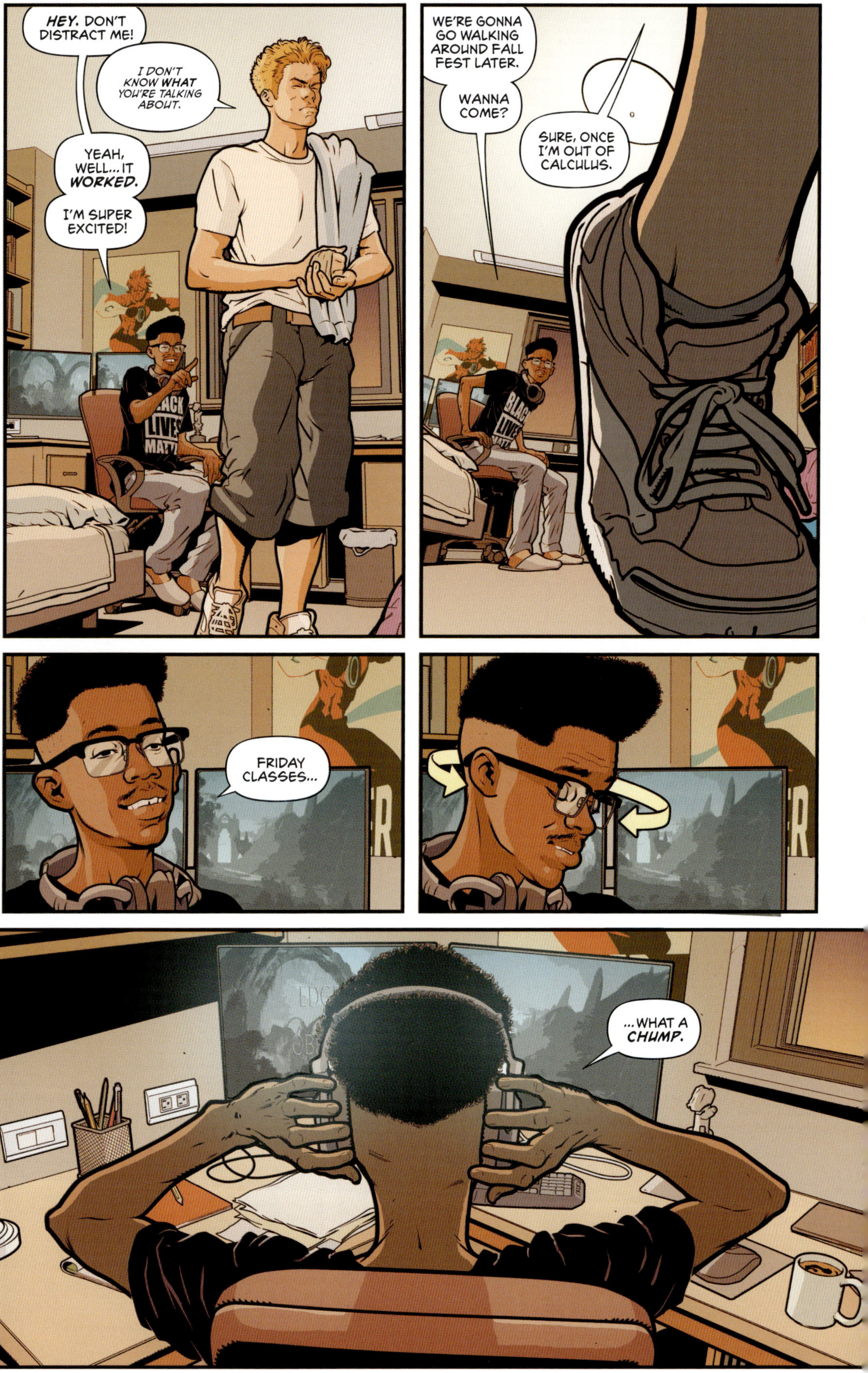
HEY. DON'T DISTRACT ME!
I DON'T KNOW WHAT YOU'RE TALKING ABOUT.
YEAH, WELL... IT WORKED.
I'M SUPER EXCITED!
WE'RE GONNA GO WALKING AROUND FALL FEST LATER.
WANNA COME?
SURE, ONCE I'M OUT OF CALCULUS.
FRIDAY CLASSES...
...WHAT A CHUMP.

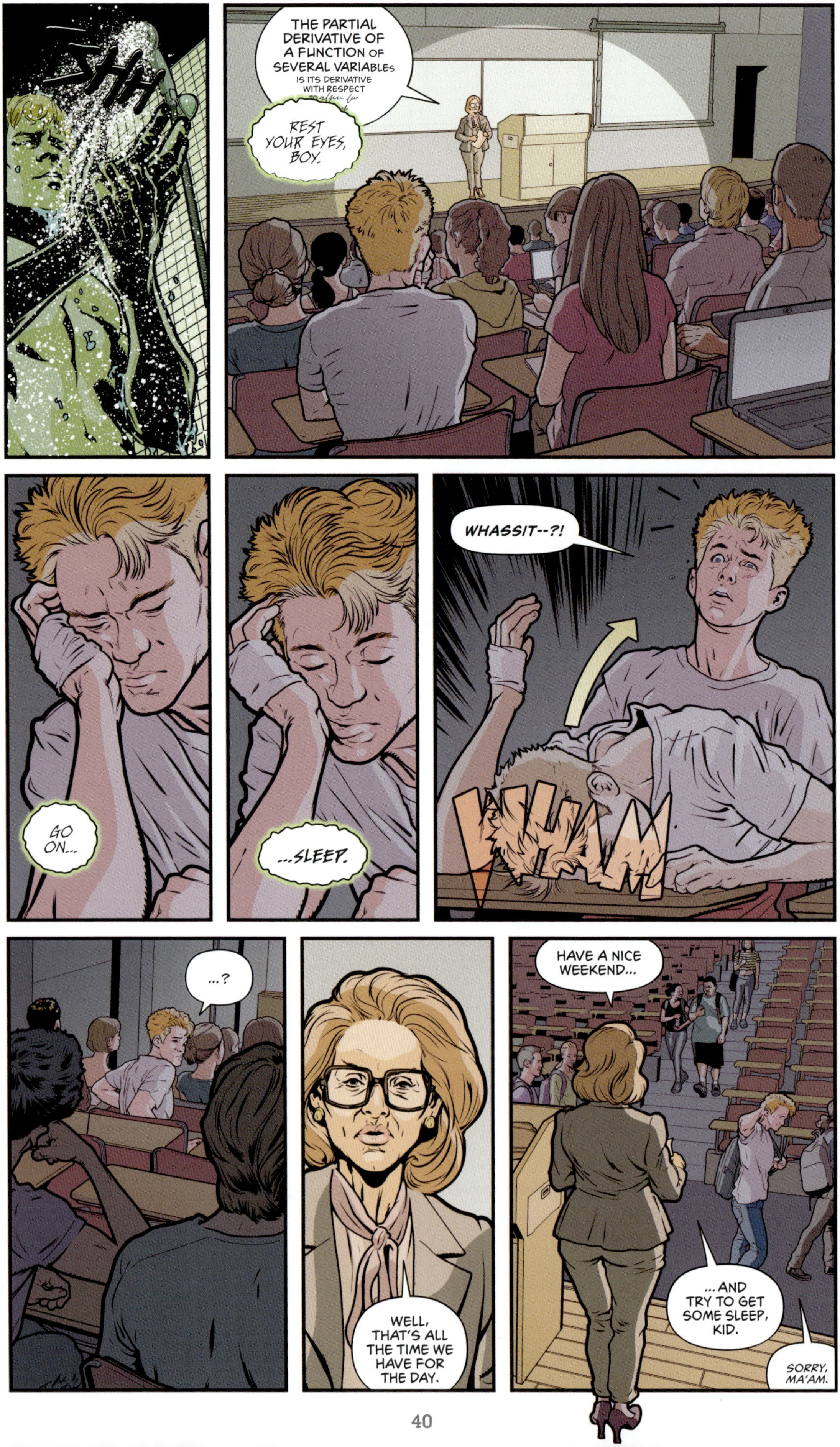
THE PARTIAL DERIVATIVE OF A FUNCTION OF SEVERAL VARIABLES IS ITS DERIVATIVE WITH RESPECT
REST YOUR EYES, BOY.
GO ON...
...SLEEP.
WHASSIT--?!
WHAM
...?
WELL, THAT'S ALL THE TIME WE HAVE FOR THE DAY.
HAVE A NICE WEEKEND...
...AND TRY TO GET SOME SLEEP, KID.
SORRY, MA'AM.

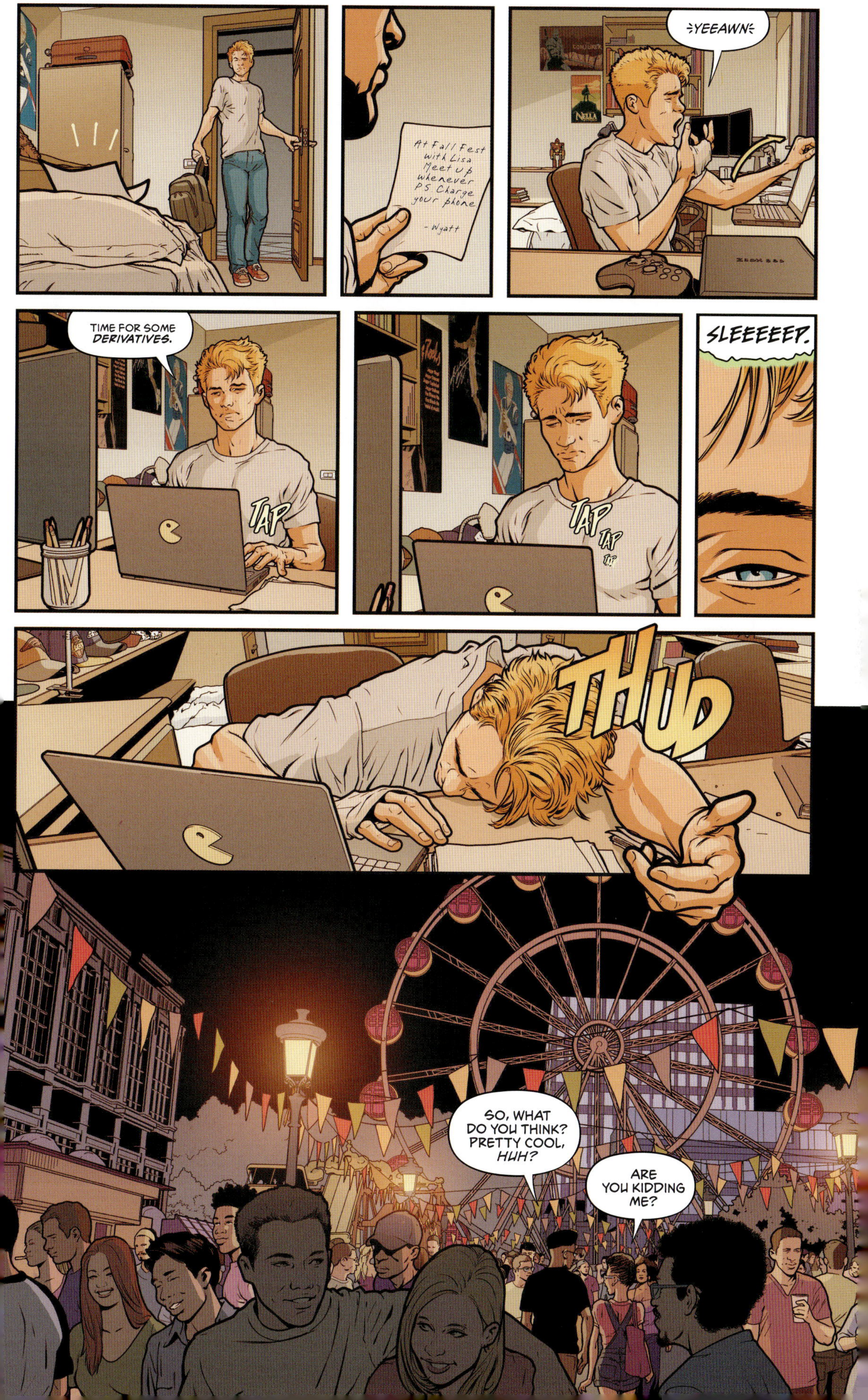
At Fall Fest
with Lisa
Meet up
whenever
PS Charge
your phone
- Wyatt
YEEAWN
TIME FOR SOME DERIVATIVES.
TAP
TAP TAP
SLEEEEEP.
THUD
SO, WHAT DO YOU THINK? PRETTY COOL, HUH?
ARE YOU KIDDING ME?

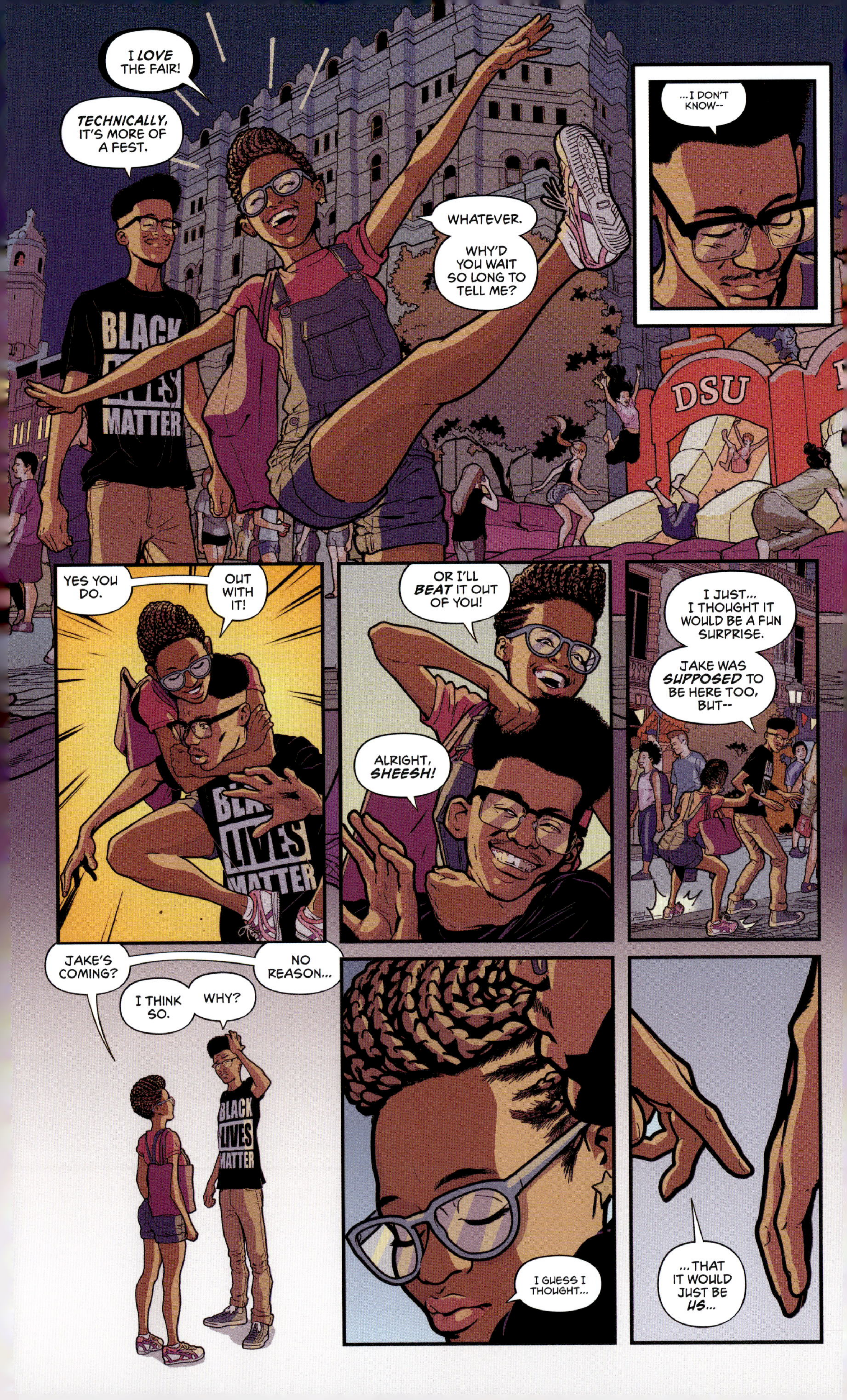
I LOVE THE FAIR!
TECHNICALLY, IT'S MORE OF A FEST.
WHATEVER.
WHY'D YOU WAIT SO LONG TO TELL ME?
...I DON'T KNOW--
BLACK LIVES MATTER
DSU
YES YOU DO.
OUT WITH IT!
OR I'LL BEAT IT OUT OF YOU!
ALRIGHT, SHEESH!
I JUST... I THOUGHT IT WOULD BE A FUN SURPRISE.
JAKE WAS SUPPOSED TO BE HERE TOO, BUT--
JAKE'S COMING?
I THINK SO.
WHY?
NO REASON...
I GUESS I THOUGHT...
...THAT IT WOULD JUST BE US...

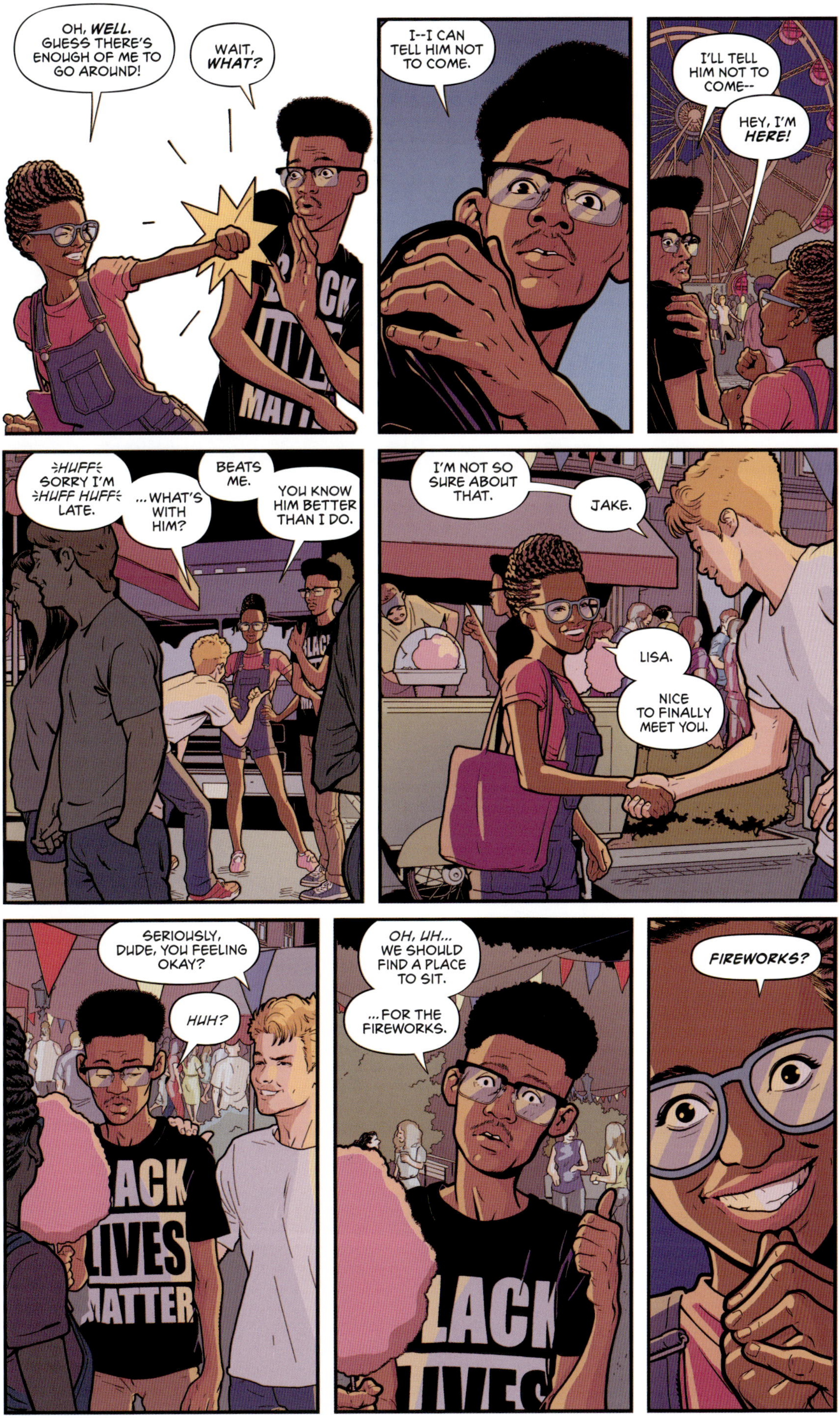

OH, WELL. GUESS THERE'S ENOUGH OF ME TO GO AROUND!
WAIT, WHAT?
BLACK LIVES MATTER
I--I CAN TELL HIM NOT TO COME.
I'LL TELL HIM NOT TO COME--
HEY, I'M HERE!
HUFF SORRY I'M HUFF HUFF LATE.
...WHAT'S WITH HIM?
BEATS ME.
YOU KNOW HIM BETTER THAN I DO.
I'M NOT SO SURE ABOUT THAT.
JAKE.
LISA.
NICE TO FINALLY MEET YOU.
SERIOUSLY, DUDE, YOU FEELING OKAY?
HUH?
BLACK LIVES MATTER
OH, UH... WE SHOULD FIND A PLACE TO SIT.
...FOR THE FIREWORKS.
FIREWORKS?

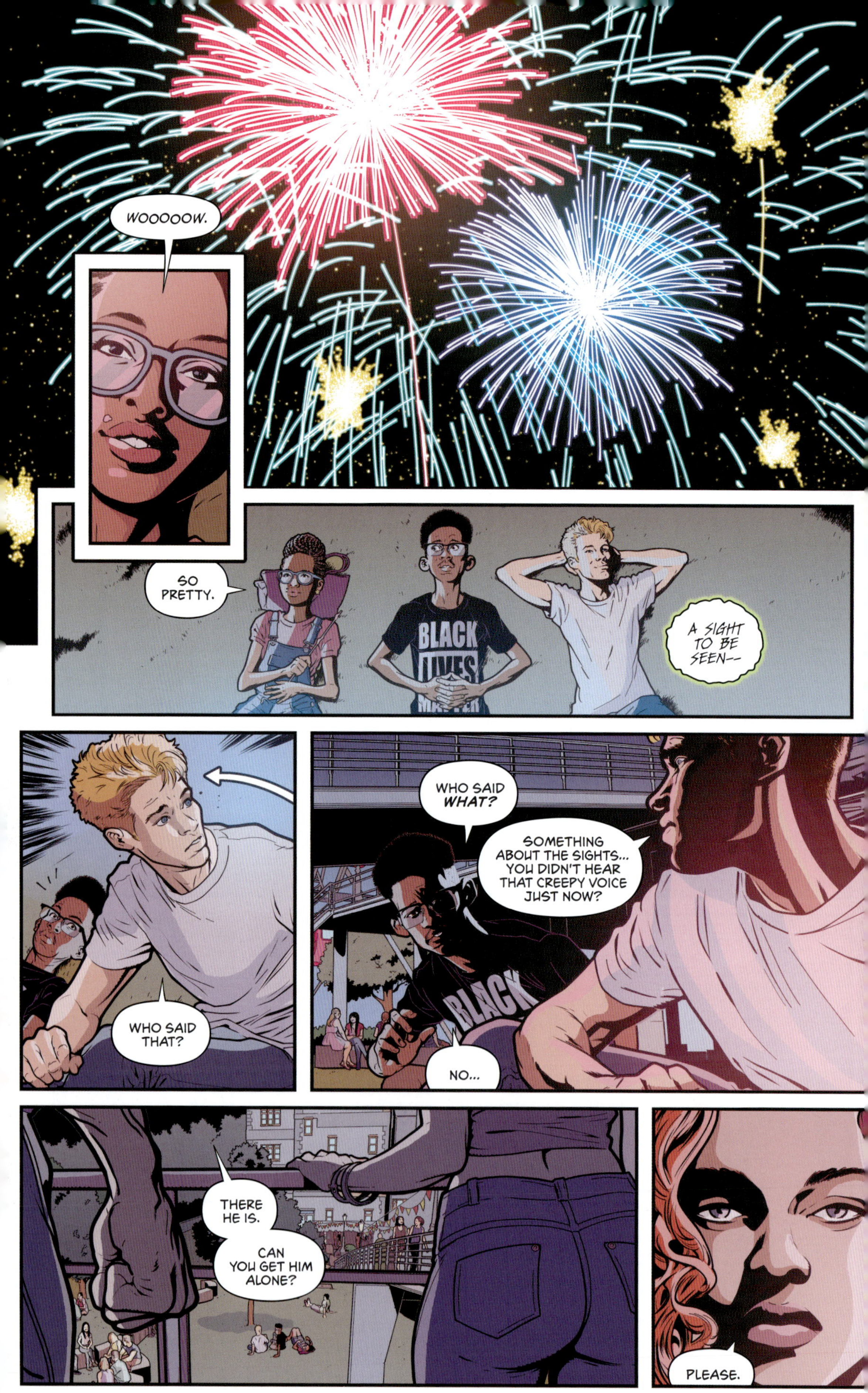
WOOOOOW.
SO PRETTY.
A SIGHT TO BE SEEN--
WHO SAID THAT?
WHO SAID *WHAT?*
SOMETHING ABOUT THE SIGHTS... YOU DIDN'T HEAR THAT CREEPY VOICE JUST NOW?
NO...
THERE HE IS.
CAN YOU GET HIM ALONE?
PLEASE.

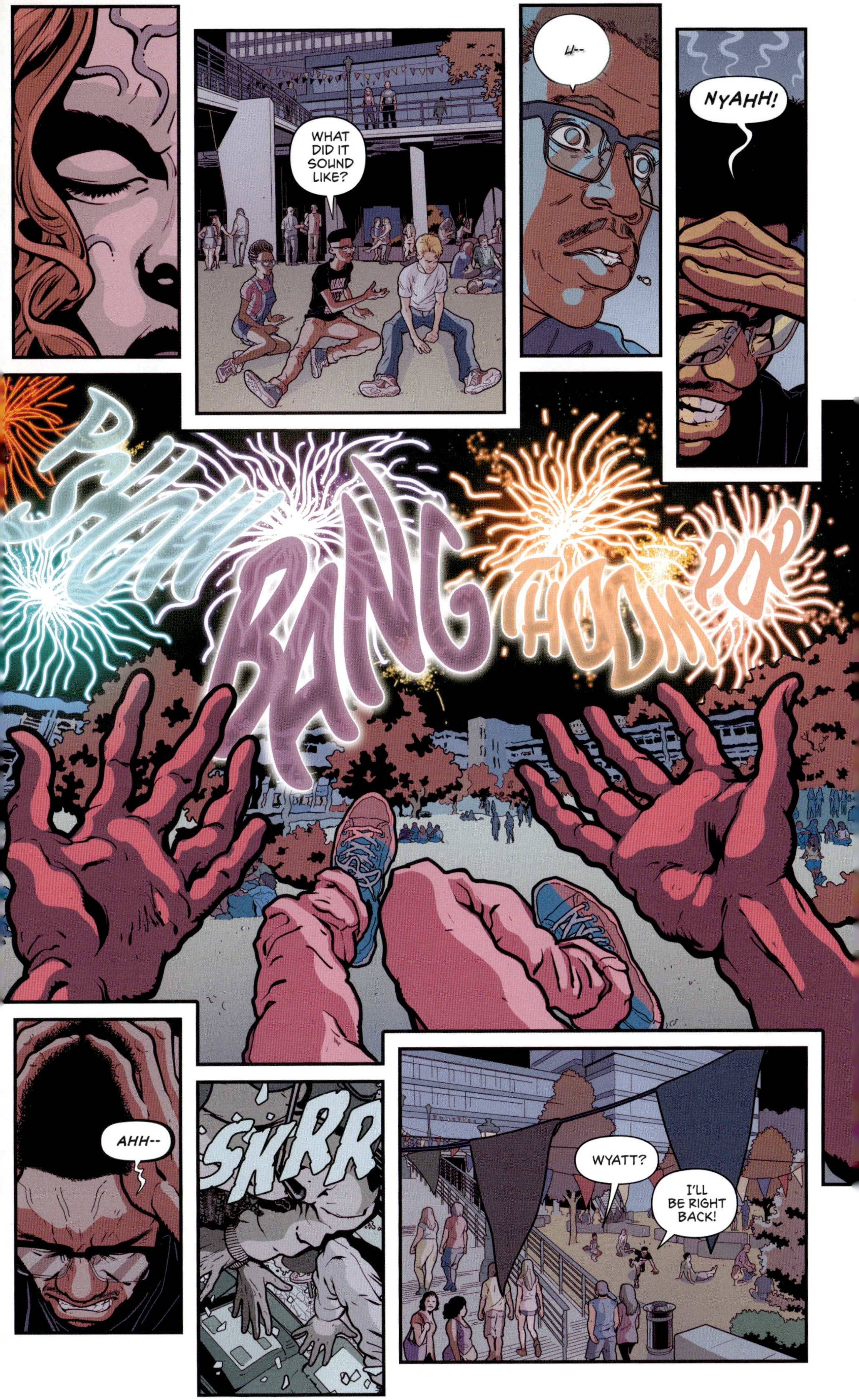
WHAT DID IT SOUND LIKE?
U--
NYAHH!
BANG
THOOM
POP
AHH--
SKRR
WYATT?
I'LL BE RIGHT BACK!

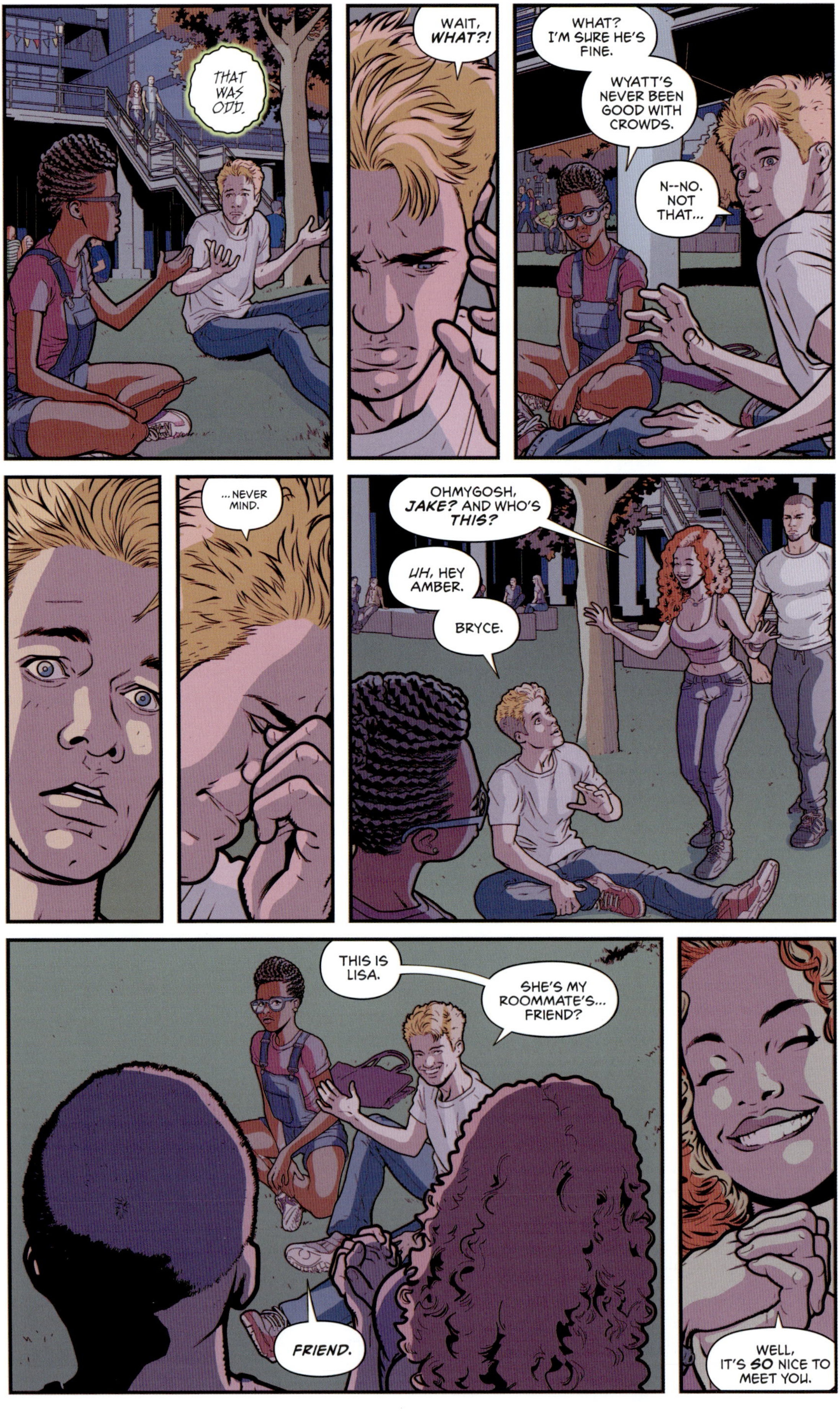
THAT WAS ODD.
WAIT, *WHAT?!*
WHAT? I'M SURE HE'S FINE.
WYATT'S NEVER BEEN GOOD WITH CROWDS.
N--NO. NOT THAT...
...NEVER MIND.
OHMYGOSH, *JAKE?* AND WHO'S *THIS?*
UH, HEY AMBER.
BRYCE.
THIS IS LISA.
SHE'S MY ROOMMATE'S... FRIEND?
FRIEND.
WELL, IT'S *SO* NICE TO MEET YOU.

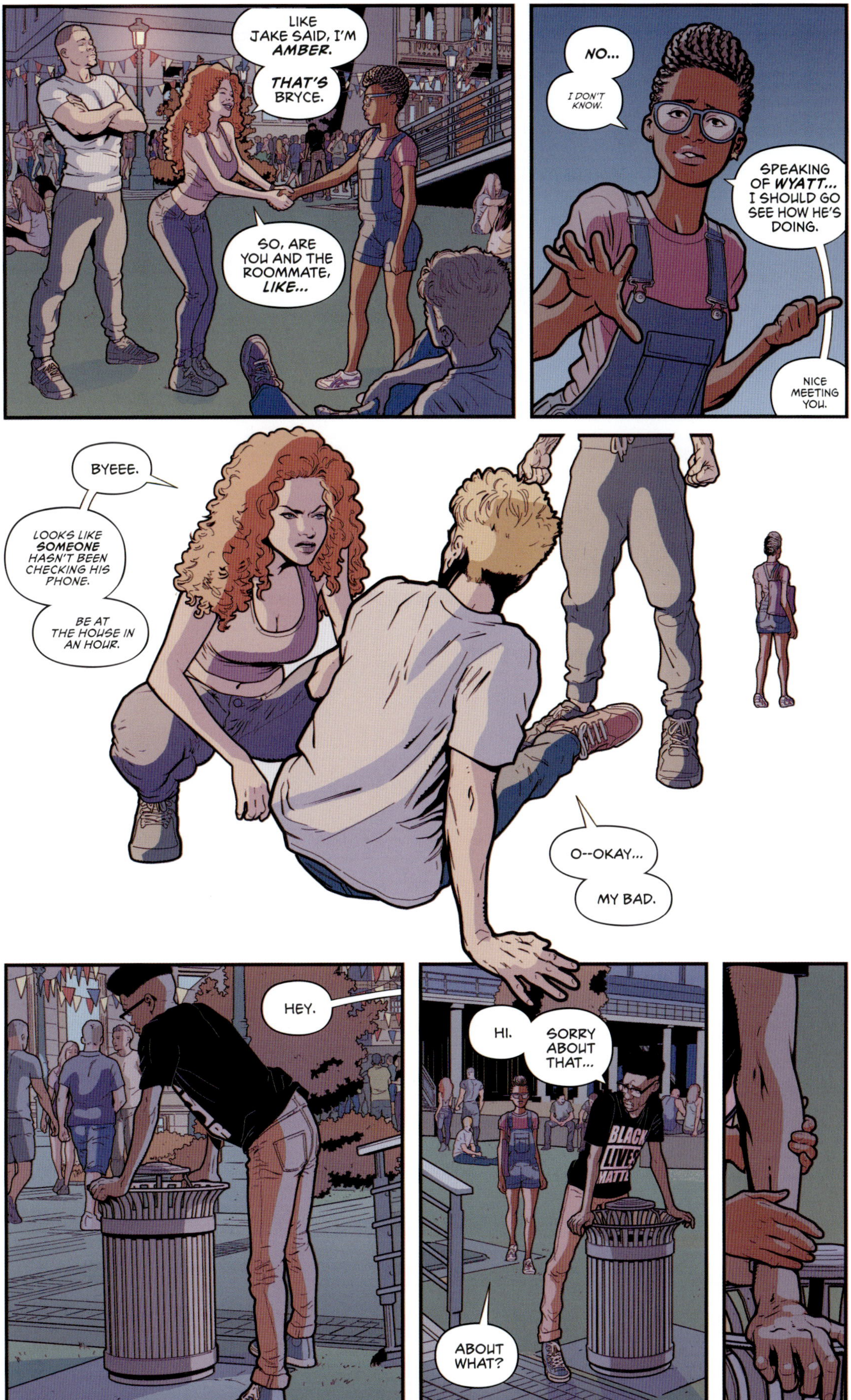

LIKE JAKE SAID, I'M AMBER.
THAT'S BRYCE.
SO, ARE YOU AND THE ROOMMATE, LIKE...
NO...
I DON'T KNOW.
SPEAKING OF WYATT... I SHOULD GO SEE HOW HE'S DOING.
NICE MEETING YOU.
BYEEE.
LOOKS LIKE SOMEONE HASN'T BEEN CHECKING HIS PHONE.
BE AT THE HOUSE IN AN HOUR.
O--OKAY...
MY BAD.
HEY.
HI.
SORRY ABOUT THAT...
ABOUT WHAT?
BLACK LIVES MATTER

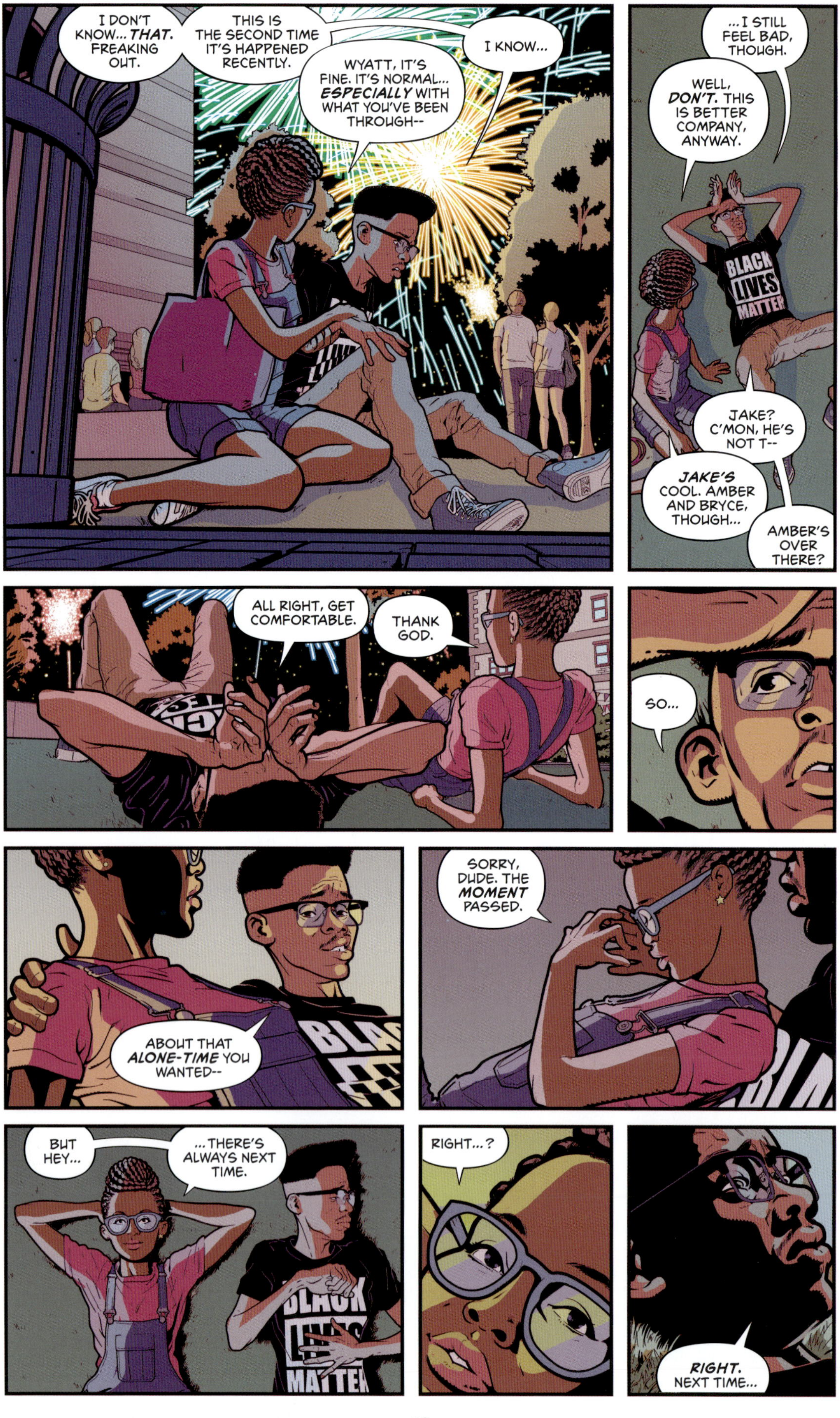
I DON'T KNOW... *THAT.* FREAKING OUT.
THIS IS THE SECOND TIME IT'S HAPPENED RECENTLY.
I KNOW...
WYATT, IT'S FINE. IT'S NORMAL... *ESPECIALLY* WITH WHAT YOU'VE BEEN THROUGH--
...I STILL FEEL BAD, THOUGH.
WELL, *DON'T.* THIS IS BETTER COMPANY, ANYWAY.
BLACK LIVES MATTER
JAKE? C'MON, HE'S NOT T--
JAKE'S COOL. AMBER AND BRYCE, THOUGH...
AMBER'S OVER THERE?
ALL RIGHT, GET COMFORTABLE.
THANK GOD.
SO...
ABOUT THAT *ALONE-TIME* YOU WANTED--
SORRY, DUDE. THE *MOMENT* PASSED.
BUT HEY...
...THERE'S ALWAYS NEXT TIME.
BLACK LIVES MATTER
RIGHT...?
RIGHT. NEXT TIME...

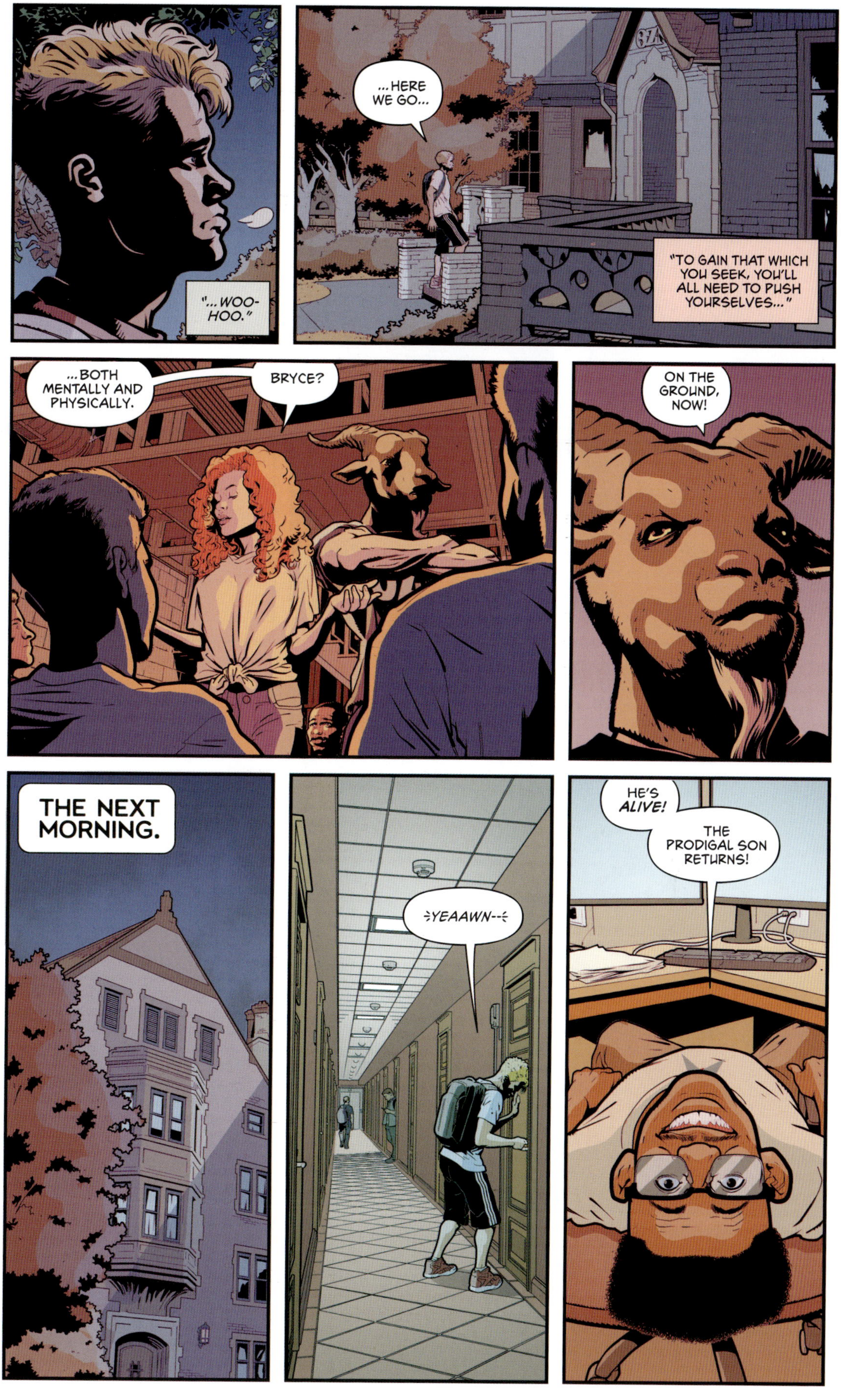
"...WOO-HOO."
...HERE WE GO...
"TO GAIN THAT WHICH YOU SEEK, YOU'LL ALL NEED TO PUSH YOURSELVES..."
...BOTH MENTALLY AND PHYSICALLY.
BRYCE?
ON THE GROUND, NOW!
THE NEXT MORNING.
YEAAWN--
HE'S ALIVE!
THE PRODIGAL SON RETURNS!

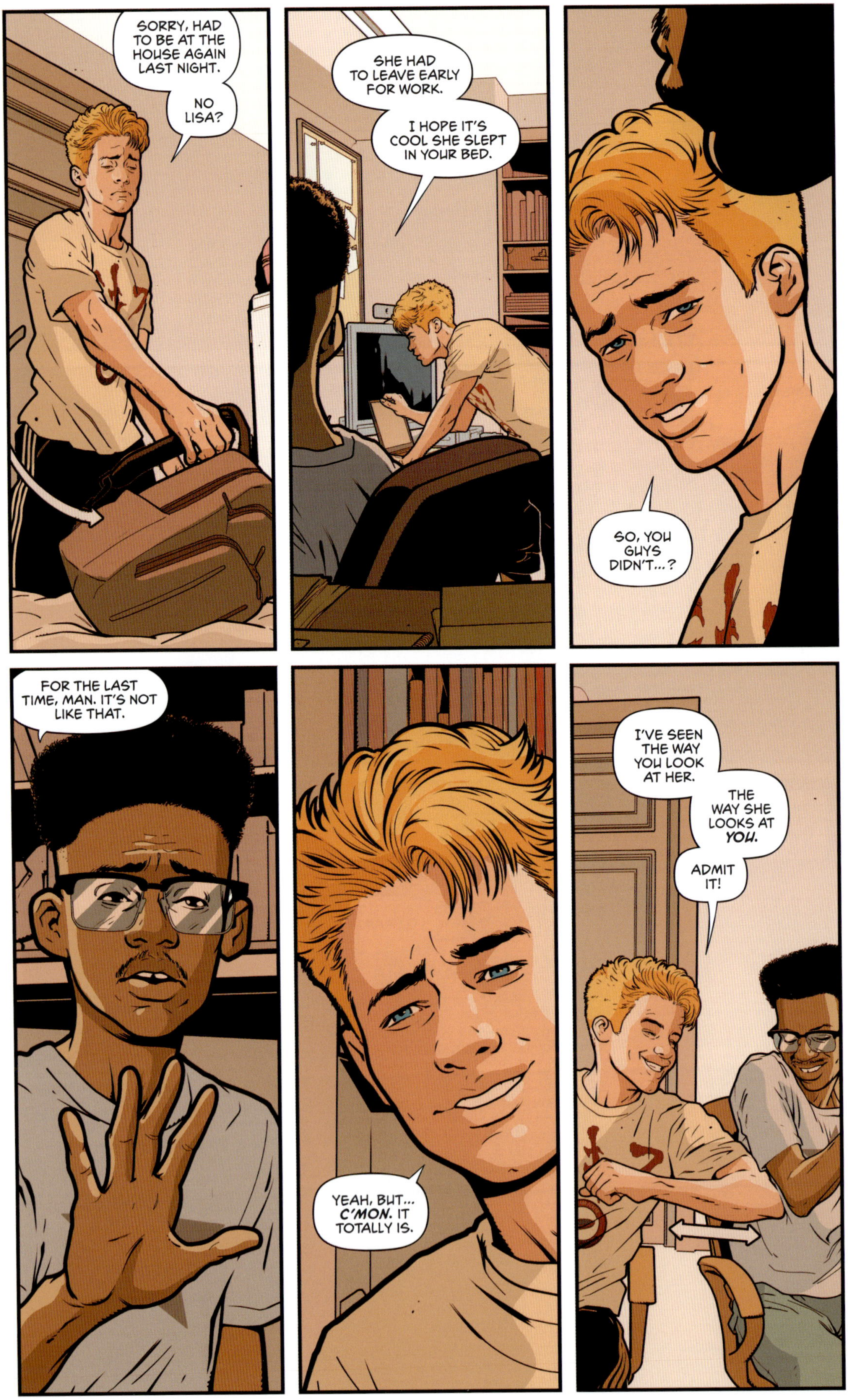

SORRY, HAD TO BE AT THE HOUSE AGAIN LAST NIGHT.
NO LISA?
SHE HAD TO LEAVE EARLY FOR WORK.
I HOPE IT'S COOL SHE SLEPT IN YOUR BED.
SO, YOU GUYS DIDN'T...?
FOR THE LAST TIME, MAN. IT'S NOT LIKE THAT.
YEAH, BUT... C'MON. IT TOTALLY IS.
I'VE SEEN THE WAY YOU LOOK AT HER.
THE WAY SHE LOOKS AT YOU.
ADMIT IT!

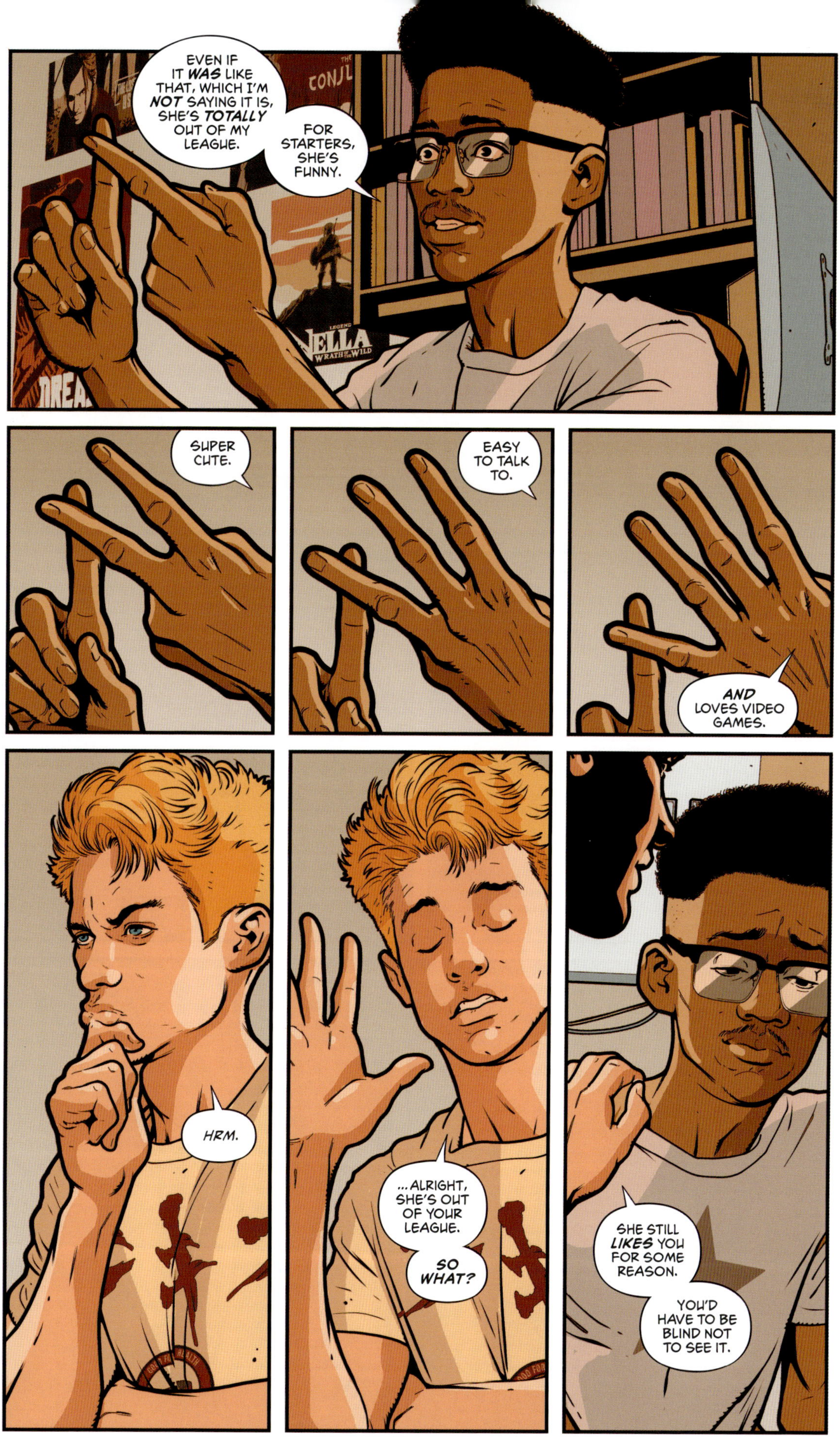
EVEN IF IT WAS LIKE THAT, WHICH I'M NOT SAYING IT IS, SHE'S TOTALLY OUT OF MY LEAGUE.
FOR STARTERS, SHE'S FUNNY.
SUPER CUTE.
EASY TO TALK TO.
AND LOVES VIDEO GAMES.
HRM.
...ALRIGHT, SHE'S OUT OF YOUR LEAGUE.
SO WHAT?
SHE STILL LIKES YOU FOR SOME REASON.
YOU'D HAVE TO BE BLIND NOT TO SEE IT.

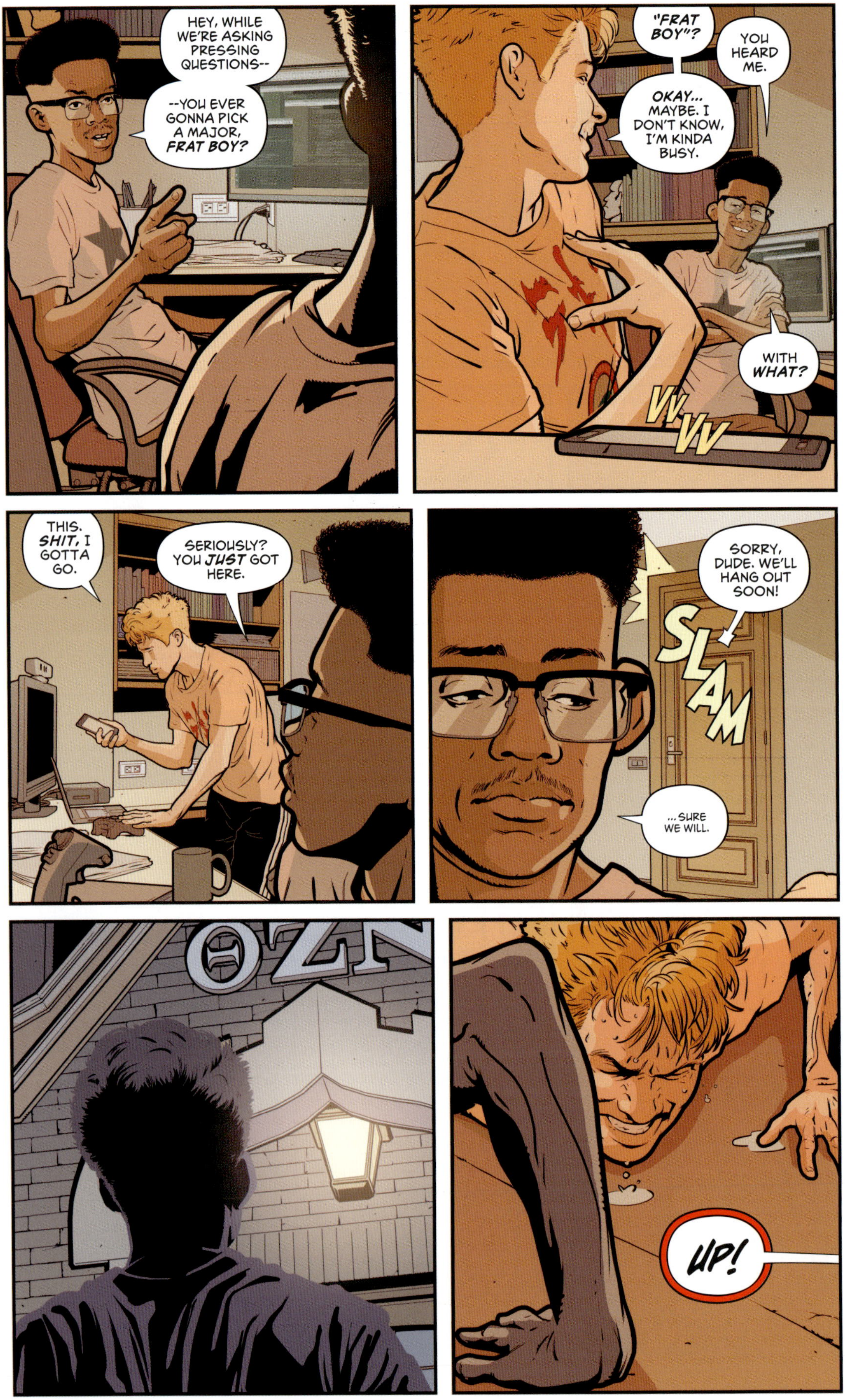
HEY, WHILE WE'RE ASKING PRESSING QUESTIONS--
--YOU EVER GONNA PICK A MAJOR, FRAT BOY?
"FRAT BOY"?
YOU HEARD ME.
OKAY... MAYBE. I DON'T KNOW, I'M KINDA BUSY.
WITH WHAT?
VVVV
THIS. SHIT, I GOTTA GO.
SERIOUSLY? YOU JUST GOT HERE.
SORRY, DUDE. WE'LL HANG OUT SOON!
SLAM
...SURE WE WILL.
UP!

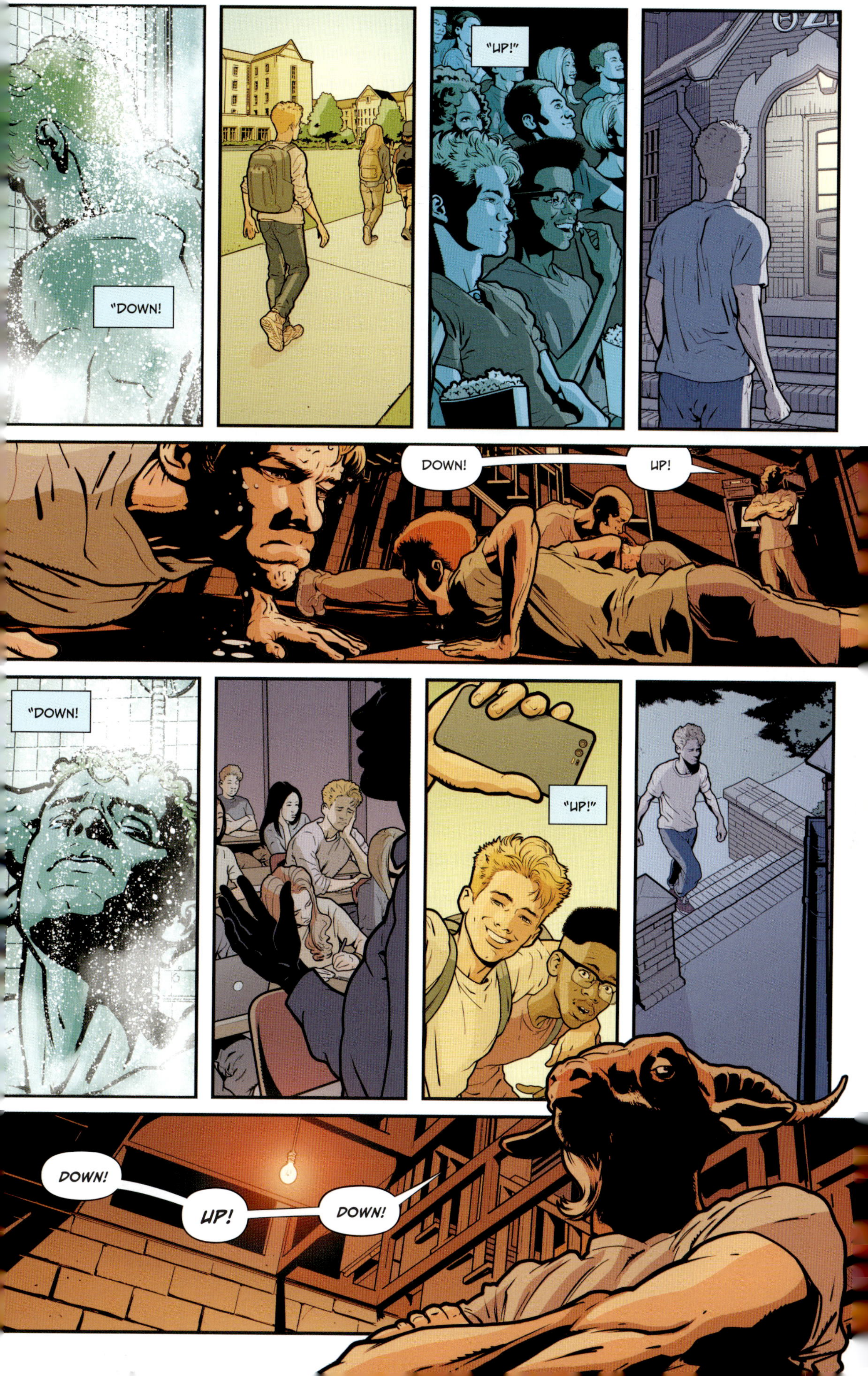
"DOWN!
"UP!"
DOWN!
UP!
"DOWN!
"UP!"
DOWN!
UP!
DOWN!

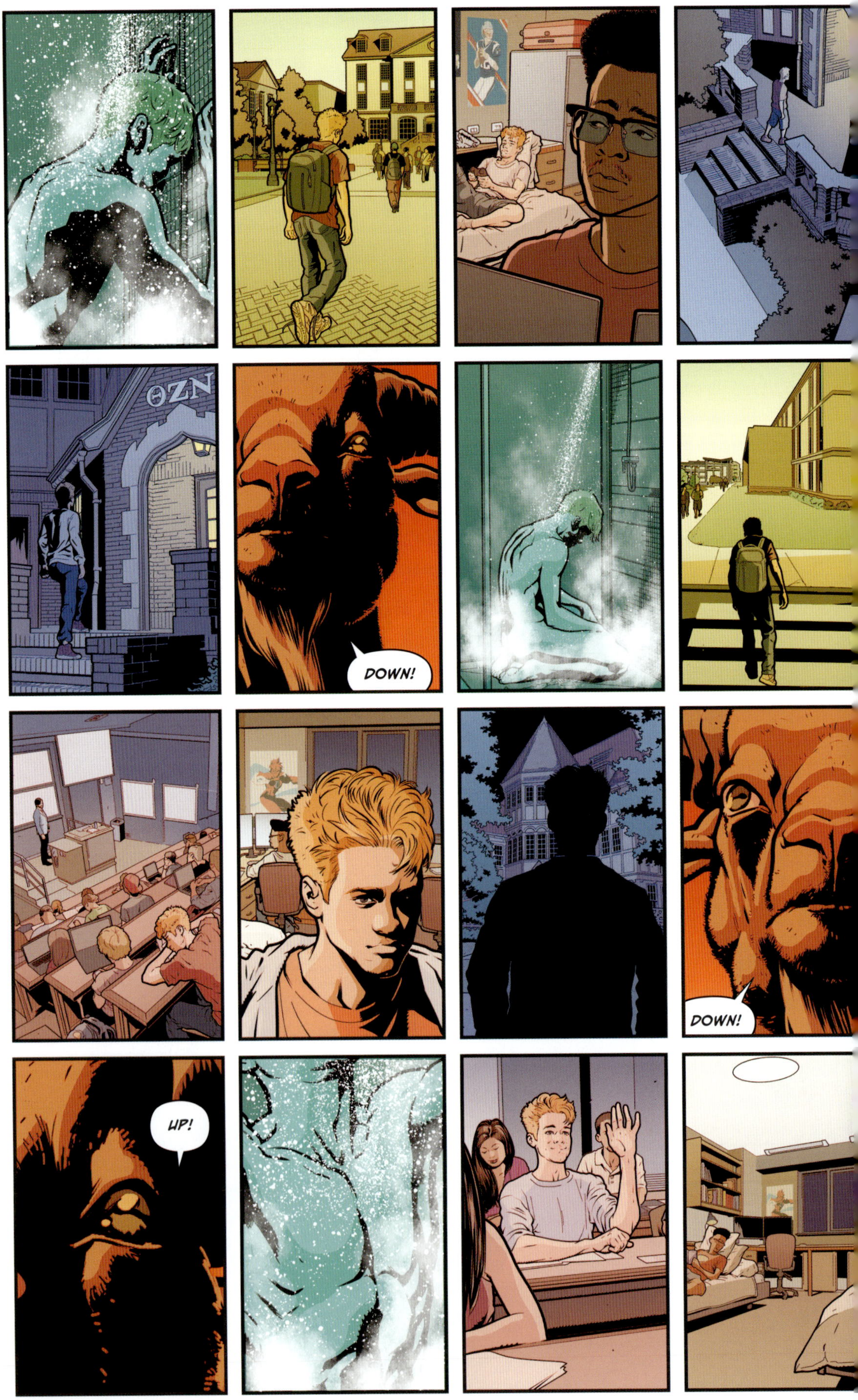
DOWN!
DOWN!
UP!

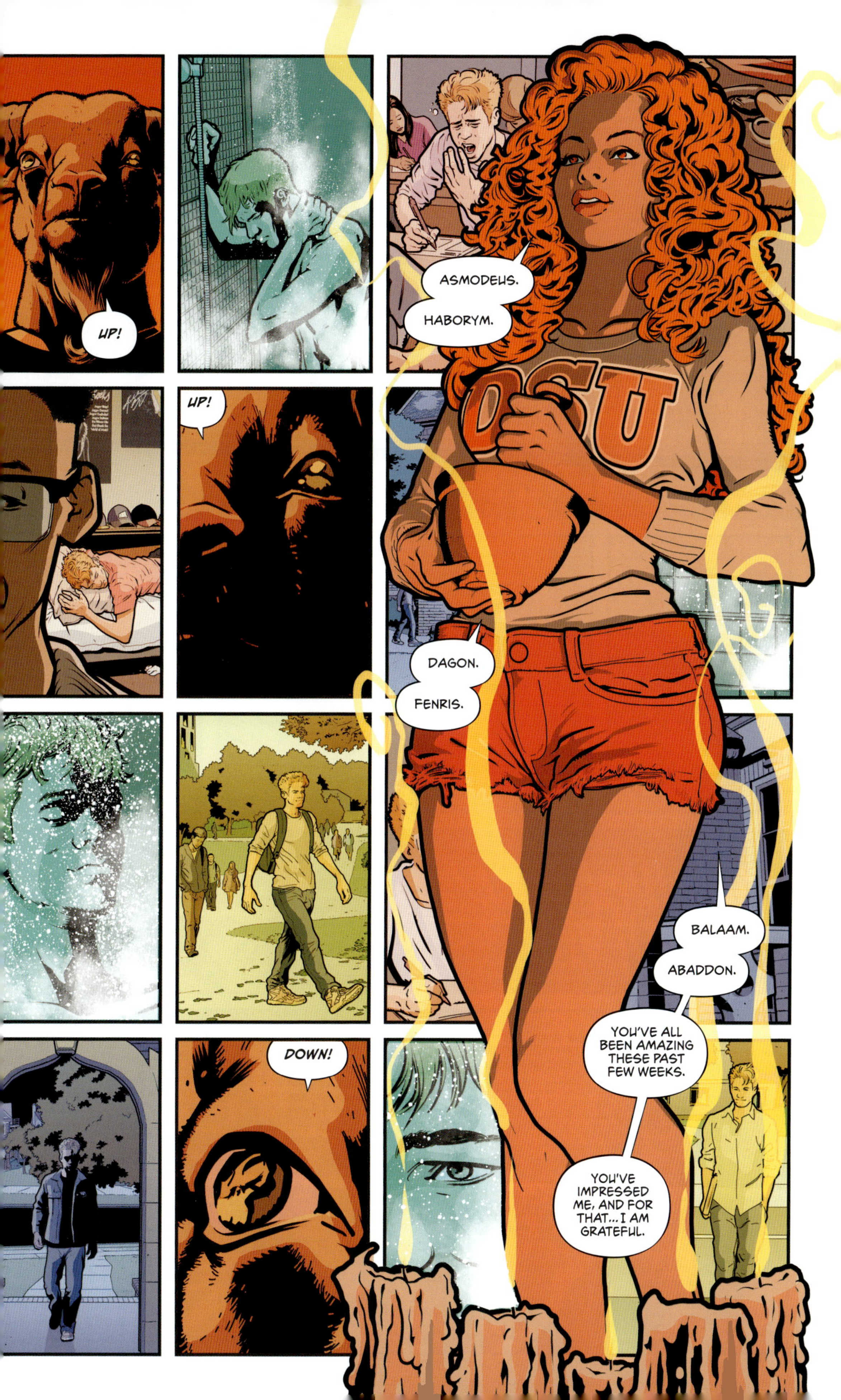
UP!
ASMODEUS.
HABORYM.
UP!
DAGON.
FENRIS.
BALAAM.
ABADDON.
YOU'VE ALL BEEN AMAZING THESE PAST FEW WEEKS.
DOWN!
YOU'VE IMPRESSED ME, AND FOR THAT... I AM GRATEFUL.

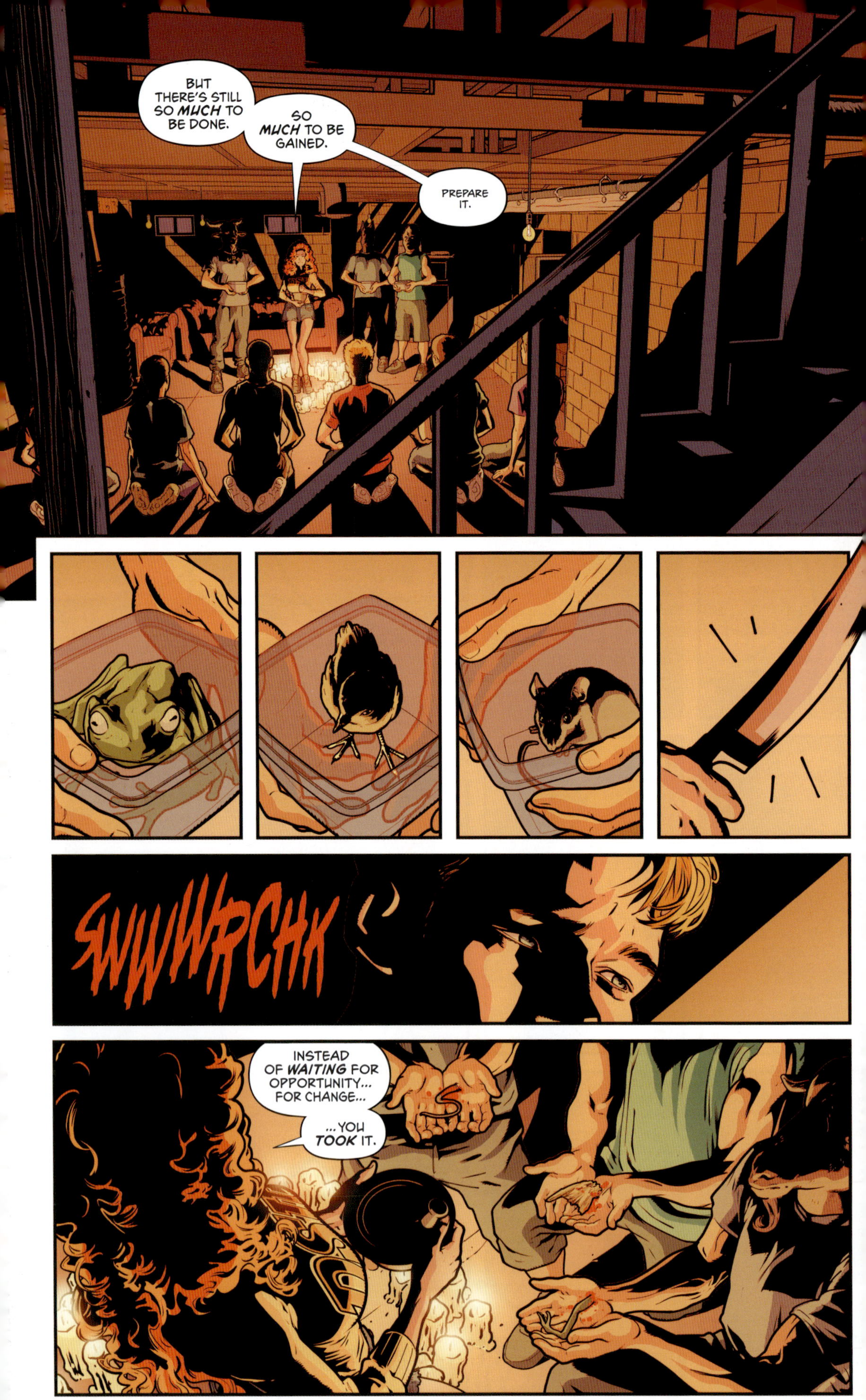

BUT THERE'S STILL SO MUCH TO BE DONE.
SO MUCH TO BE GAINED.
PREPARE IT.
SWWRCHK
INSTEAD OF WAITING FOR OPPORTUNITY... FOR CHANGE...
...YOU TOOK IT.

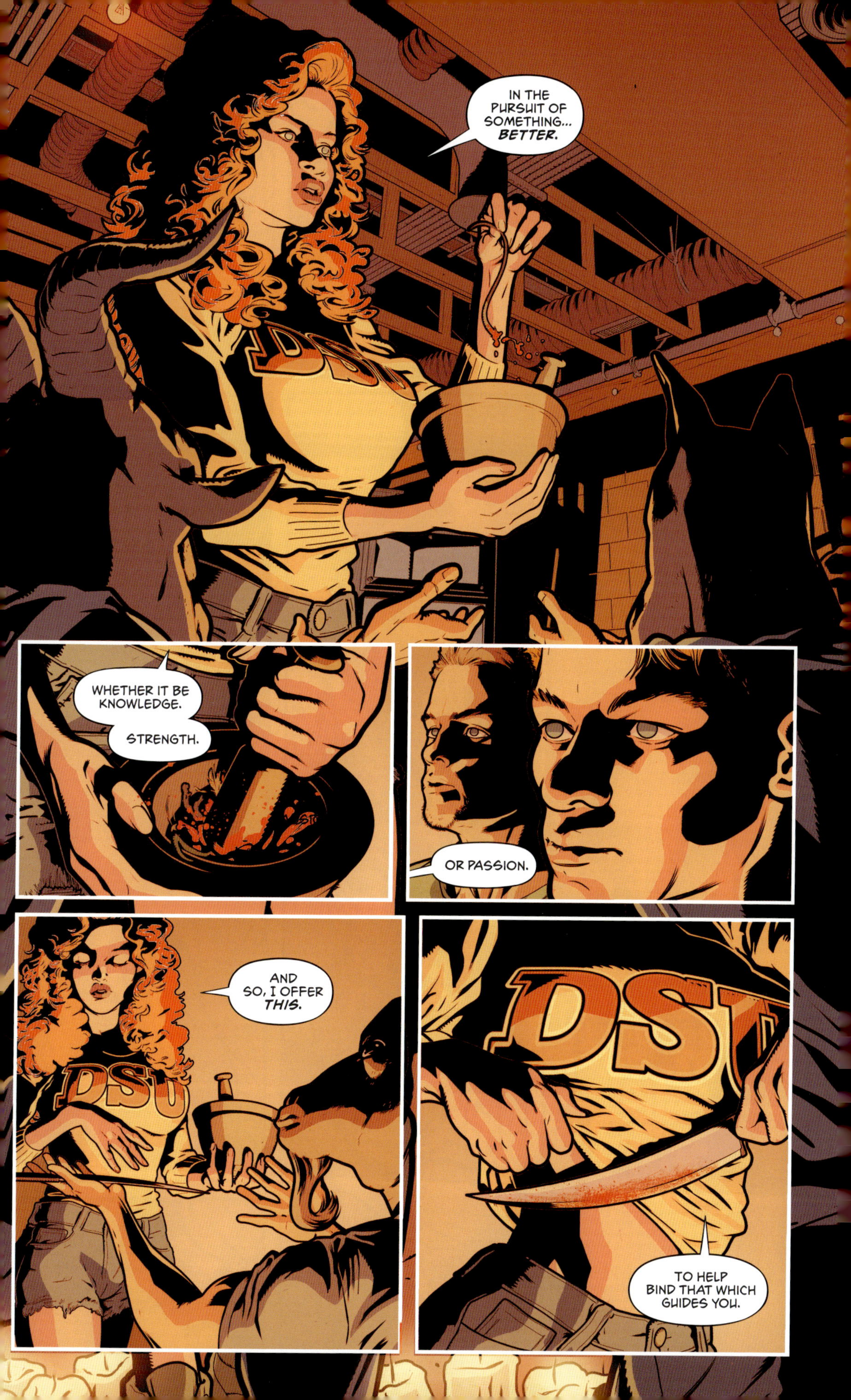
IN THE PURSUIT OF SOMETHING... *BETTER.*
WHETHER IT BE KNOWLEDGE.
STRENGTH.
OR PASSION.
AND SO, I OFFER *THIS.*
DSU
DS
TO HELP BIND THAT WHICH GUIDES YOU.

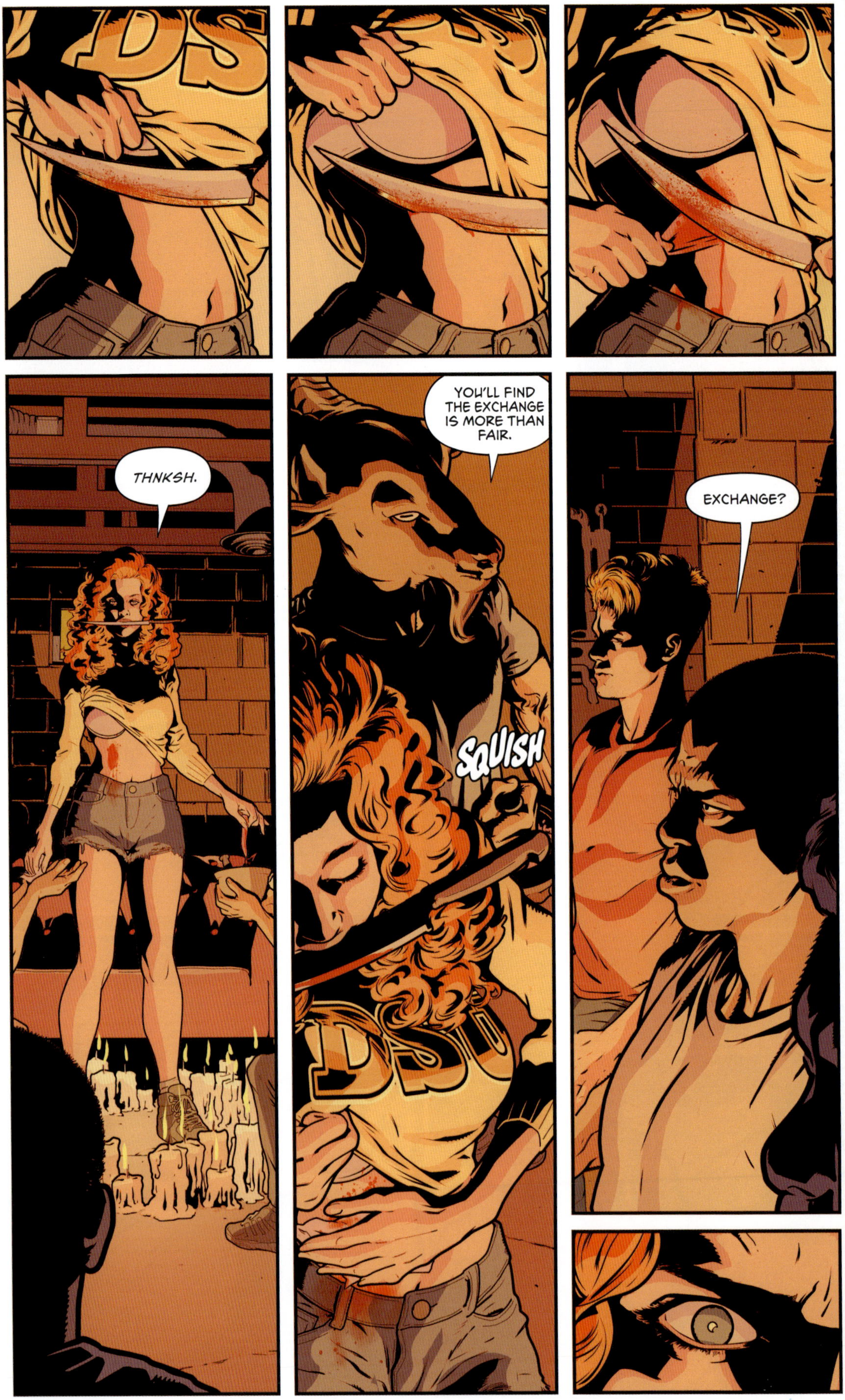
THNKSH.
YOU'LL FIND THE EXCHANGE IS MORE THAN FAIR.
SQUISH
EXCHANGE?

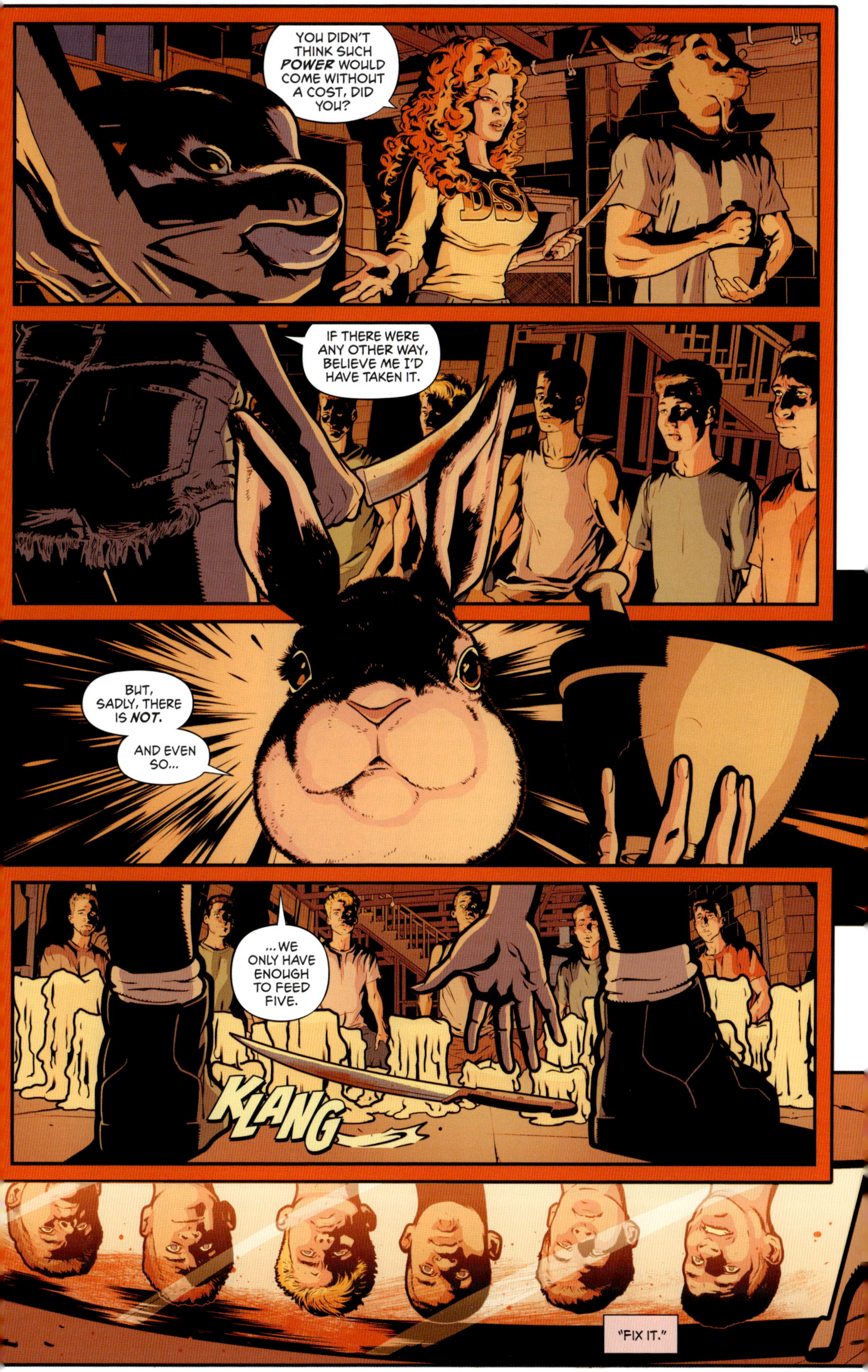
YOU DIDN'T THINK SUCH *POWER* WOULD COME WITHOUT A COST, DID YOU?
IF THERE WERE ANY OTHER WAY, BELIEVE ME I'D HAVE TAKEN IT.
BUT, SADLY, THERE IS *NOT.*
AND EVEN SO...
...WE ONLY HAVE ENOUGH TO FEED FIVE.
KLANG
"FIX IT."

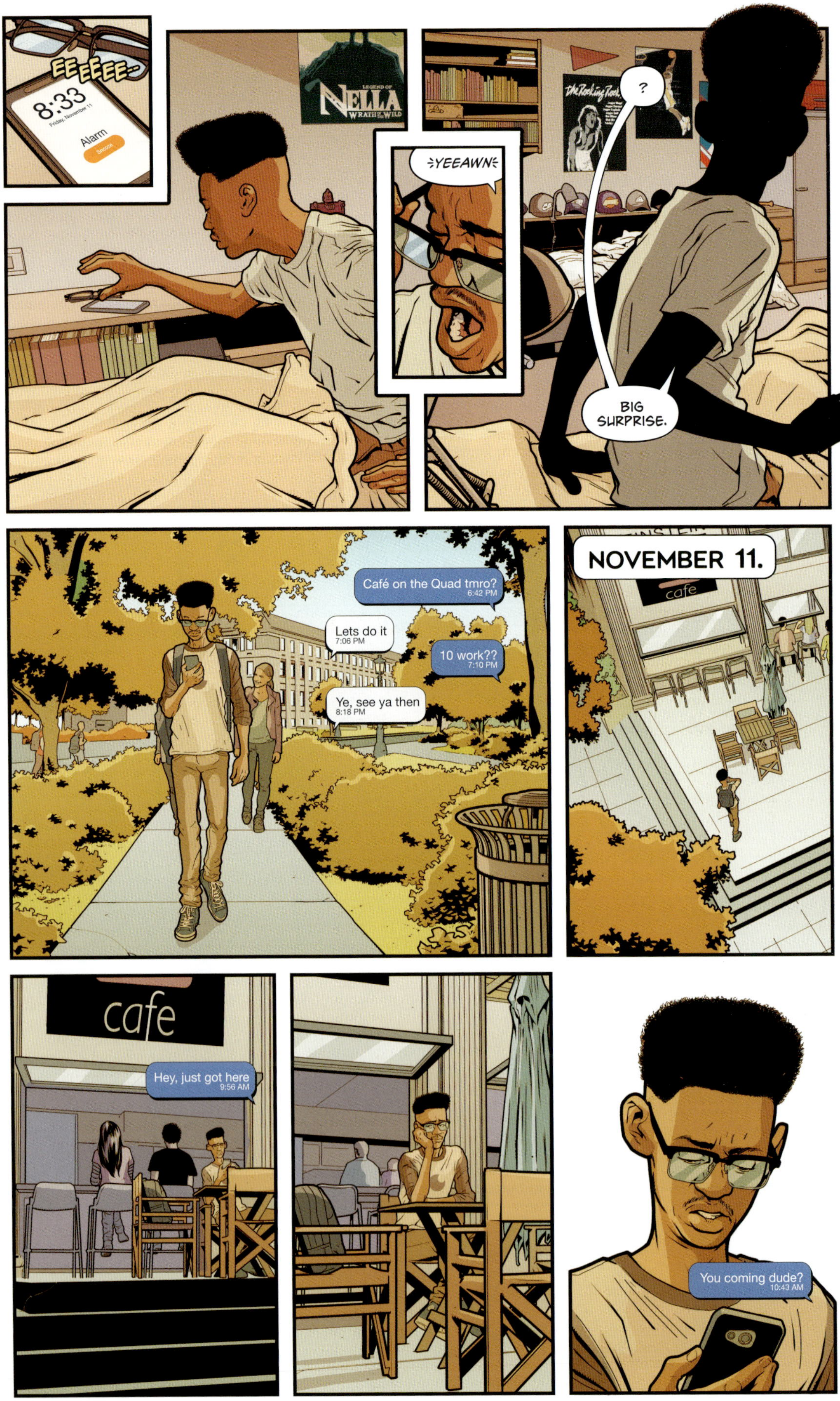
EEEEEE--
8:33
Friday, November 11
Alarm
LEGEND OF
NELLA
WRATH OF THE WILD
YEEAWN
?
BIG SURPRISE.
Café on the Quad tmro?
6:42 PM
Lets do it
7:06 PM
10 work??
7:10 PM
Ye, see ya then
8:18 PM
NOVEMBER 11.
cafe
cafe
Hey, just got here
9:56 AM
You coming dude?
10:43 AM

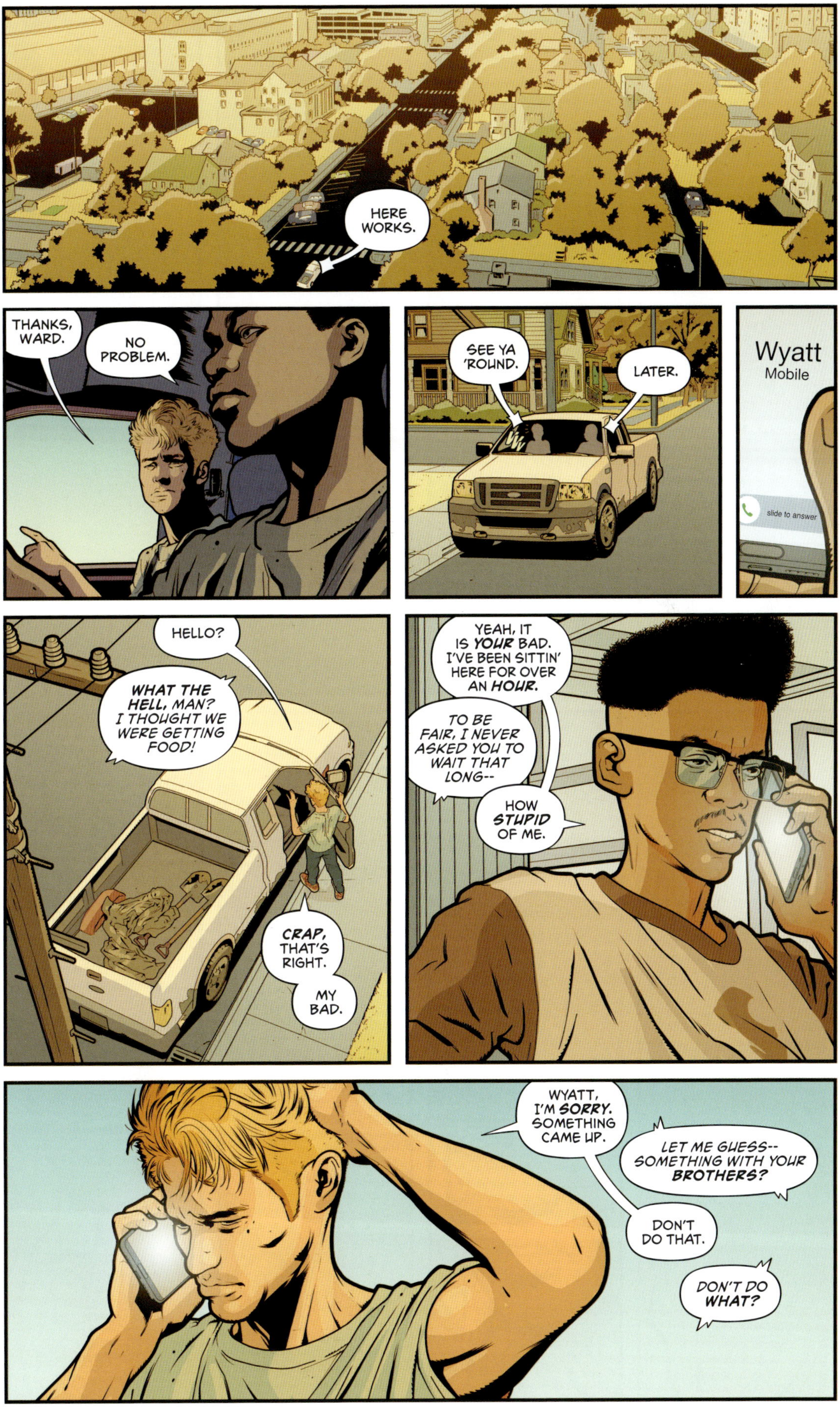
HERE WORKS.
THANKS, WARD.
NO PROBLEM.
SEE YA 'ROUND.
LATER.
Wyatt
Mobile
slide to answer
HELLO?
WHAT THE HELL, MAN? I THOUGHT WE WERE GETTING FOOD!
CRAP, THAT'S RIGHT.
MY BAD.
YEAH, IT IS YOUR BAD. I'VE BEEN SITTIN' HERE FOR OVER AN HOUR.
TO BE FAIR, I NEVER ASKED YOU TO WAIT THAT LONG--
HOW STUPID OF ME.
WYATT, I'M SORRY. SOMETHING CAME UP.
LET ME GUESS-- SOMETHING WITH YOUR BROTHERS?
DON'T DO THAT.
DON'T DO WHAT?

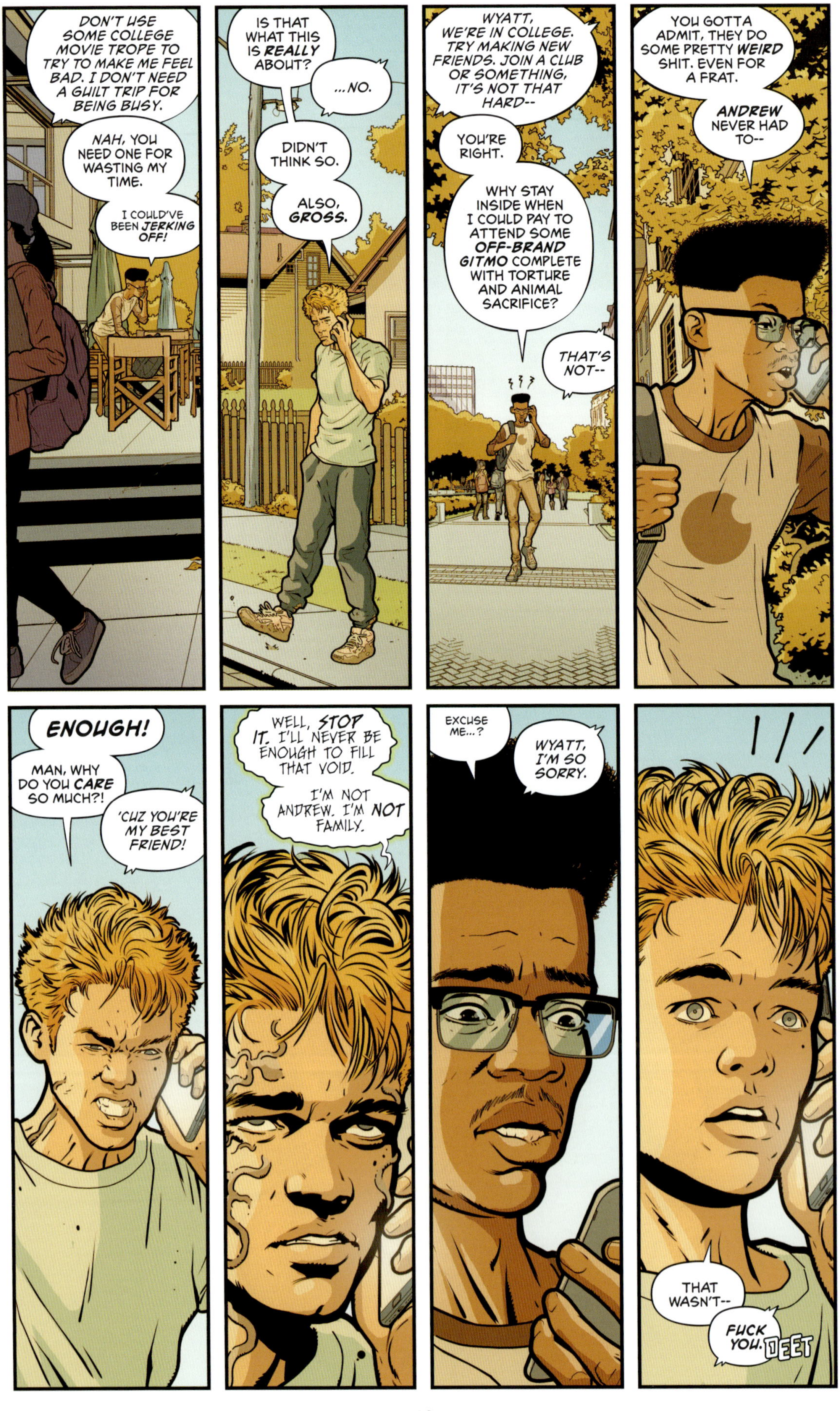
DON'T USE SOME COLLEGE MOVIE TROPE TO TRY TO MAKE ME FEEL BAD. I DON'T NEED A GUILT TRIP FOR BEING BUSY.
NAH, YOU NEED ONE FOR WASTING MY TIME.
I COULD'VE BEEN JERKING OFF!
IS THAT WHAT THIS IS REALLY ABOUT?
...NO.
DIDN'T THINK SO.
ALSO, GROSS.
WYATT, WE'RE IN COLLEGE. TRY MAKING NEW FRIENDS. JOIN A CLUB OR SOMETHING, IT'S NOT THAT HARD--
YOU'RE RIGHT.
WHY STAY INSIDE WHEN I COULD PAY TO ATTEND SOME OFF-BRAND GITMO COMPLETE WITH TORTURE AND ANIMAL SACRIFICE?
THAT'S NOT--
YOU GOTTA ADMIT, THEY DO SOME PRETTY WEIRD SHIT. EVEN FOR A FRAT.
ANDREW NEVER HAD TO--
ENOUGH!
MAN, WHY DO YOU CARE SO MUCH?!
'CUZ YOU'RE MY BEST FRIEND!
WELL, STOP IT. I'LL NEVER BE ENOUGH TO FILL THAT VOID.
I'M NOT ANDREW. I'M NOT FAMILY.
EXCUSE ME...?
WYATT, I'M SO SORRY.
THAT WASN'T--
FUCK YOU.
DEET

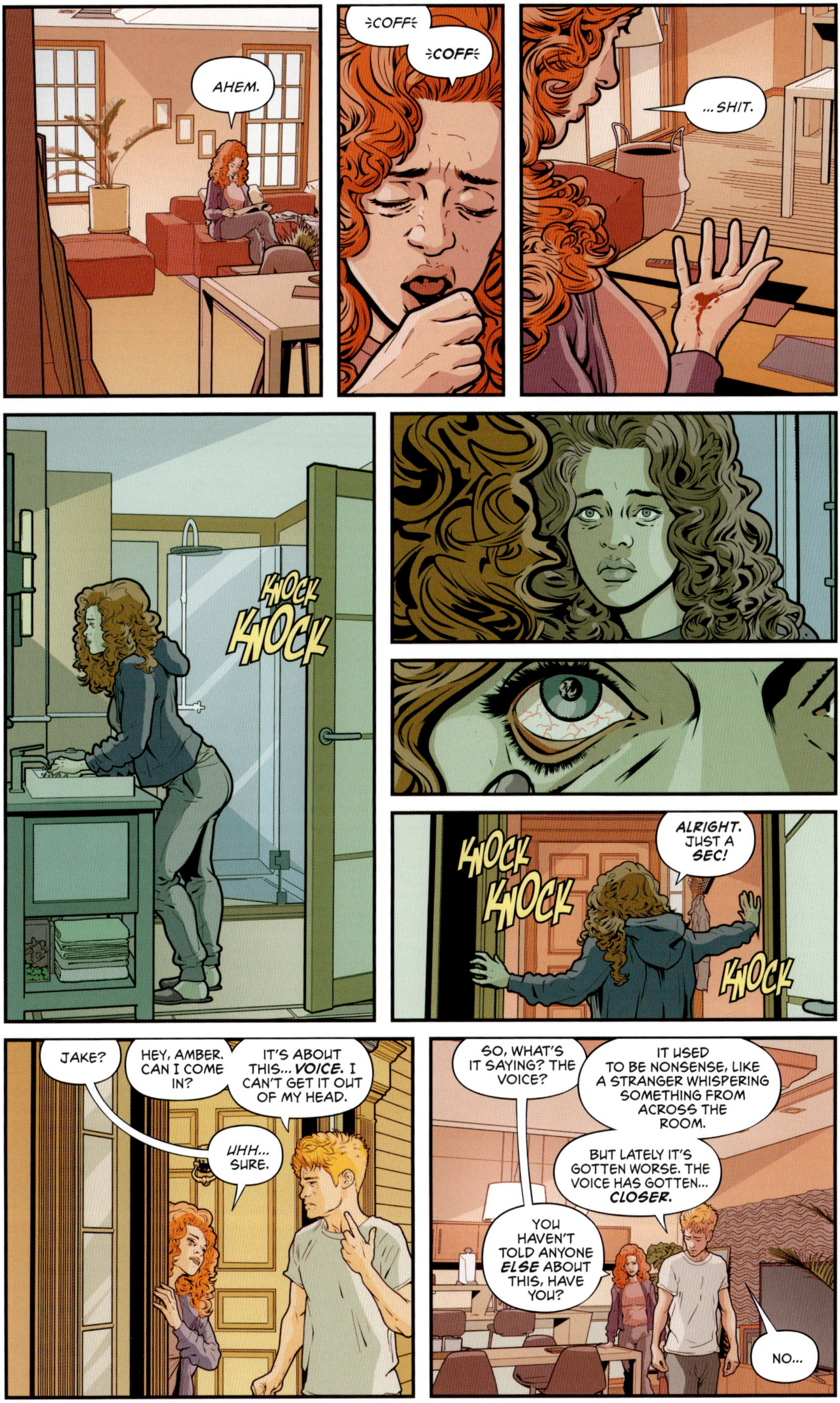
AHEM.
COFF
COFF
...SHIT.
KNOCK
KNOCK
KNOCK
KNOCK
ALRIGHT. JUST A SEC!
KNOCK
JAKE?
HEY, AMBER. CAN I COME IN?
IT'S ABOUT THIS... VOICE. I CAN'T GET IT OUT OF MY HEAD.
UHH... SURE.
SO, WHAT'S IT SAYING? THE VOICE?
IT USED TO BE NONSENSE, LIKE A STRANGER WHISPERING SOMETHING FROM ACROSS THE ROOM.
BUT LATELY IT'S GOTTEN WORSE. THE VOICE HAS GOTTEN... CLOSER.
YOU HAVEN'T TOLD ANYONE ELSE ABOUT THIS, HAVE YOU?
NO...

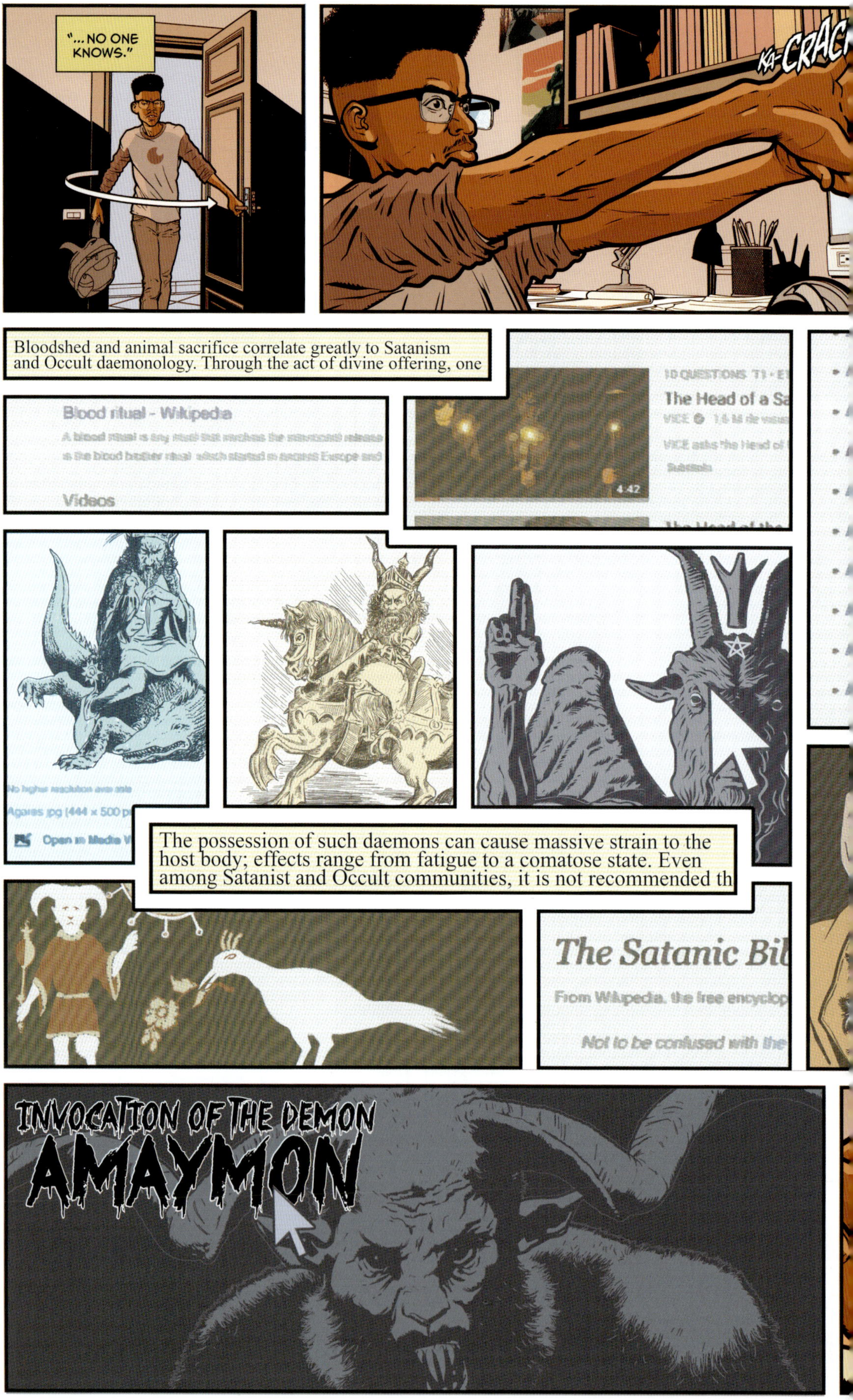
"...NO ONE KNOWS."
KA-CRAC
Bloodshed and animal sacrifice correlate greatly to Satanism and Occult daemonology. Through the act of divine offering, one
Blood ritual - Wikipedia
Videos
The Head of a Sa
4:42
The possession of such daemons can cause massive strain to the host body; effects range from fatigue to a comatose state. Even among Satanist and Occult communities, it is not recommended th
The Satanic Bi
From Wikipedia, the free encyclop
Not to be confused with the
INVOCATION OF THE DEMON
AMAYMON

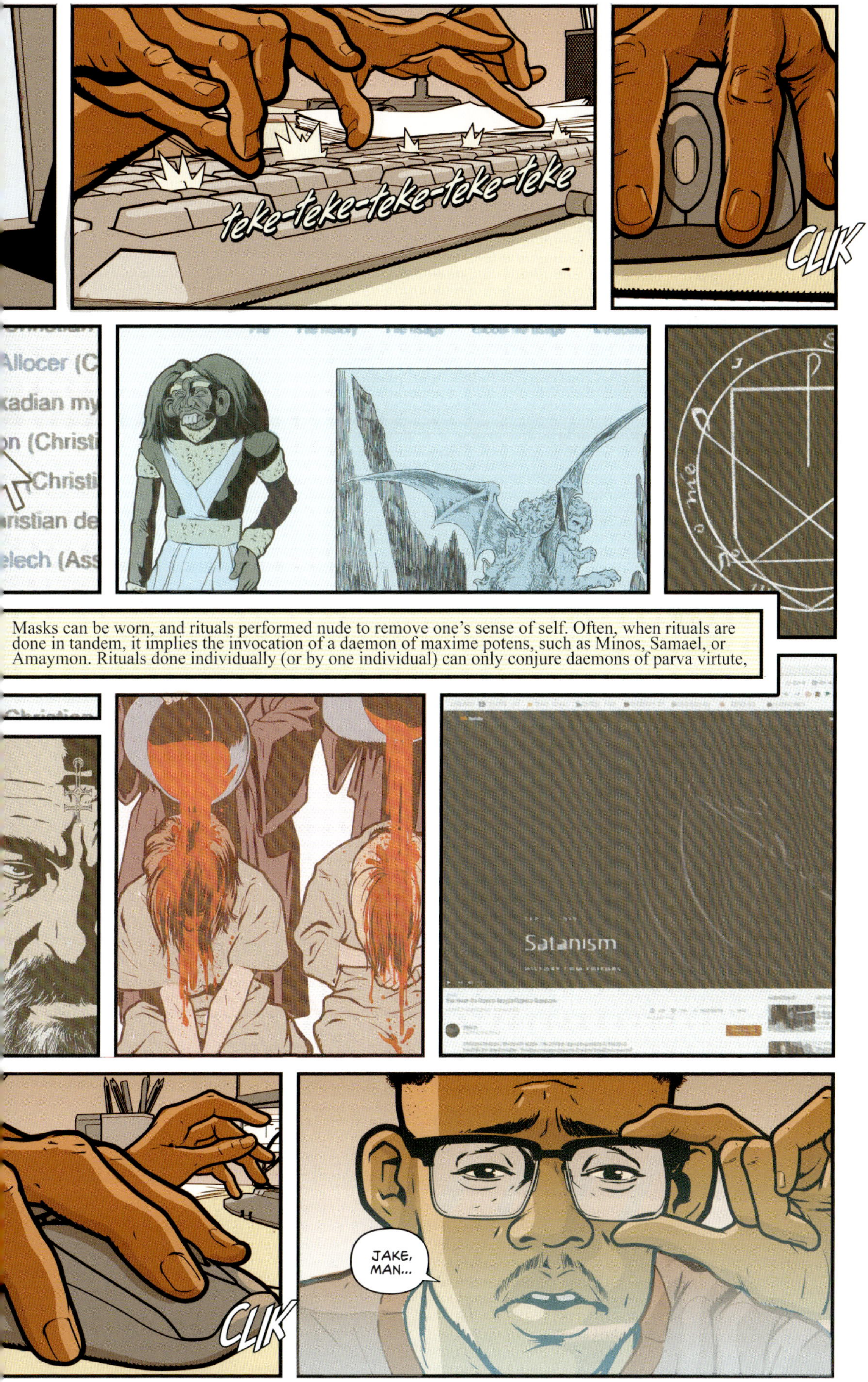
teke-teke-teke-teke-teke
CLIK
Allocer (C
kadian my
on (Christi
Christi
ristian de
elech (Ass
Masks can be worn, and rituals performed nude to remove one's sense of self. Often, when rituals are done in tandem, it implies the invocation of a daemon of maxime potens, such as Minos, Samael, or Amaymon. Rituals done individually (or by one individual) can only conjure daemons of parva virtute,
Satanism
CLIK
JAKE, MAN...

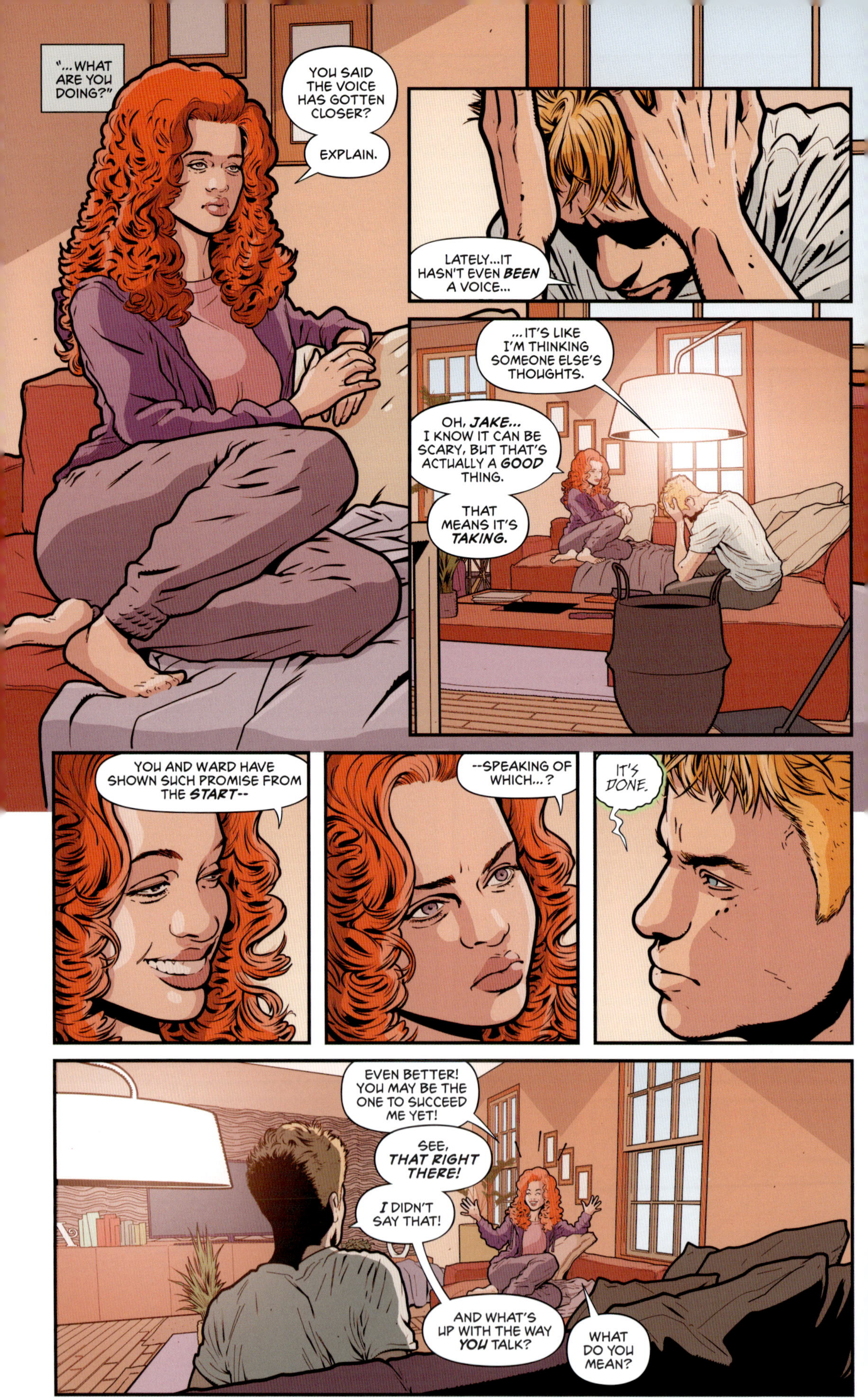
"...WHAT ARE YOU DOING?"
YOU SAID THE VOICE HAS GOTTEN CLOSER?
EXPLAIN.
LATELY...IT HASN'T EVEN BEEN A VOICE...
...IT'S LIKE I'M THINKING SOMEONE ELSE'S THOUGHTS.
OH, JAKE... I KNOW IT CAN BE SCARY, BUT THAT'S ACTUALLY A GOOD THING.
THAT MEANS IT'S TAKING.
YOU AND WARD HAVE SHOWN SUCH PROMISE FROM THE START--
--SPEAKING OF WHICH...?
IT'S DONE.
EVEN BETTER! YOU MAY BE THE ONE TO SUCCEED ME YET!
SEE, THAT RIGHT THERE!
I DIDN'T SAY THAT!
AND WHAT'S UP WITH THE WAY YOU TALK?
WHAT DO YOU MEAN?

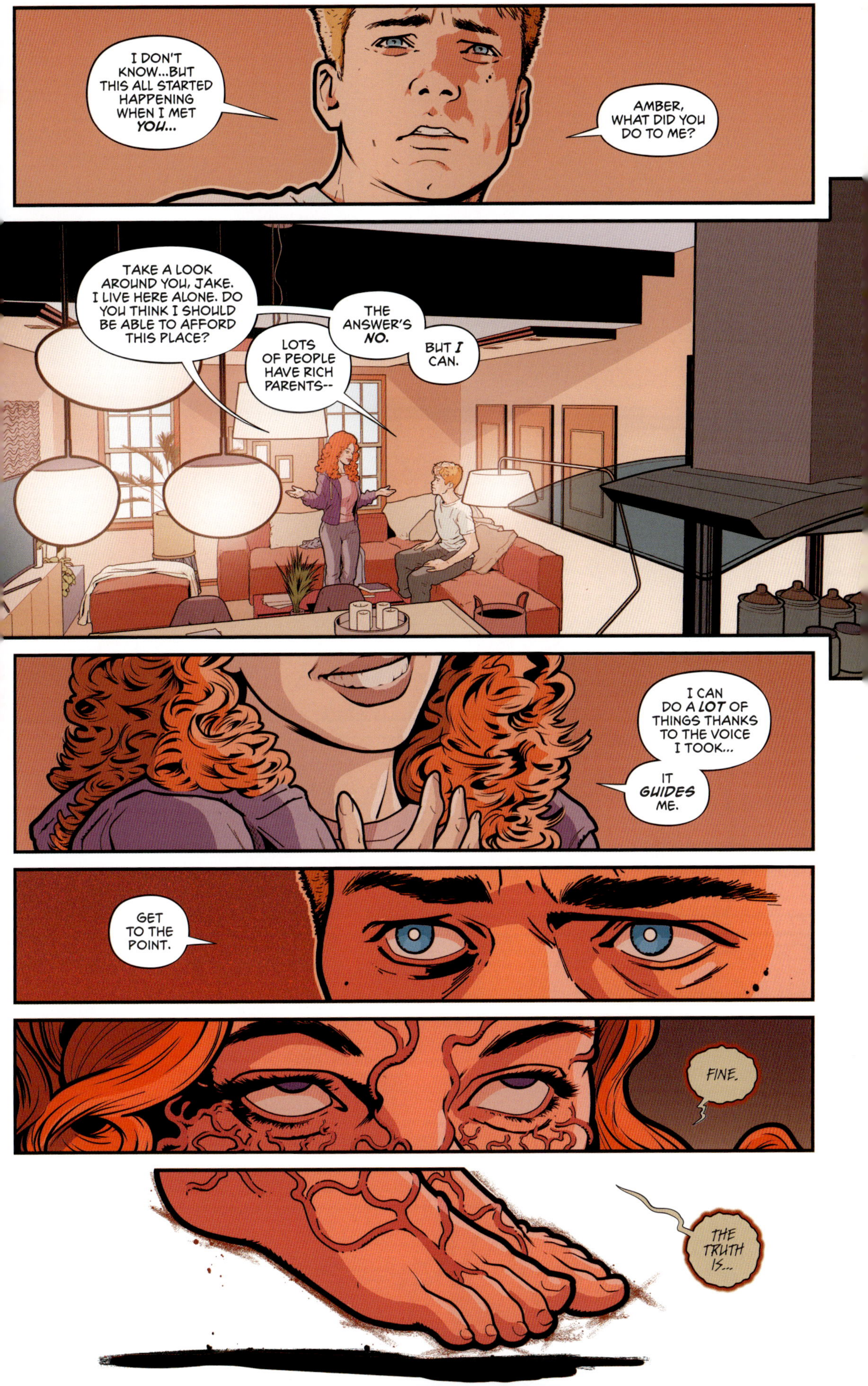
I DON'T KNOW...BUT THIS ALL STARTED HAPPENING WHEN I MET YOU...
AMBER, WHAT DID YOU DO TO ME?
TAKE A LOOK AROUND YOU, JAKE. I LIVE HERE ALONE. DO YOU THINK I SHOULD BE ABLE TO AFFORD THIS PLACE?
LOTS OF PEOPLE HAVE RICH PARENTS--
THE ANSWER'S NO.
BUT I CAN.
I CAN DO A LOT OF THINGS THANKS TO THE VOICE I TOOK...
IT GUIDES ME.
GET TO THE POINT.
FINE.
THE TRUTH IS...

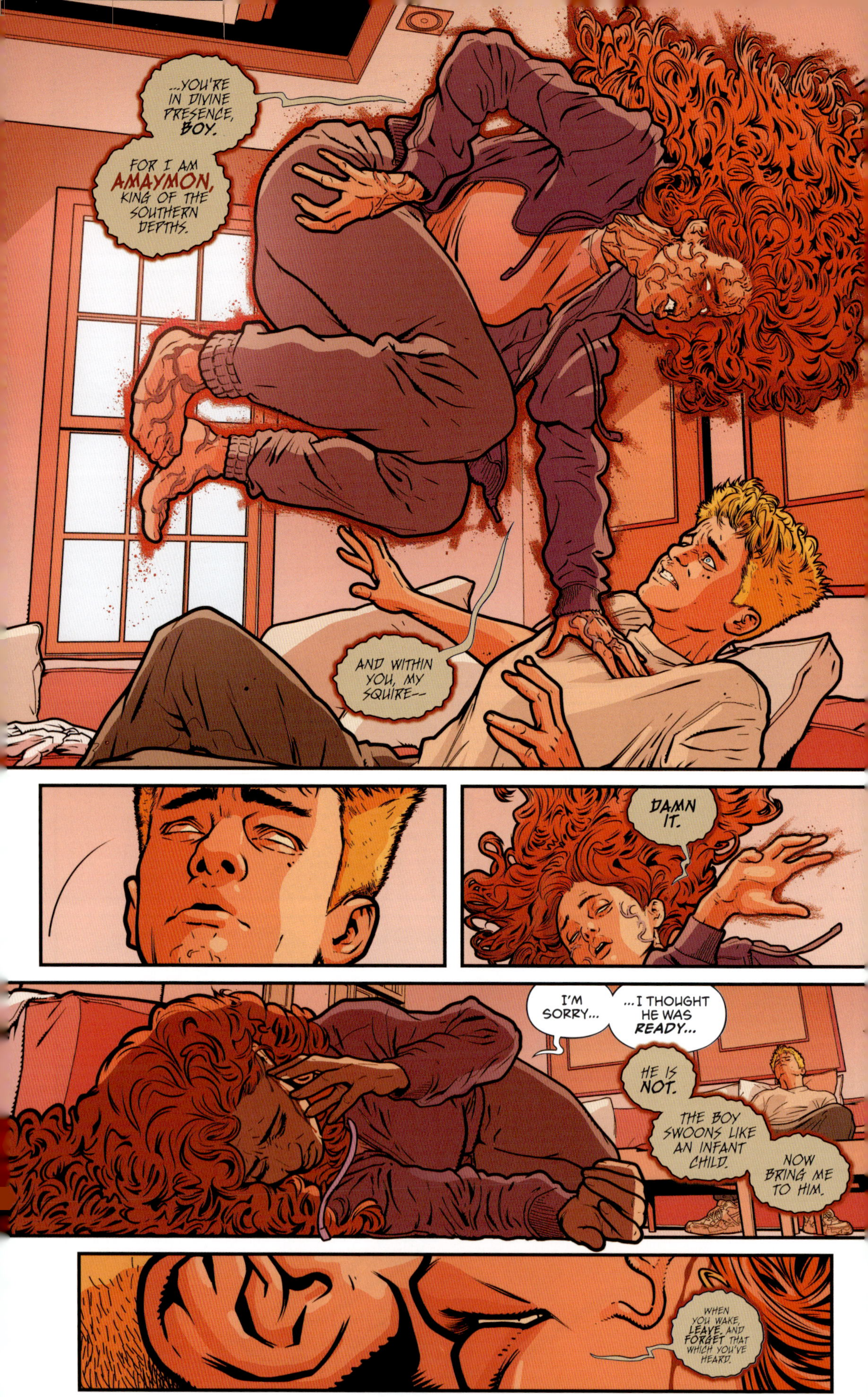
...YOU'RE IN DIVINE PRESENCE, BOY.
FOR I AM AMAYMON, KING OF THE SOUTHERN DEPTHS.
AND WITHIN YOU, MY SQUIRE--
DAMN IT.
I'M SORRY...
...I THOUGHT HE WAS READY...
HE IS NOT.
THE BOY SWOONS LIKE AN INFANT CHILD.
NOW BRING ME TO HIM.
WHEN YOU WAKE, LEAVE. AND FORGET THAT WHICH YOU'VE HEARD.

CHAPTER THREE
THE APPOINTMENT

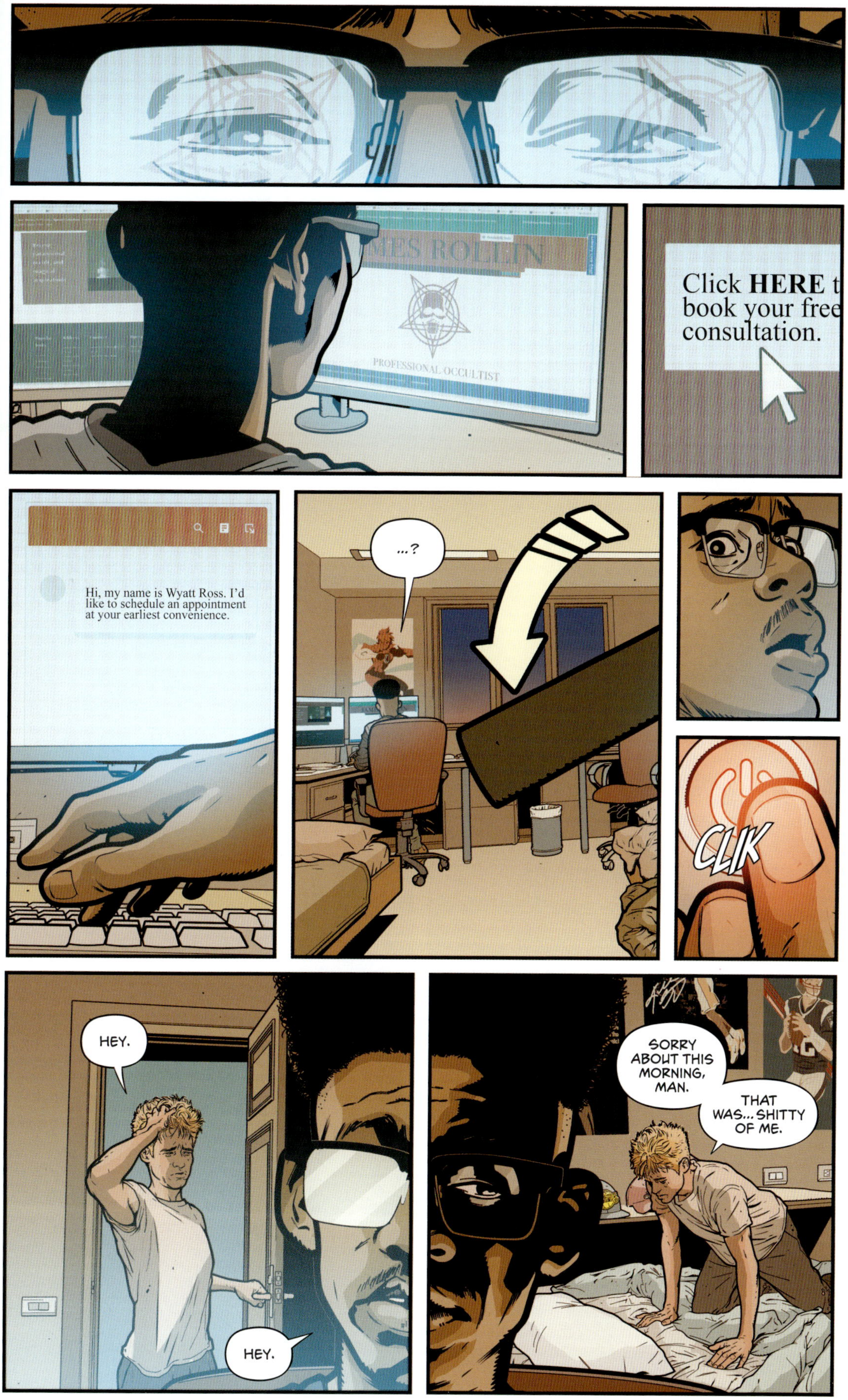
MES ROLLIN
PROFESSIONAL OCCULTIST
Click HERE t
book your free
consultation.
Hi, my name is Wyatt Ross. I'd like to schedule an appointment at your earliest convenience.
...?
CLIK
HEY.
HEY.
SORRY ABOUT THIS MORNING, MAN.
THAT WAS... SHITTY OF ME.

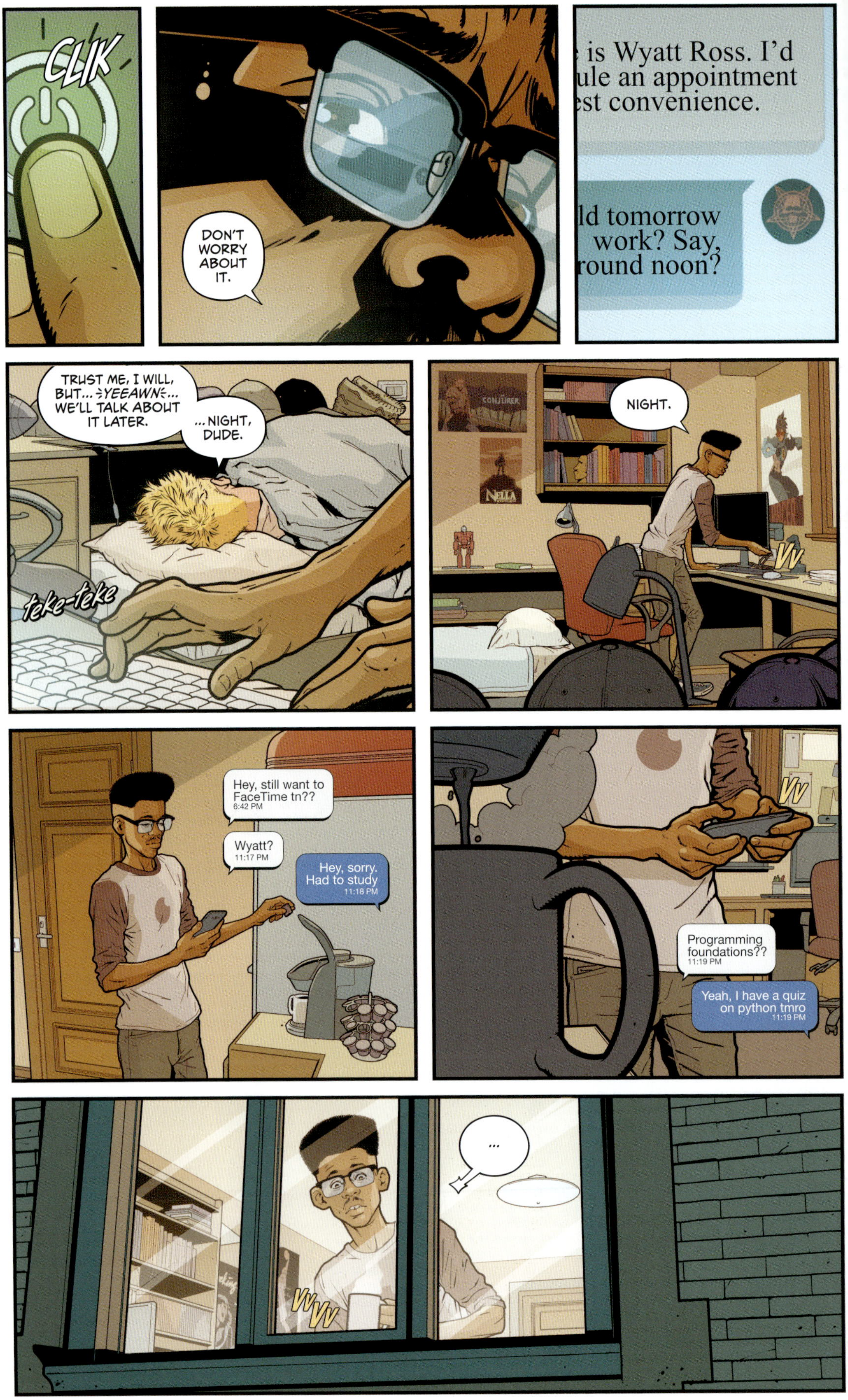
CLIK
DON'T WORRY ABOUT IT.
e is Wyatt Ross. I'd
ule an appointment
est convenience.
ld tomorrow
work? Say,
round noon?
TRUST ME, I WILL, BUT... ≈YEEAWN≈... WE'LL TALK ABOUT IT LATER.
...NIGHT, DUDE.
teke-teke
CONJURER
NELLA
NIGHT.
VV
Hey, still want to FaceTime tn?? 6:42 PM
Wyatt? 11:17 PM
Hey, sorry. Had to study 11:18 PM
VV
Programming foundations?? 11:19 PM
Yeah, I have a quiz on python tmro 11:19 PM
...
VVVV

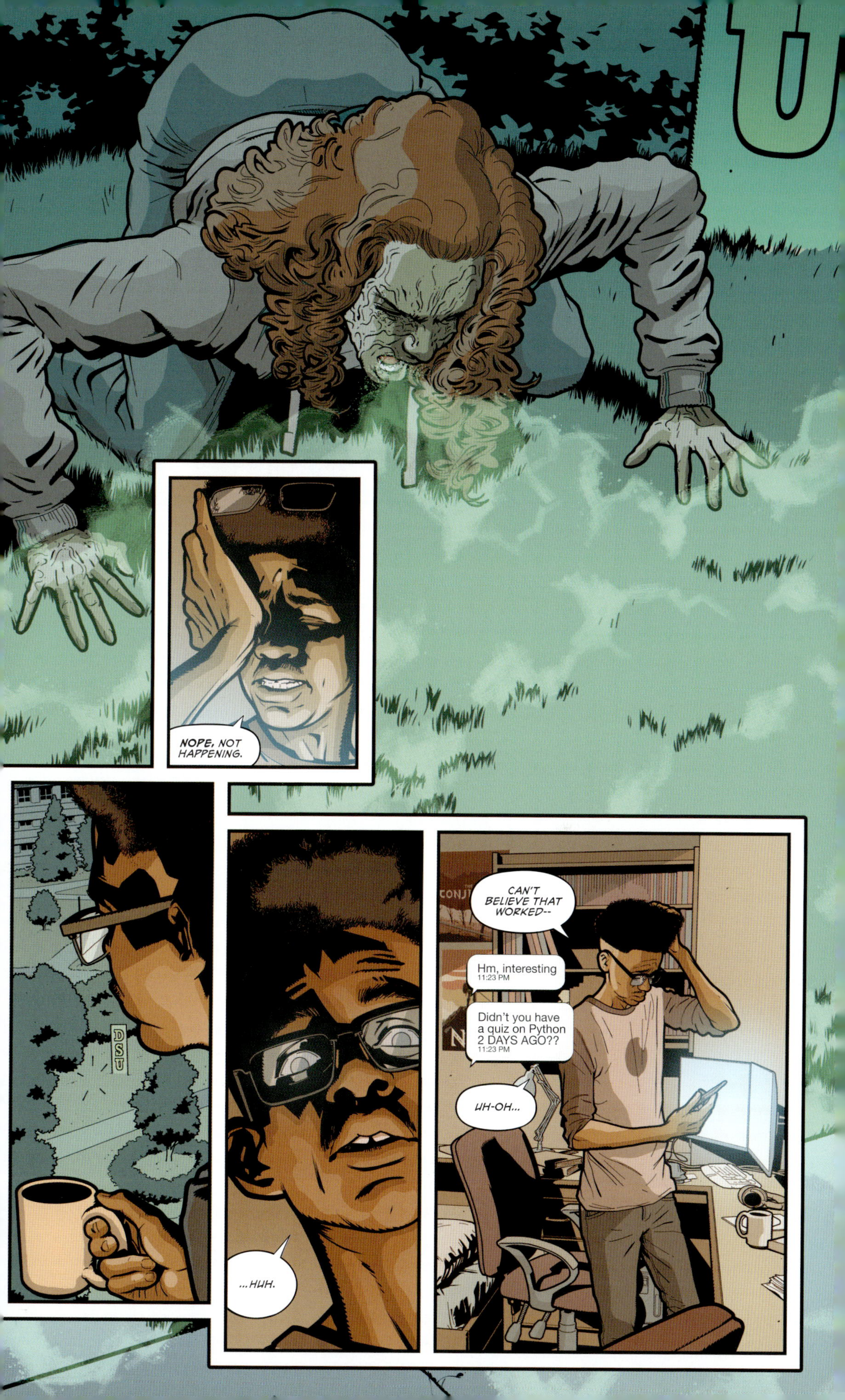
NOPE, NOT HAPPENING.
DSU
...HUH.
CAN'T BELIEVE THAT WORKED--
Hm, interesting
11:23 PM
Didn't you have a quiz on Python 2 DAYS AGO??
11:23 PM
UH-OH...

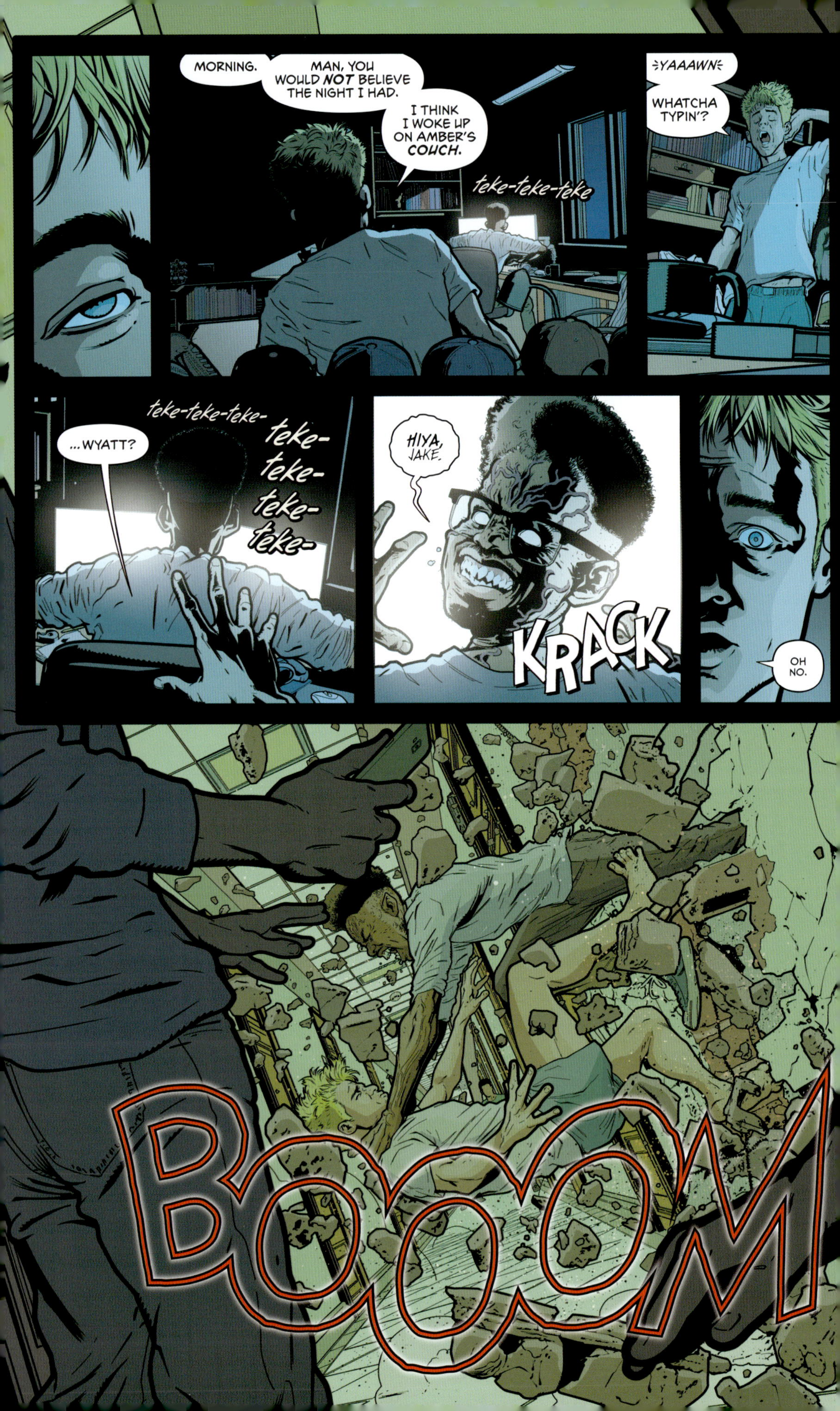
MORNING.
MAN, YOU WOULD NOT BELIEVE THE NIGHT I HAD.
I THINK I WOKE UP ON AMBER'S COUCH.
teke-teke-teke
YAAAWN
WHATCHA TYPIN'?
...WYATT?
teke-teke-teke-
teke-
teke-
teke-
teke-
HIYA, JAKE.
KRACK
OH NO.
BOOOM

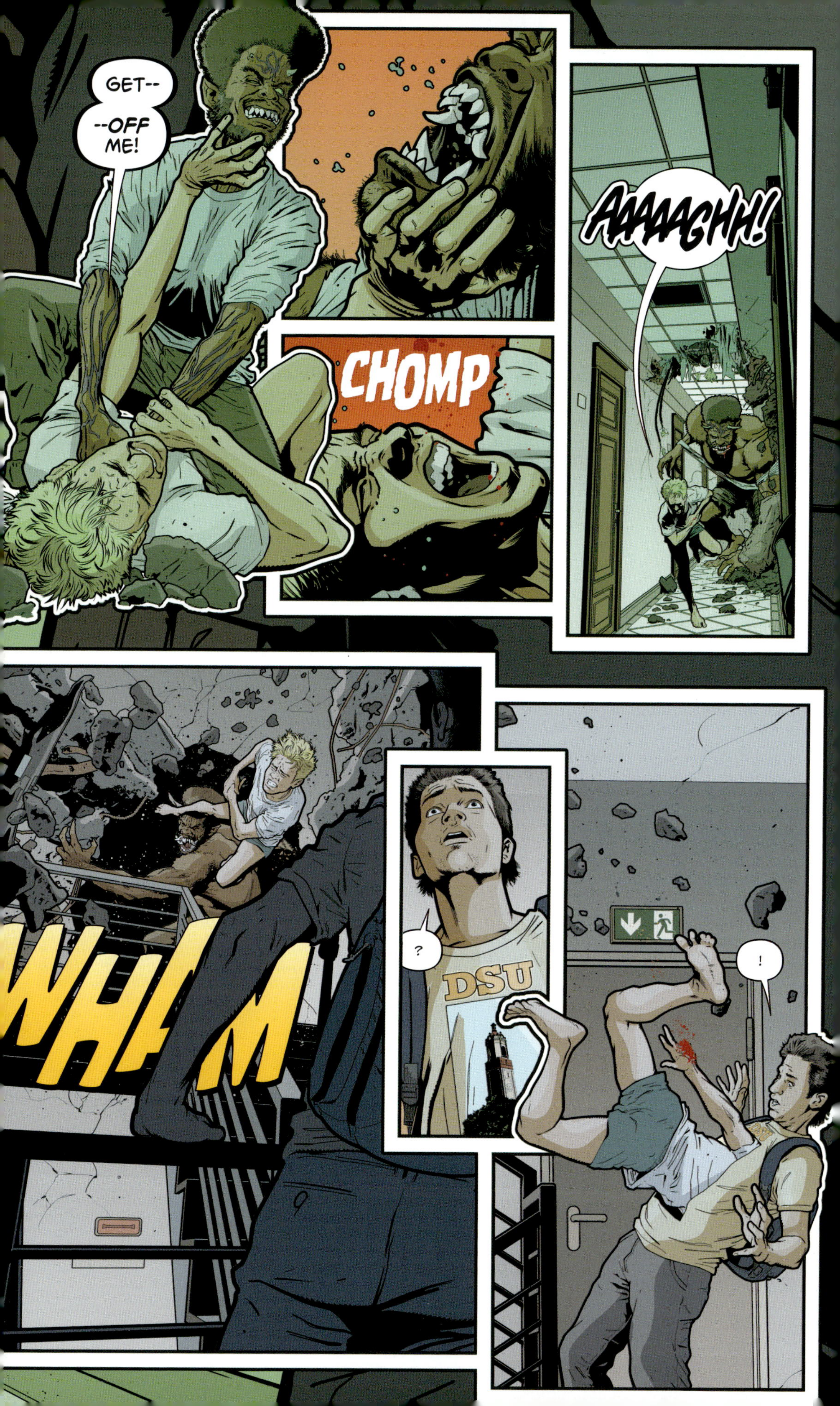
GET--
--OFF ME!
CHOMP
AAAAAGHH!
WHAM
?
DSU
!

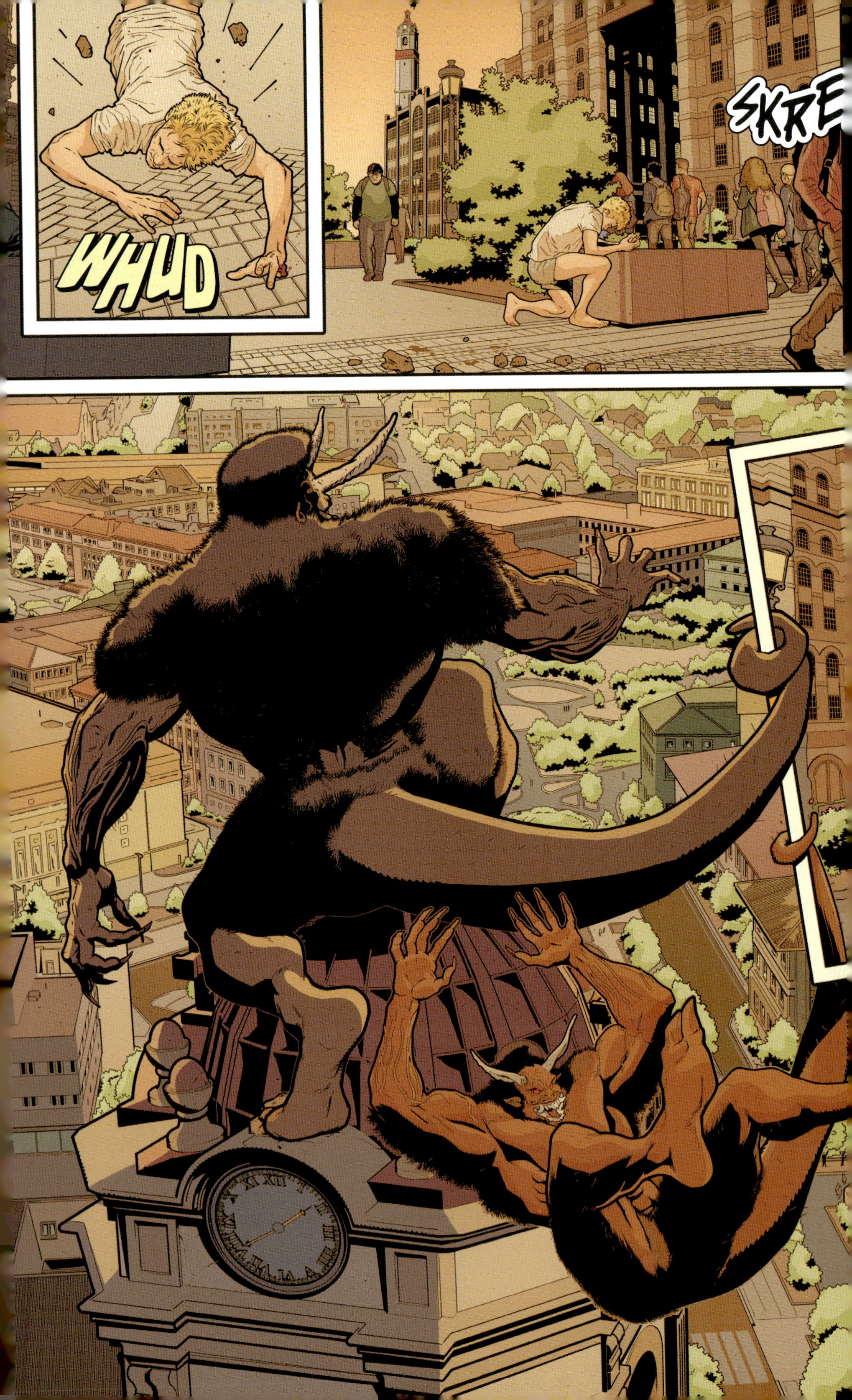
WHUD
SKRE

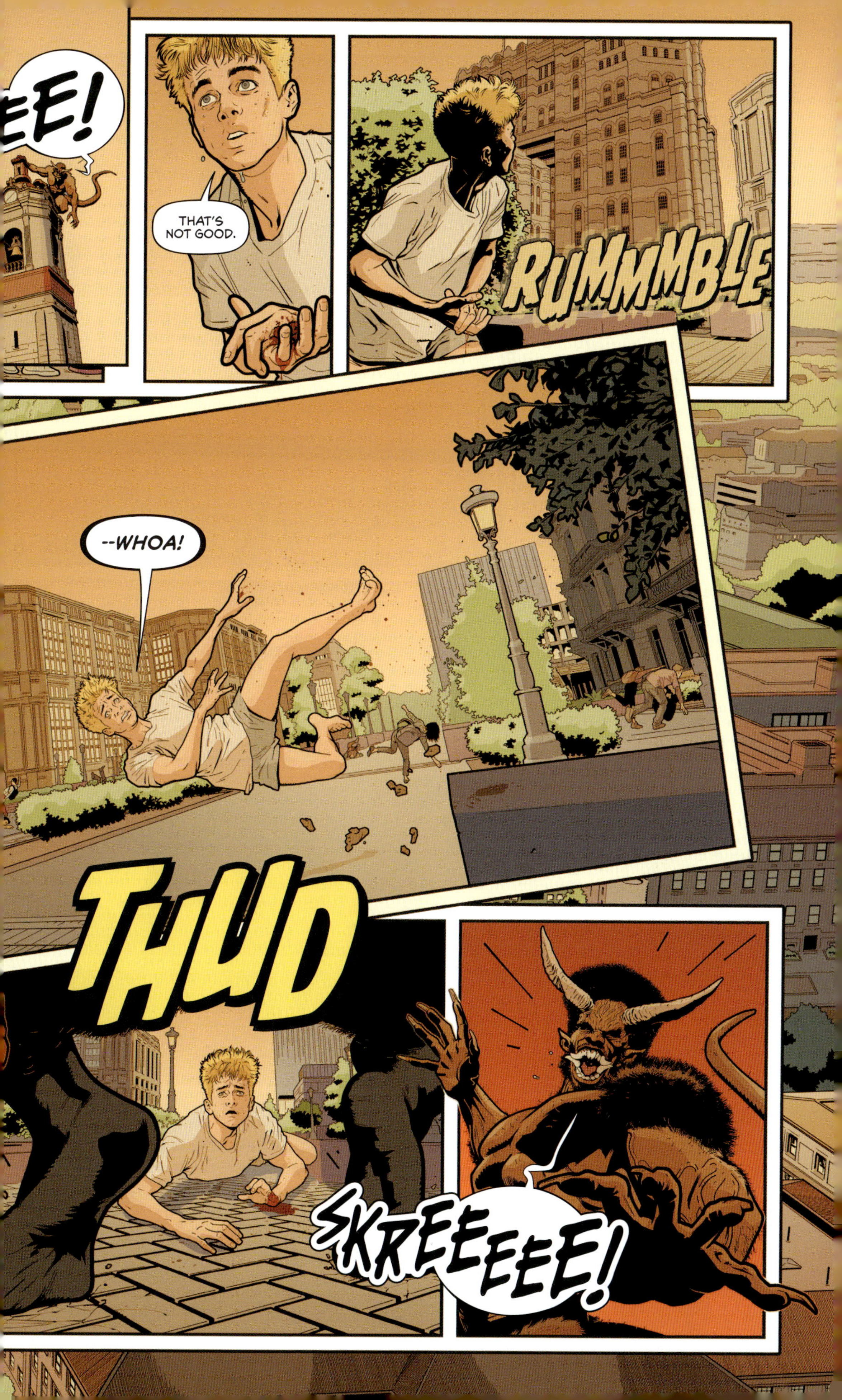
EE!
THAT'S NOT GOOD.
RUMMMBLE
--WHOA!
THUD
SKREEEEEE!

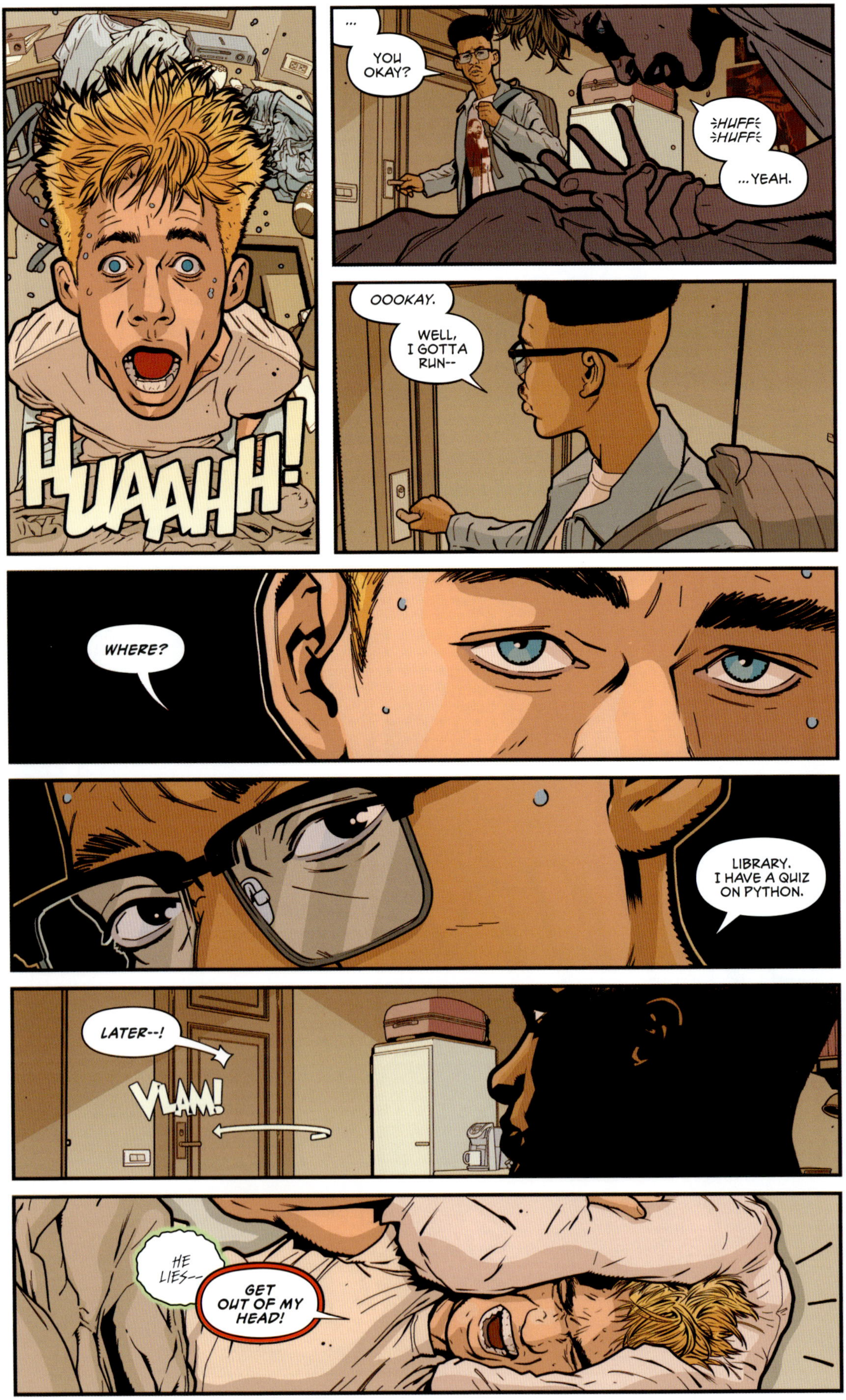
HUAAHH!
...
YOU OKAY?
HUFF HUFF
...YEAH.
OOOKAY.
WELL, I GOTTA RUN--
WHERE?
LIBRARY. I HAVE A QUIZ ON PYTHON.
LATER--!
VLAM!
HE LIES--
GET OUT OF MY HEAD!

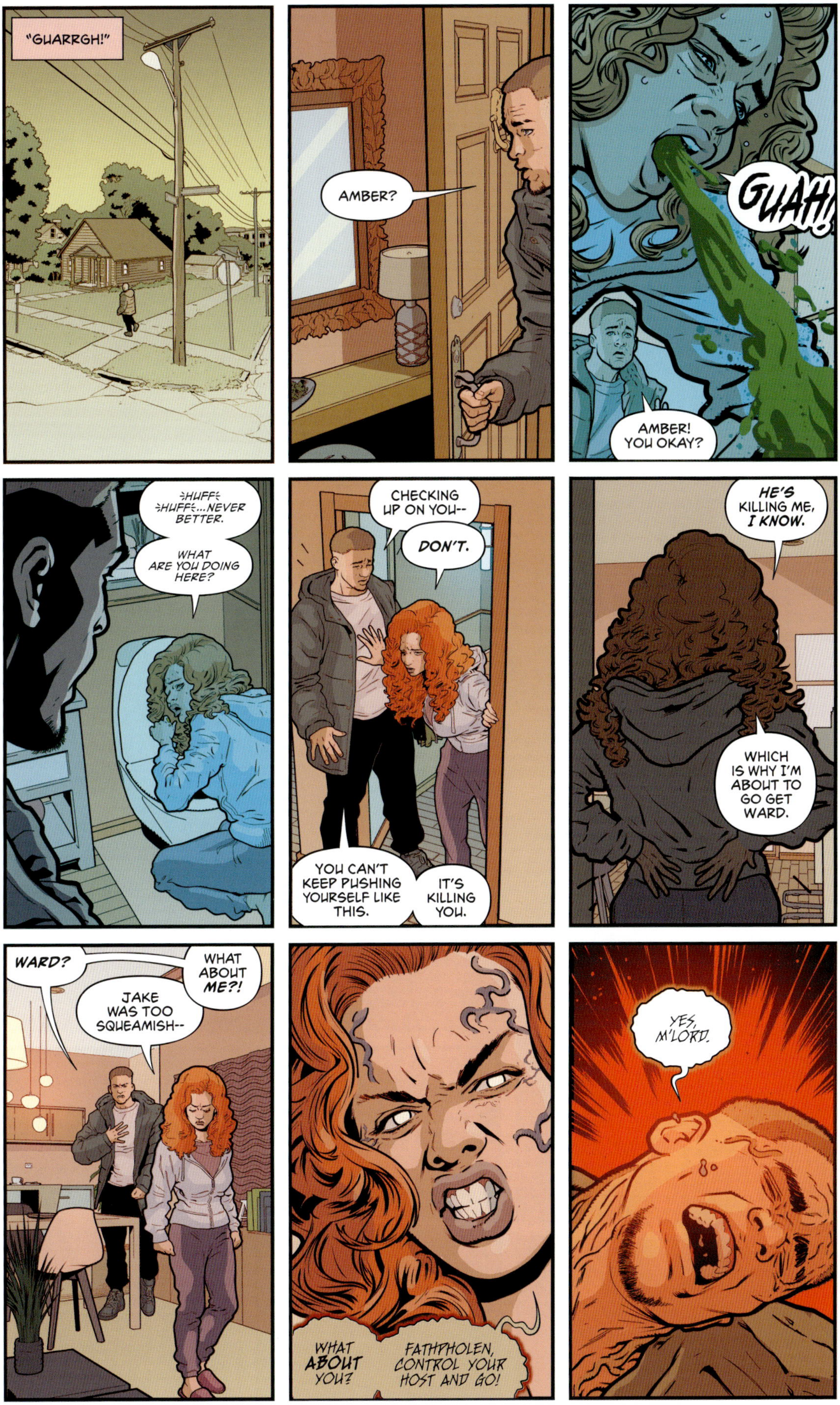
"GUARRGH!"
AMBER?
GUAH!
AMBER! YOU OKAY?
≷HUFF≶ ≷HUFF≶...NEVER BETTER.
WHAT ARE YOU DOING HERE?
CHECKING UP ON YOU--
DON'T.
YOU CAN'T KEEP PUSHING YOURSELF LIKE THIS.
IT'S KILLING YOU.
HE'S KILLING ME, I KNOW.
WHICH IS WHY I'M ABOUT TO GO GET WARD.
WARD?
WHAT ABOUT ME?!
JAKE WAS TOO SQUEAMISH--
WHAT ABOUT YOU?
FATHPHOLEN, CONTROL YOUR HOST AND GO!
YES, M'LORD.

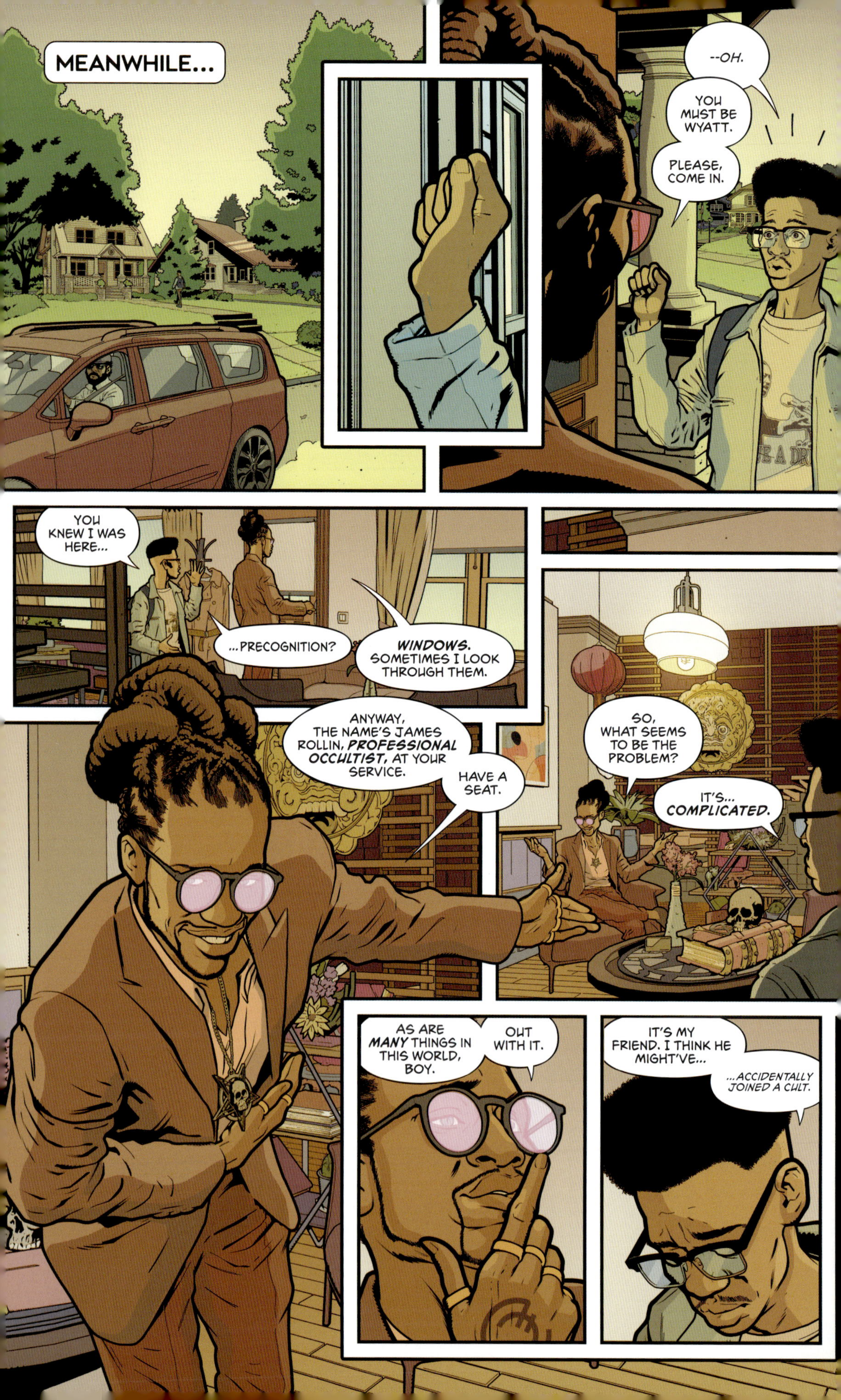
MEANWHILE...
--OH.
YOU MUST BE WYATT.
PLEASE, COME IN.
YOU KNEW I WAS HERE...
...PRECOGNITION?
WINDOWS. SOMETIMES I LOOK THROUGH THEM.
ANYWAY, THE NAME'S JAMES ROLLIN, PROFESSIONAL OCCULTIST, AT YOUR SERVICE.
HAVE A SEAT.
SO, WHAT SEEMS TO BE THE PROBLEM?
IT'S... COMPLICATED.
AS ARE MANY THINGS IN THIS WORLD, BOY.
OUT WITH IT.
IT'S MY FRIEND. I THINK HE MIGHT'VE...
...ACCIDENTALLY JOINED A CULT.

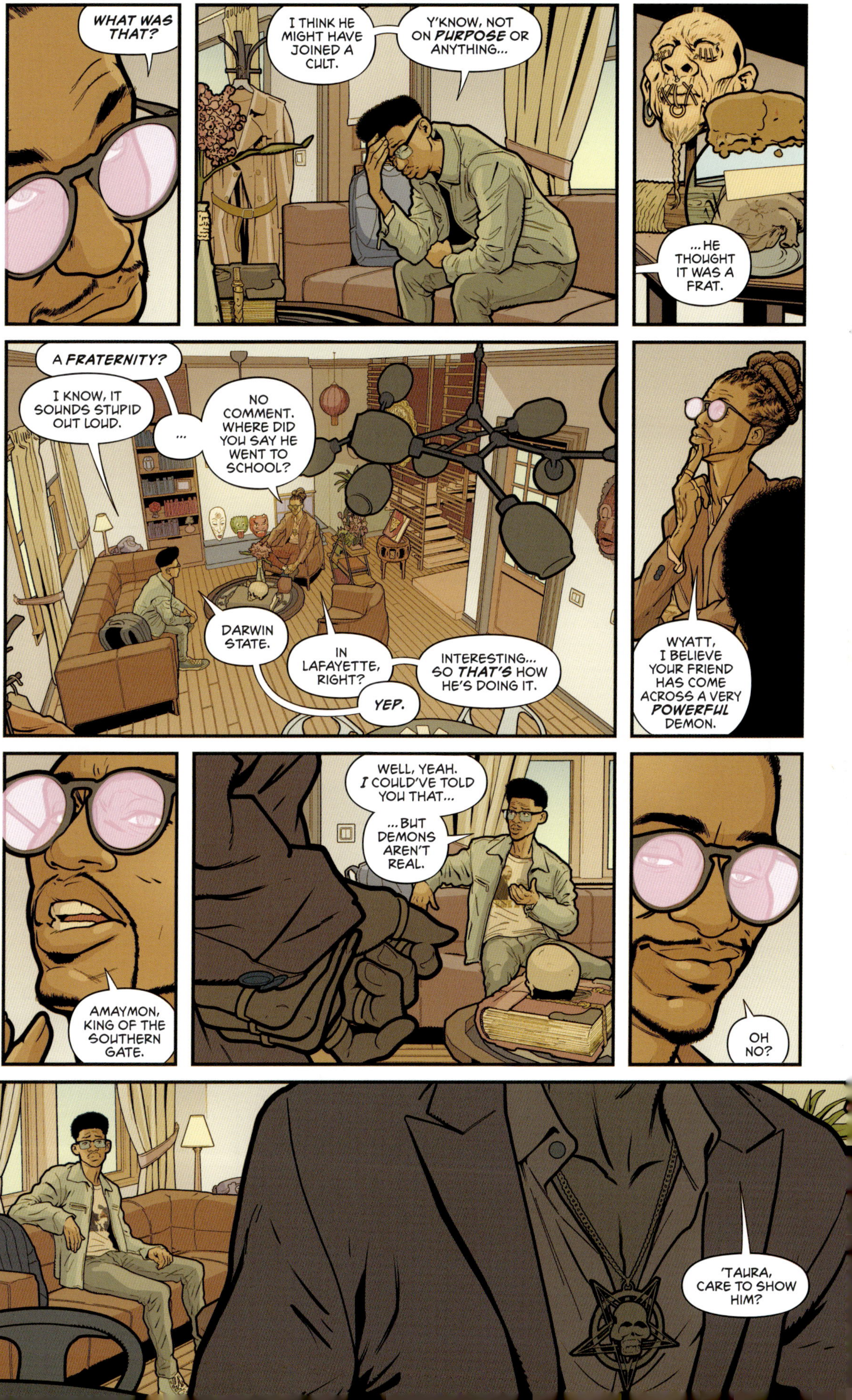
WHAT WAS THAT?
I THINK HE MIGHT HAVE JOINED A CULT.
Y'KNOW, NOT ON PURPOSE OR ANYTHING...
...HE THOUGHT IT WAS A FRAT.
A FRATERNITY?
I KNOW, IT SOUNDS STUPID OUT LOUD.
...
NO COMMENT. WHERE DID YOU SAY HE WENT TO SCHOOL?
DARWIN STATE.
IN LAFAYETTE, RIGHT?
YEP.
INTERESTING... SO THAT'S HOW HE'S DOING IT.
WYATT, I BELIEVE YOUR FRIEND HAS COME ACROSS A VERY POWERFUL DEMON.
AMAYMON, KING OF THE SOUTHERN GATE.
WELL, YEAH. I COULD'VE TOLD YOU THAT...
...BUT DEMONS AREN'T REAL.
OH NO?
'TAURA, CARE TO SHOW HIM?

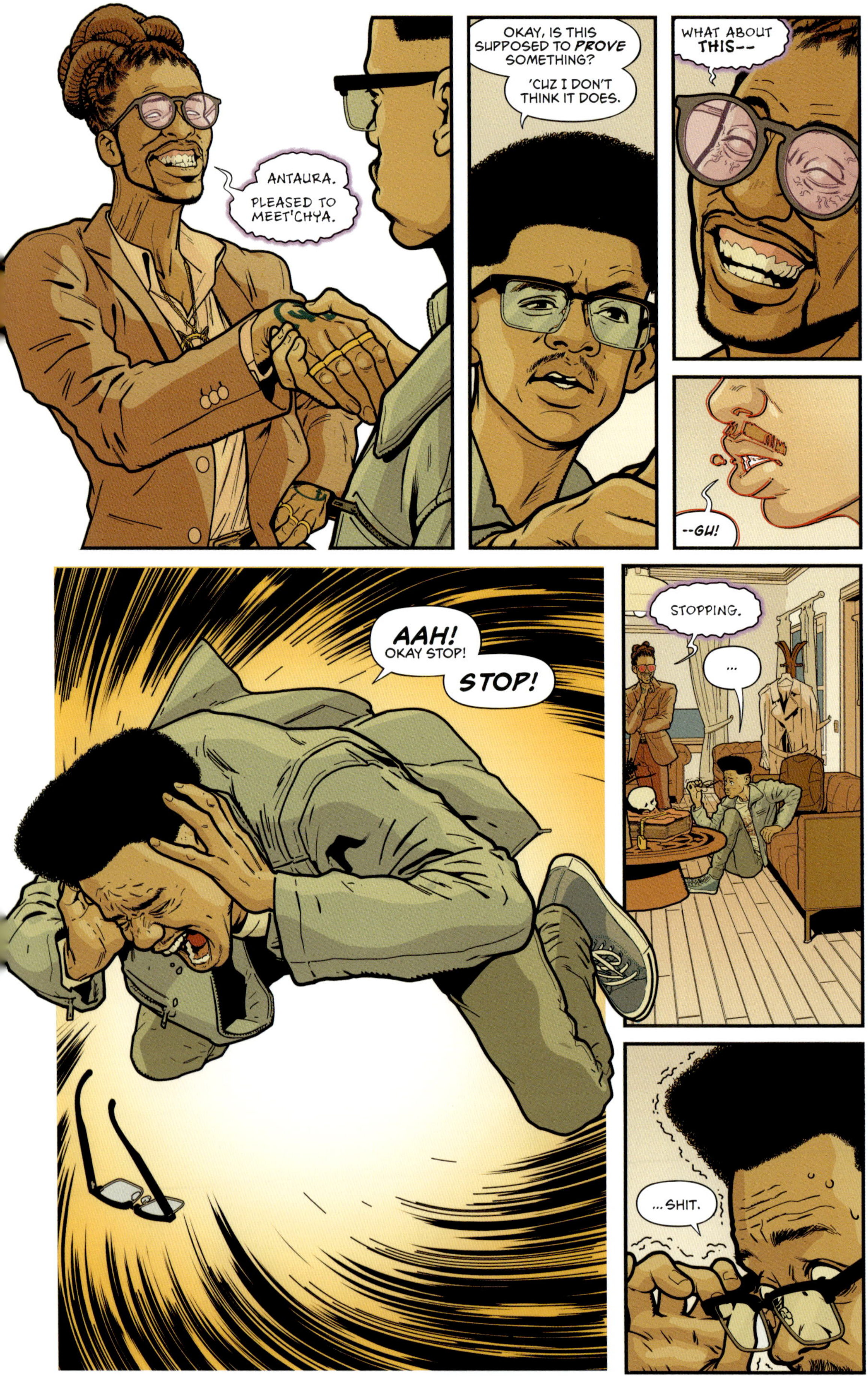
ANTAURA.
PLEASED TO MEET'CHYA.
OKAY, IS THIS SUPPOSED TO *PROVE* SOMETHING?
'CUZ I DON'T THINK IT DOES.
WHAT ABOUT **THIS--**
--GH!
AAH! OKAY STOP!
STOP!
STOPPING.
...
...SHIT.

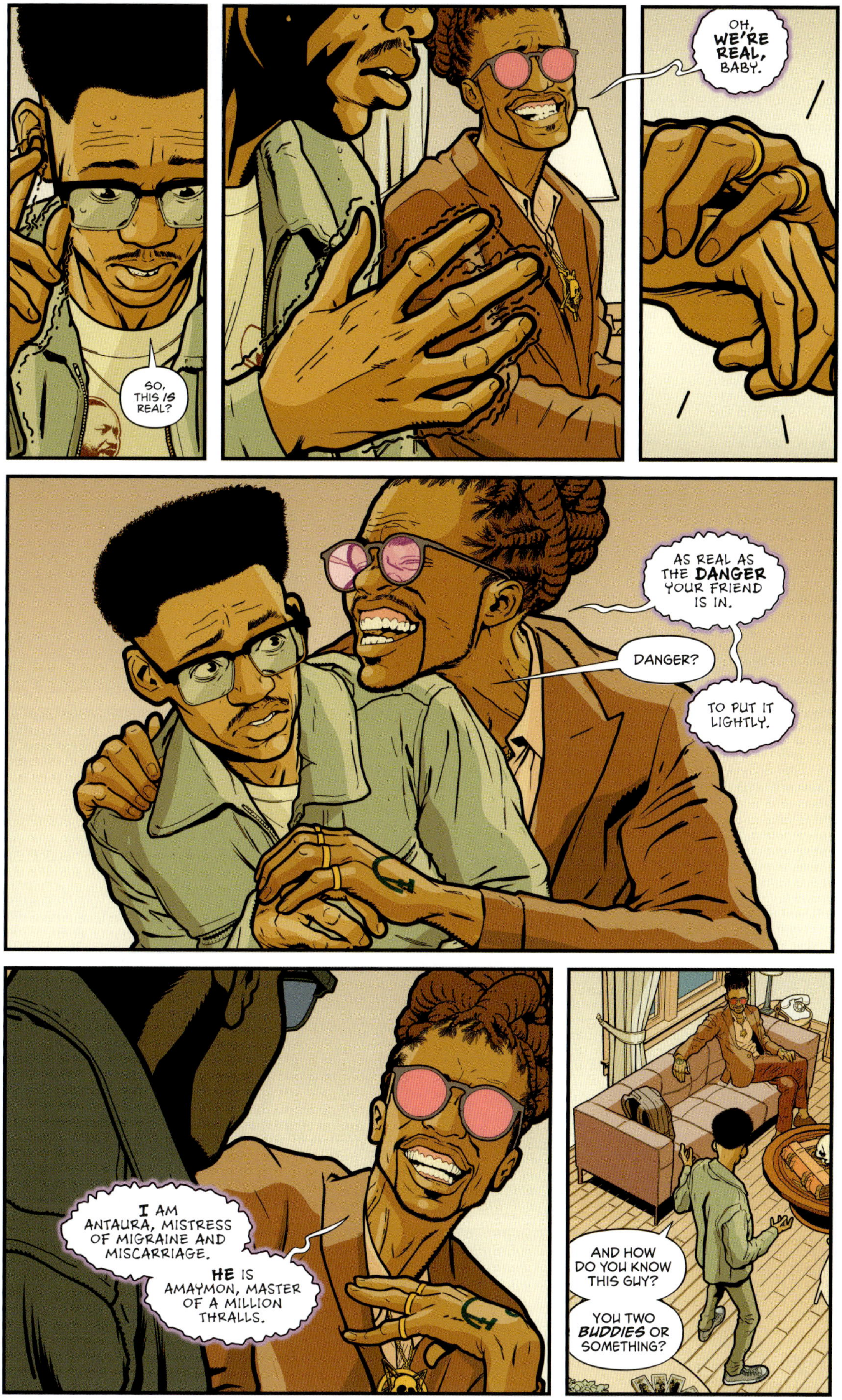
SO, THIS IS REAL?
OH, WE'RE REAL, BABY.
AS REAL AS THE DANGER YOUR FRIEND IS IN.
DANGER?
TO PUT IT LIGHTLY.
I AM ANTAURA, MISTRESS OF MIGRAINE AND MISCARRIAGE.
HE IS AMAYMON, MASTER OF A MILLION THRALLS.
AND HOW DO YOU KNOW THIS GUY?
YOU TWO BUDDIES OR SOMETHING?

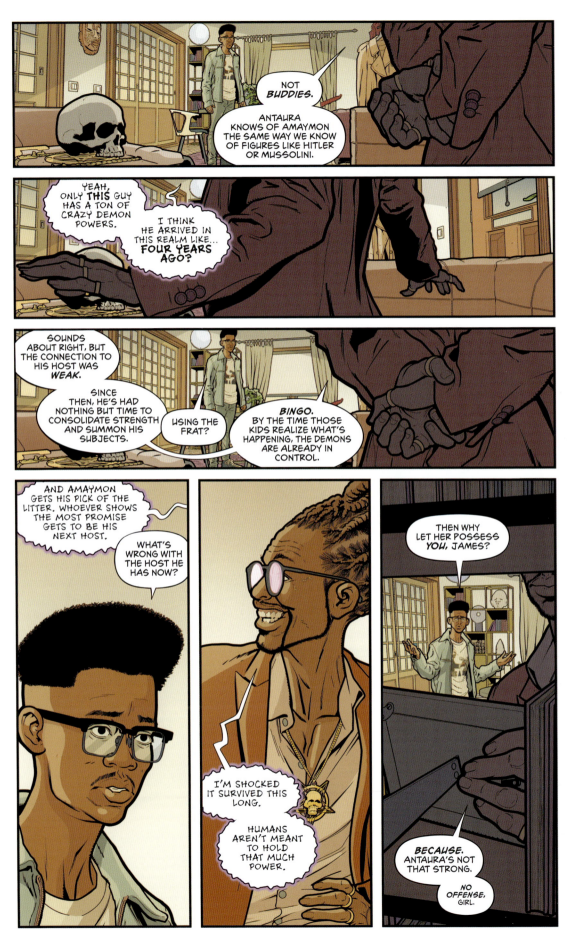

NOT *BUDDIES*.

ANTAURA KNOWS OF AMAYMON THE SAME WAY WE KNOW OF FIGURES LIKE HITLER OR MUSSOLINI.

YEAH, ONLY **THIS** GUY HAS A TON OF CRAZY DEMON POWERS.

I THINK HE ARRIVED IN THIS REALM LIKE... **FOUR YEARS AGO?**

SOUNDS ABOUT RIGHT, BUT THE CONNECTION TO HIS HOST WAS *WEAK*.

SINCE THEN, HE'S HAD NOTHING BUT TIME TO CONSOLIDATE STRENGTH AND SUMMON HIS SUBJECTS.

USING THE FRAT?

BINGO. BY THE TIME THOSE KIDS REALIZE WHAT'S HAPPENING, THE DEMONS ARE ALREADY IN CONTROL.

AND AMAYMON GETS HIS PICK OF THE LITTER. WHOEVER SHOWS THE MOST PROMISE GETS TO BE HIS NEXT HOST.

WHAT'S WRONG WITH THE HOST HE HAS NOW?

I'M SHOCKED IT SURVIVED THIS LONG.

HUMANS AREN'T MEANT TO HOLD THAT MUCH POWER.

THEN WHY LET HER POSSESS *YOU*, JAMES?

BECAUSE. ANTAURA'S NOT THAT STRONG.

NO OFFENSE, GIRL.

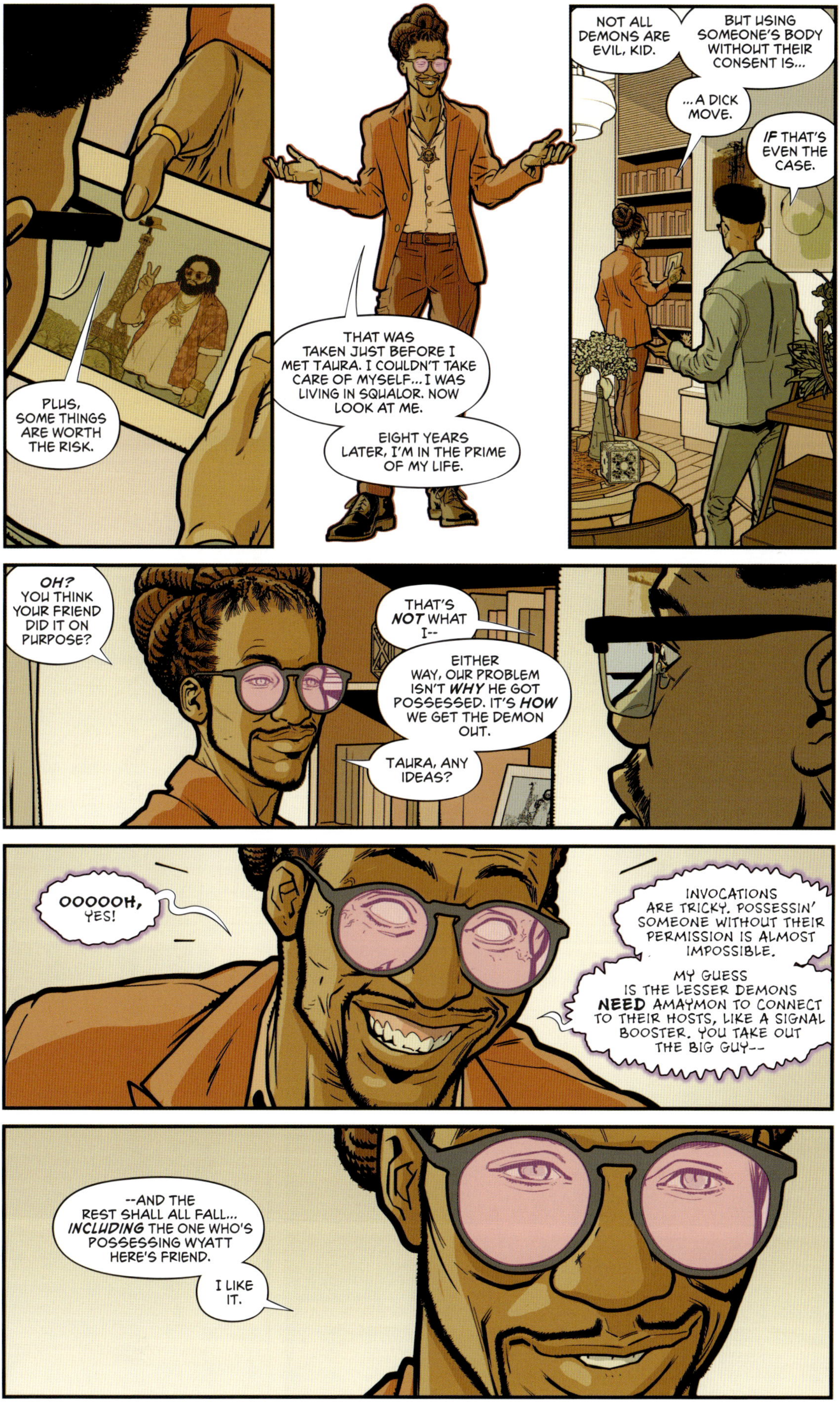
PLUS, SOME THINGS ARE WORTH THE RISK.
THAT WAS TAKEN JUST BEFORE I MET TAURA. I COULDN'T TAKE CARE OF MYSELF... I WAS LIVING IN SQUALOR. NOW LOOK AT ME.
EIGHT YEARS LATER, I'M IN THE PRIME OF MY LIFE.
NOT ALL DEMONS ARE EVIL, KID.
BUT USING SOMEONE'S BODY WITHOUT THEIR CONSENT IS...
...A DICK MOVE.
IF THAT'S EVEN THE CASE.
OH? YOU THINK YOUR FRIEND DID IT ON PURPOSE?
THAT'S NOT WHAT I--
EITHER WAY, OUR PROBLEM ISN'T WHY HE GOT POSSESSED. IT'S HOW WE GET THE DEMON OUT.
TAURA, ANY IDEAS?
OOOOOH, YES!
INVOCATIONS ARE TRICKY. POSSESSIN' SOMEONE WITHOUT THEIR PERMISSION IS ALMOST IMPOSSIBLE.
MY GUESS IS THE LESSER DEMONS NEED AMAYMON TO CONNECT TO THEIR HOSTS, LIKE A SIGNAL BOOSTER. YOU TAKE OUT THE BIG GUY--
--AND THE REST SHALL ALL FALL... INCLUDING THE ONE WHO'S POSSESSING WYATT HERE'S FRIEND.
I LIKE IT.

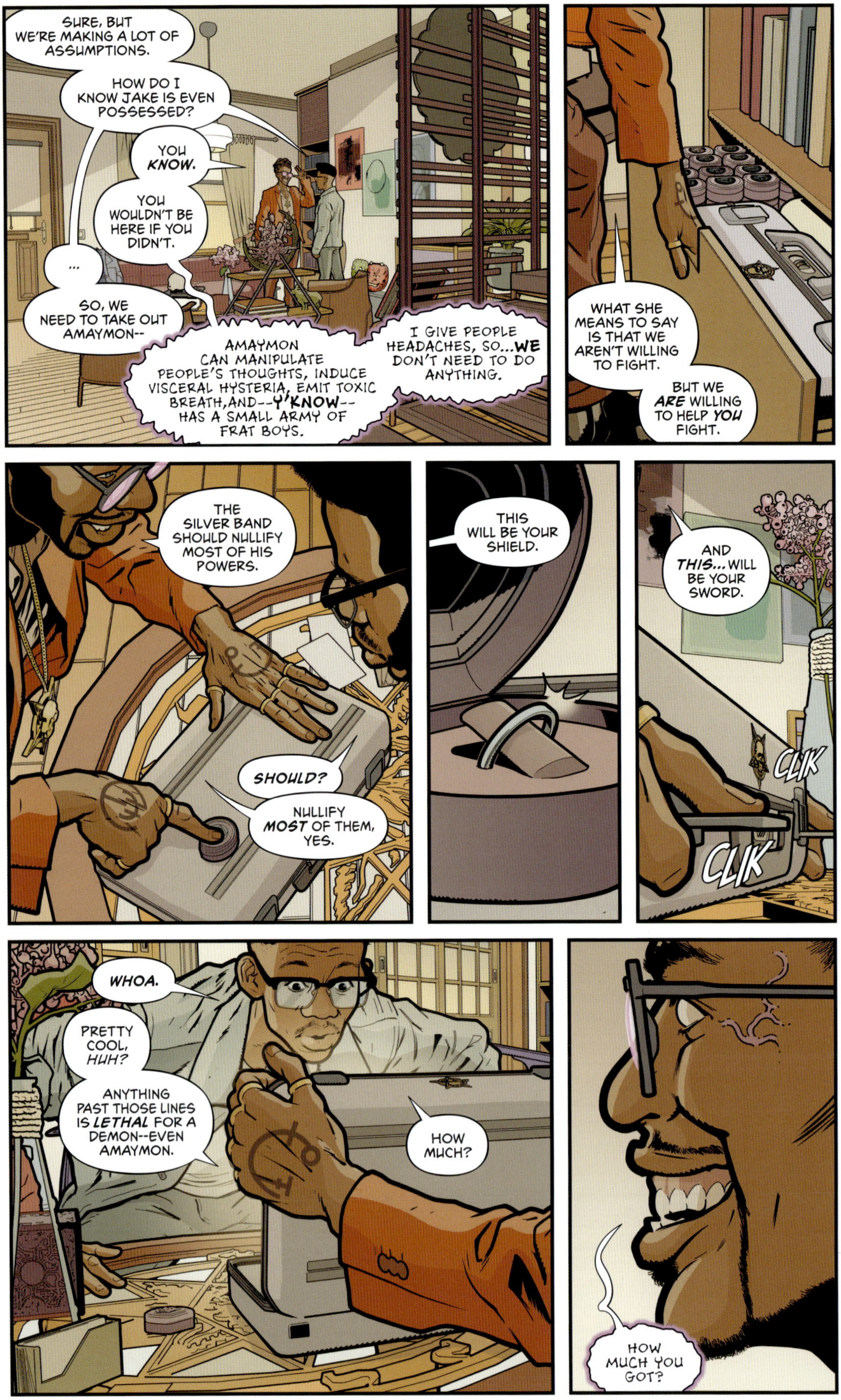
SURE, BUT WE'RE MAKING A LOT OF ASSUMPTIONS.
HOW DO I KNOW JAKE IS EVEN POSSESSED?
YOU *KNOW.*
YOU WOULDN'T BE HERE IF YOU DIDN'T.
...
SO, WE NEED TO TAKE OUT AMAYMON--
AMAYMON CAN MANIPULATE PEOPLE'S THOUGHTS, INDUCE VISCERAL HYSTERIA, EMIT TOXIC BREATH, AND--*Y'KNOW*--HAS A SMALL ARMY OF FRAT BOYS.
I GIVE PEOPLE HEADACHES, SO...*WE* DON'T NEED TO DO ANYTHING.
WHAT SHE MEANS TO SAY IS THAT WE AREN'T WILLING TO FIGHT.
BUT WE *ARE* WILLING TO HELP *YOU* FIGHT.
THE SILVER BAND SHOULD NULLIFY MOST OF HIS POWERS.
SHOULD?
NULLIFY *MOST* OF THEM, YES.
THIS WILL BE YOUR SHIELD.
AND *THIS*... WILL BE YOUR SWORD.
CLIK
CLIK
WHOA.
PRETTY COOL, *HUH?*
ANYTHING PAST THOSE LINES IS *LETHAL* FOR A DEMON--EVEN AMAYMON.
HOW MUCH?
HOW MUCH YOU GOT?

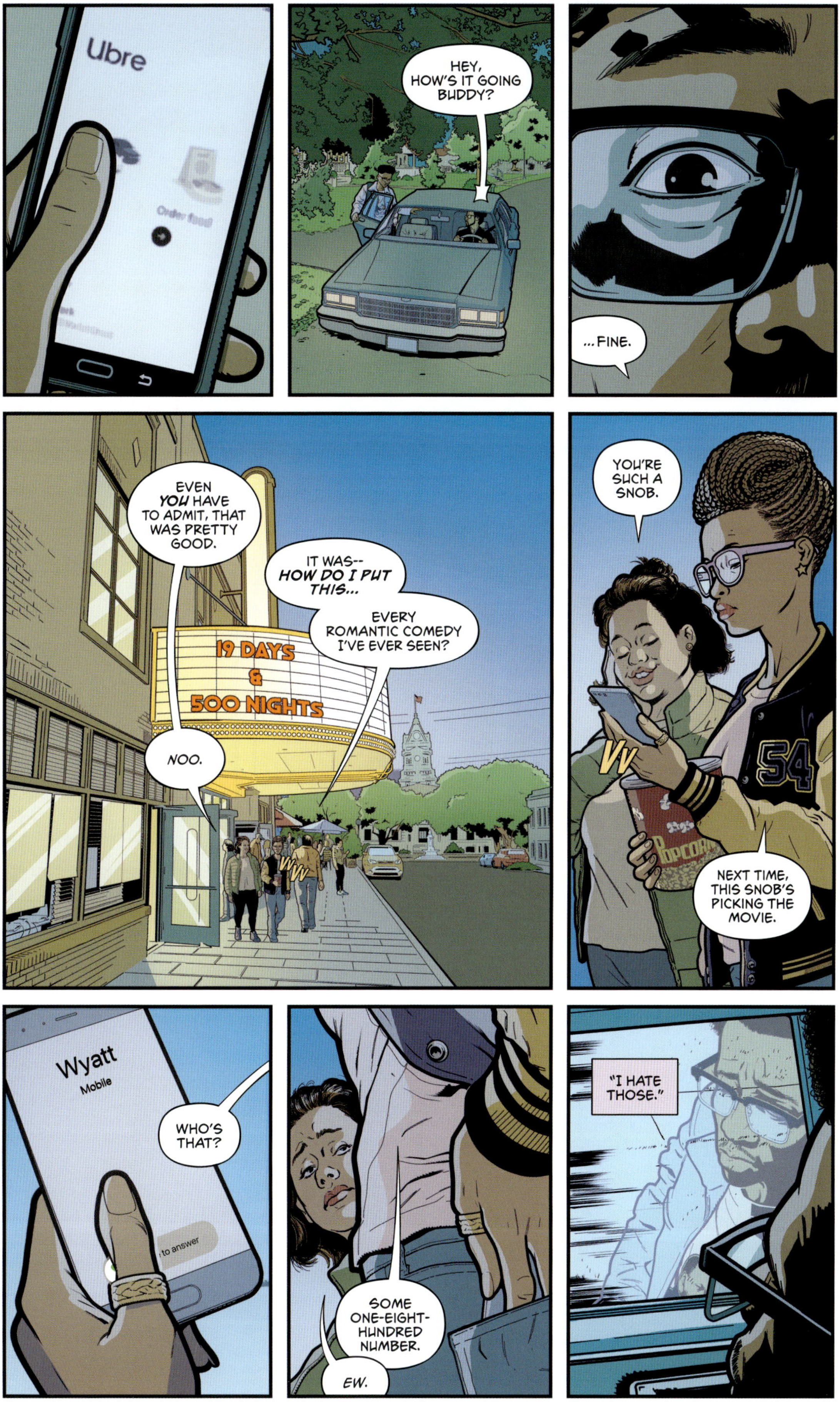
Ubre
HEY, HOW'S IT GOING BUDDY?
...FINE.
19 DAYS & 500 NIGHTS
EVEN *YOU* HAVE TO ADMIT, THAT WAS PRETTY GOOD.
NOO.
IT WAS-- *HOW DO I PUT THIS...*
EVERY ROMANTIC COMEDY I'VE EVER SEEN?
YOU'RE SUCH A SNOB.
NEXT TIME, THIS SNOB'S PICKING THE MOVIE.
Wyatt
Mobile
WHO'S THAT?
SOME ONE-EIGHT-HUNDRED NUMBER.
EW.
"I HATE THOSE."

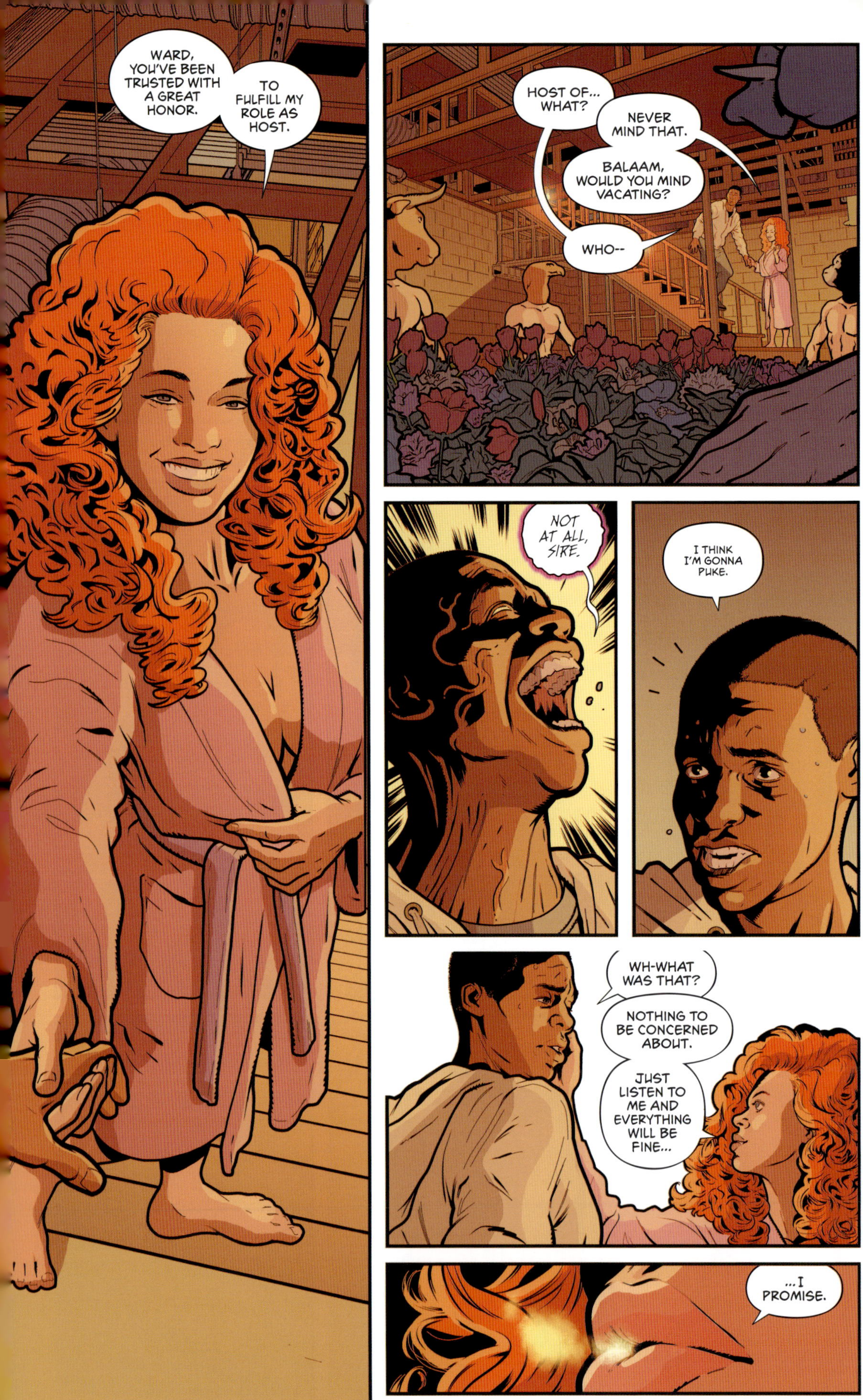
WARD, YOU'VE BEEN TRUSTED WITH A GREAT HONOR.
TO FULFILL MY ROLE AS HOST.
HOST OF... WHAT?
NEVER MIND THAT.
BALAAM, WOULD YOU MIND VACATING?
WHO--
NOT AT ALL, SIRE.
I THINK I'M GONNA PUKE.
WH-WHAT WAS THAT?
NOTHING TO BE CONCERNED ABOUT.
JUST LISTEN TO ME AND EVERYTHING WILL BE FINE...
...I PROMISE.

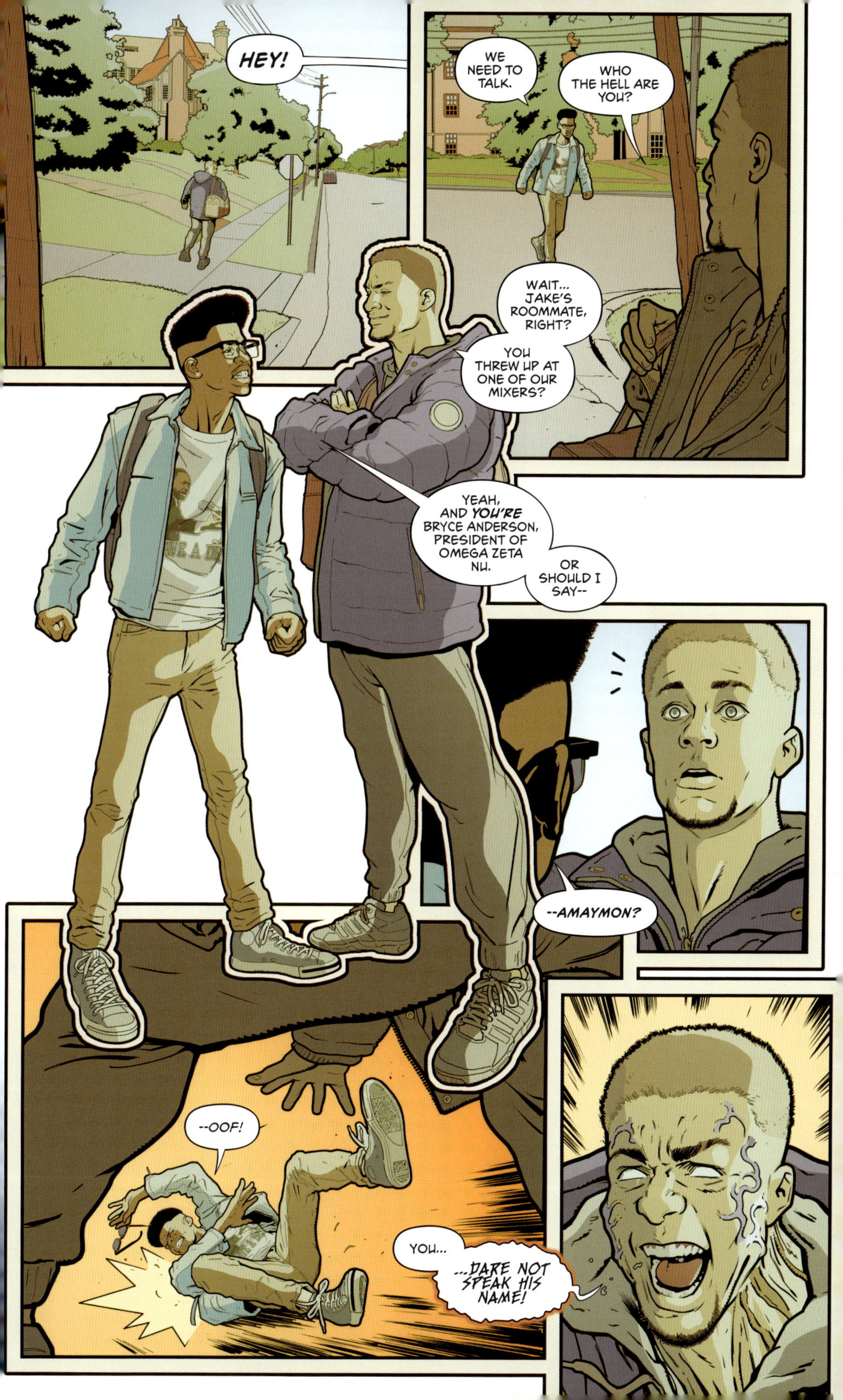
HEY!
WE NEED TO TALK.
WHO THE HELL ARE YOU?
WAIT... JAKE'S ROOMMATE, RIGHT?
YOU THREW UP AT ONE OF OUR MIXERS?
YEAH, AND *YOU'RE* BRYCE ANDERSON, PRESIDENT OF OMEGA ZETA NU.
OR SHOULD I SAY--
--AMAYMON?
--OOF!
YOU...
...DARE NOT SPEAK HIS NAME!

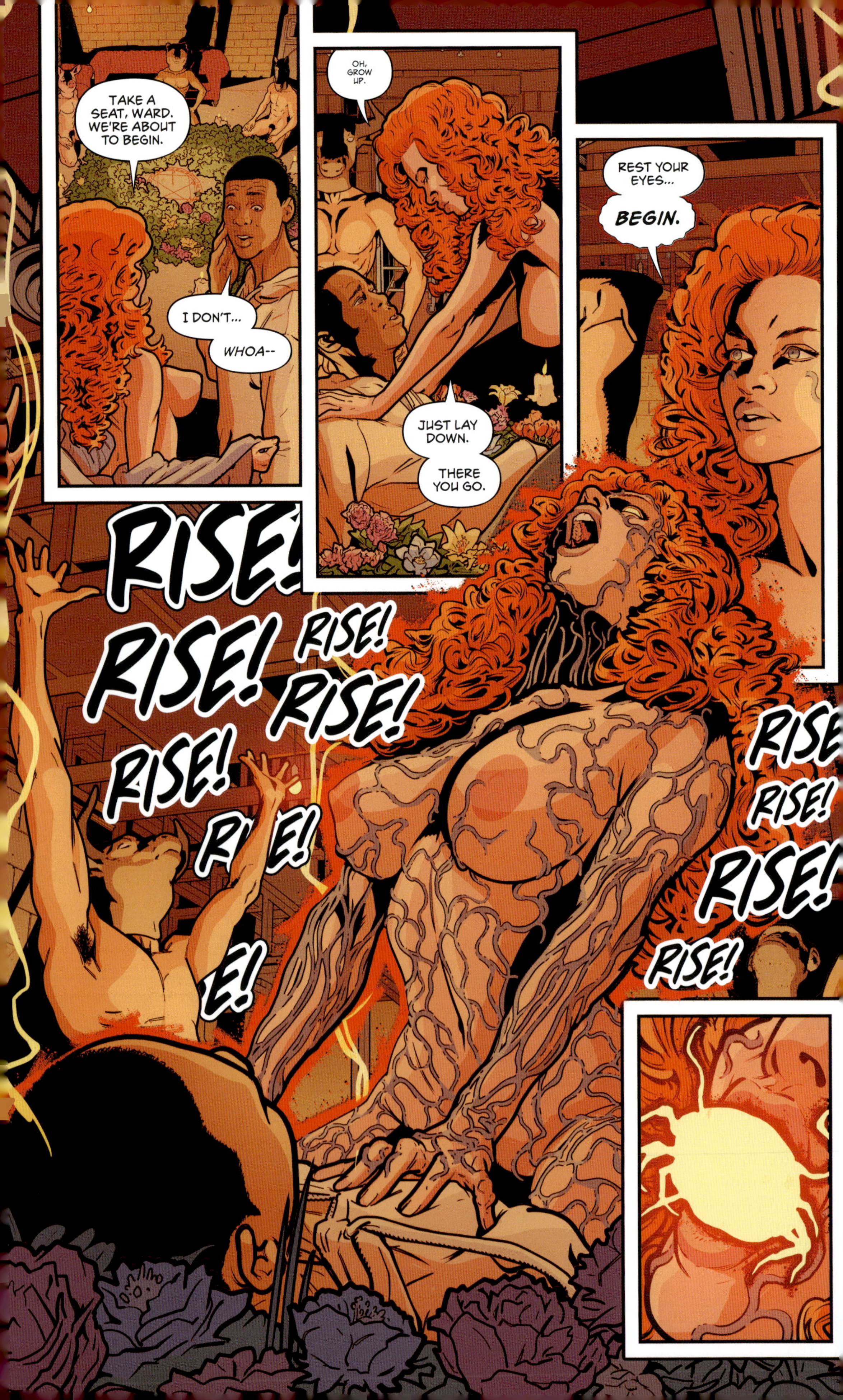
TAKE A SEAT, WARD. WE'RE ABOUT TO BEGIN.
I DON'T...
WHOA--
OH, GROW UP.
JUST LAY DOWN.
THERE YOU GO.
REST YOUR EYES...
BEGIN.
RISE!
RISE!
RISE!
RISE!
RISE!
RISE!
RISE!
RISE!
RISE!

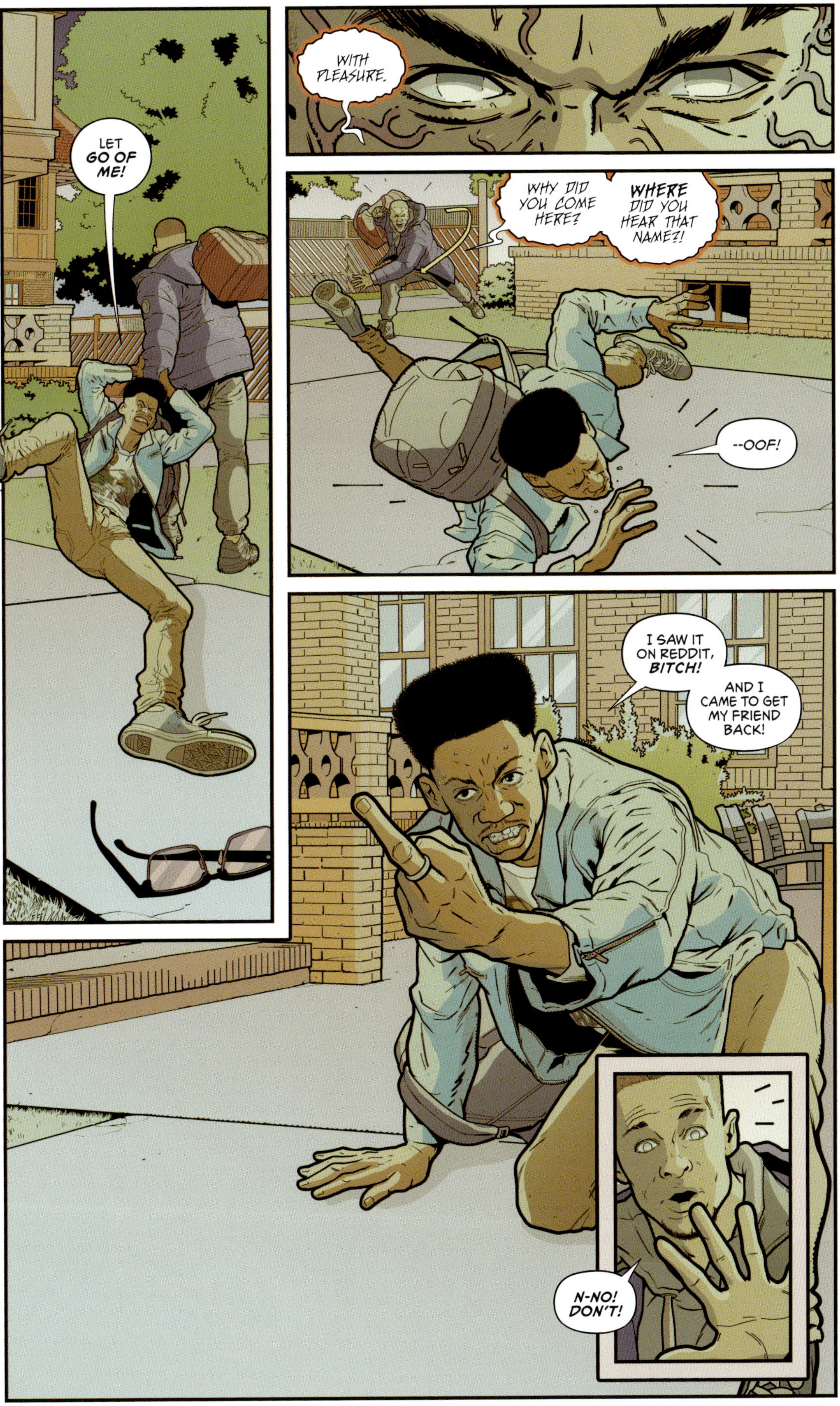
LET GO OF ME!
WITH PLEASURE.
WHY DID YOU COME HERE?
WHERE DID YOU HEAR THAT NAME?!
--OOF!
I SAW IT ON REDDIT, BITCH!
AND I CAME TO GET MY FRIEND BACK!
N-NO! DON'T!

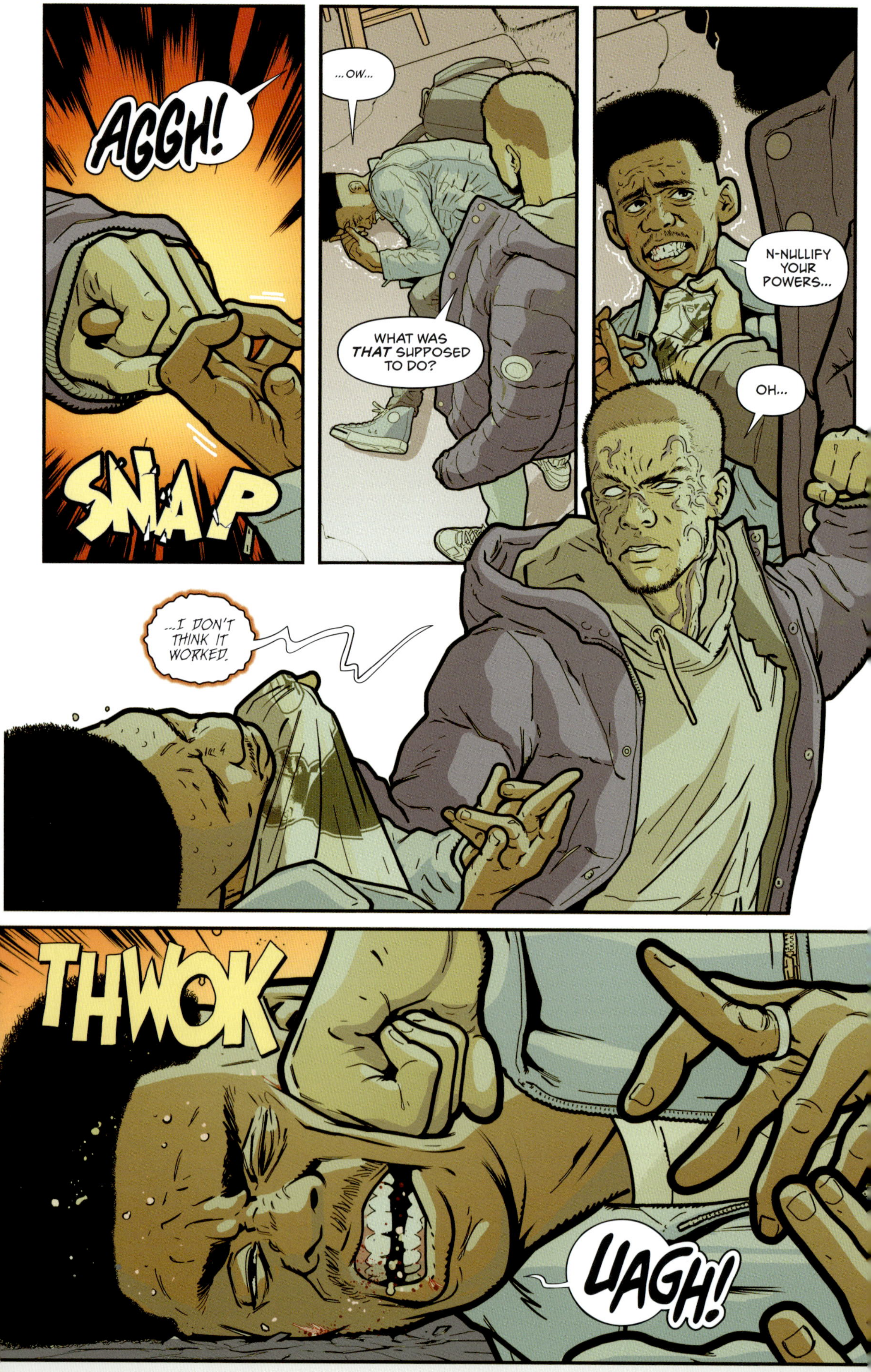
AGGH!
SNAP
...OW...
WHAT WAS THAT SUPPOSED TO DO?
N-NULLIFY YOUR POWERS...
OH...
...I DON'T THINK IT WORKED.
THWOK
UAGH!

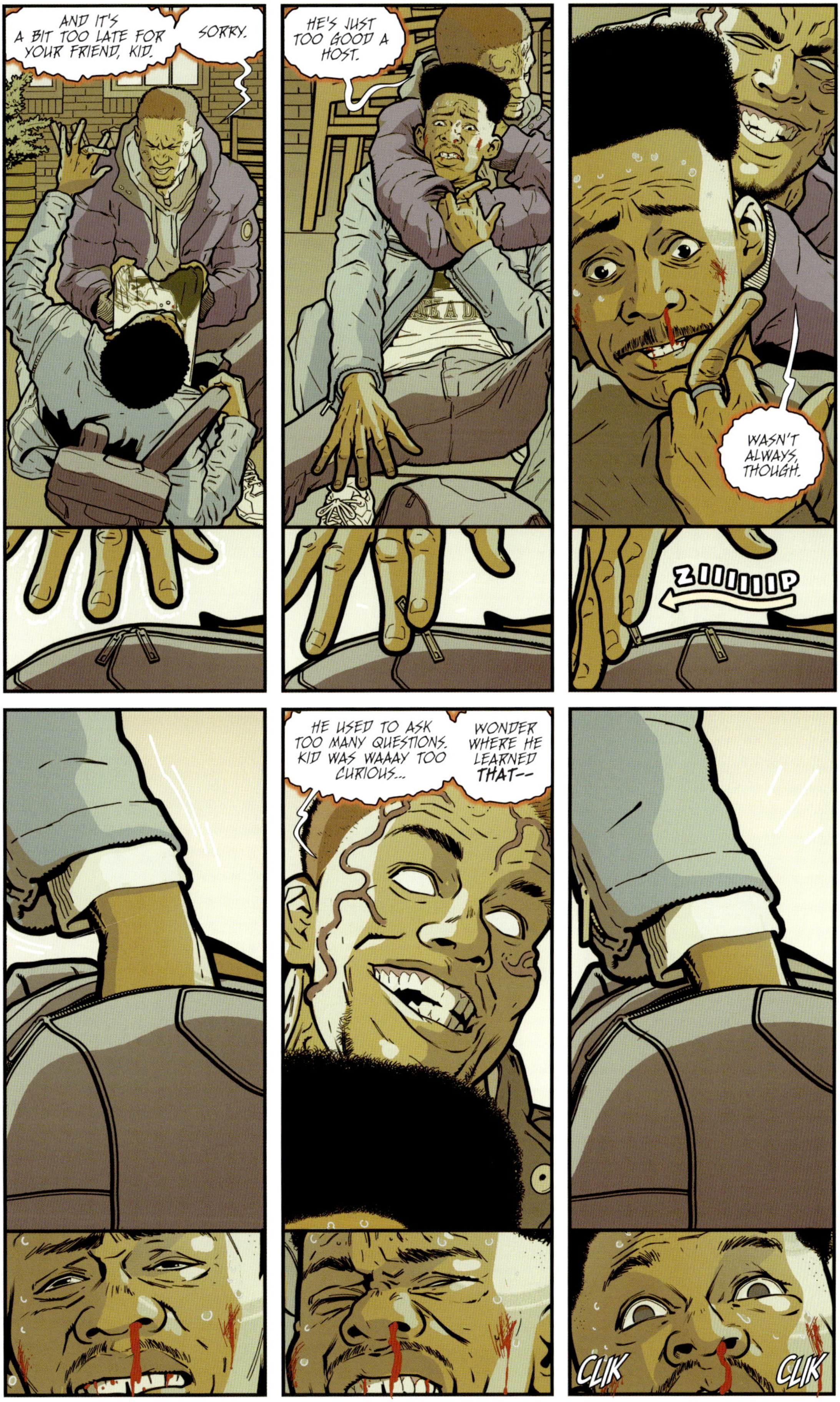
AND IT'S A BIT TOO LATE FOR YOUR FRIEND, KID.
SORRY.
HE'S JUST TOO GOOD A HOST.
WASN'T ALWAYS, THOUGH.
ZIIIIIIIP
HE USED TO ASK TOO MANY QUESTIONS. KID WAS WAAAY TOO CURIOUS...
WONDER WHERE HE LEARNED THAT--
CLIK
CLIK

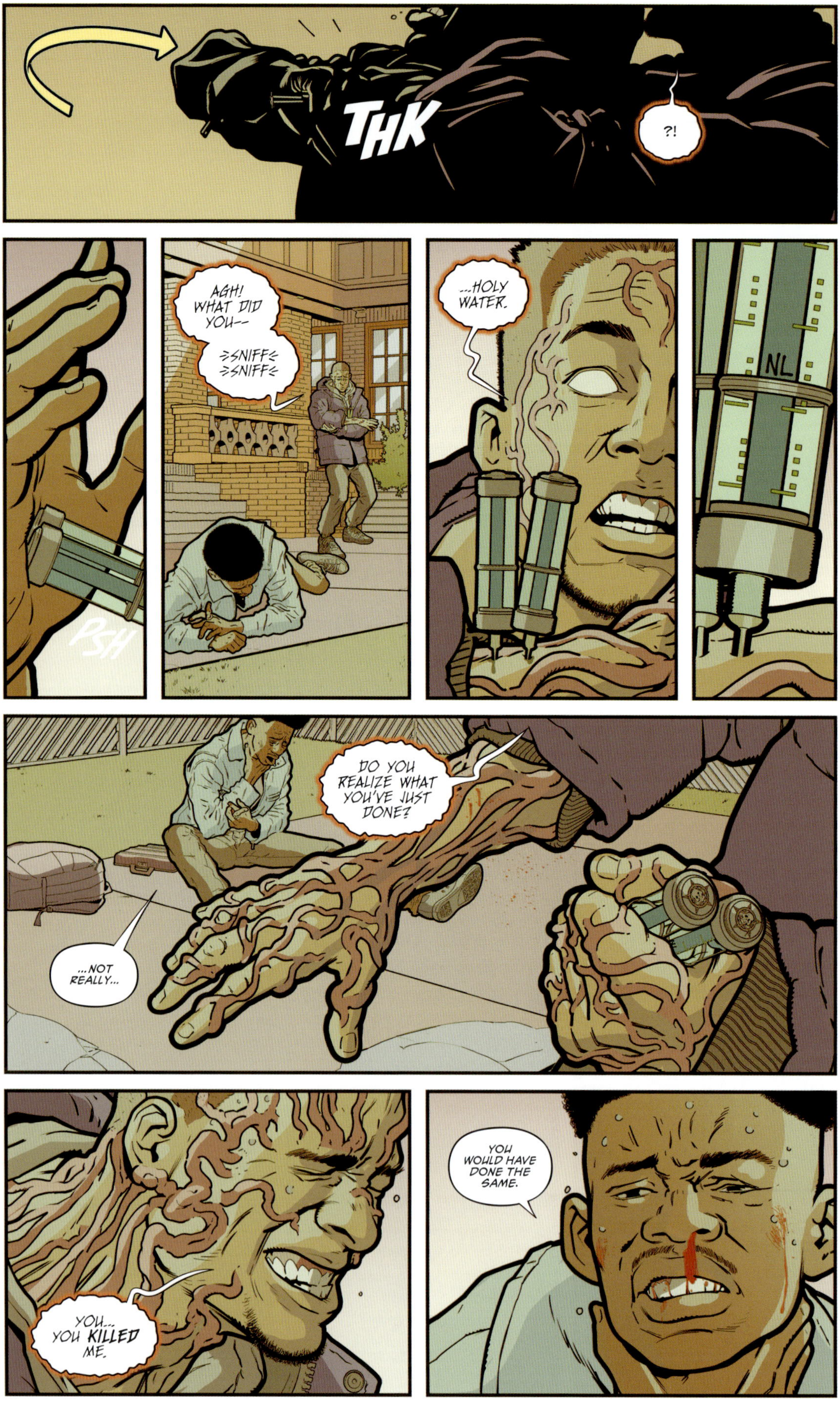
THK
?!
PSH
AGH! WHAT DID YOU--
≥SNIFF≤ ≥SNIFF≤
...HOLY WATER.
NL
DO YOU REALIZE WHAT YOU'VE JUST DONE?
...NOT REALLY...
YOU... YOU KILLED ME.
YOU WOULD HAVE DONE THE SAME.

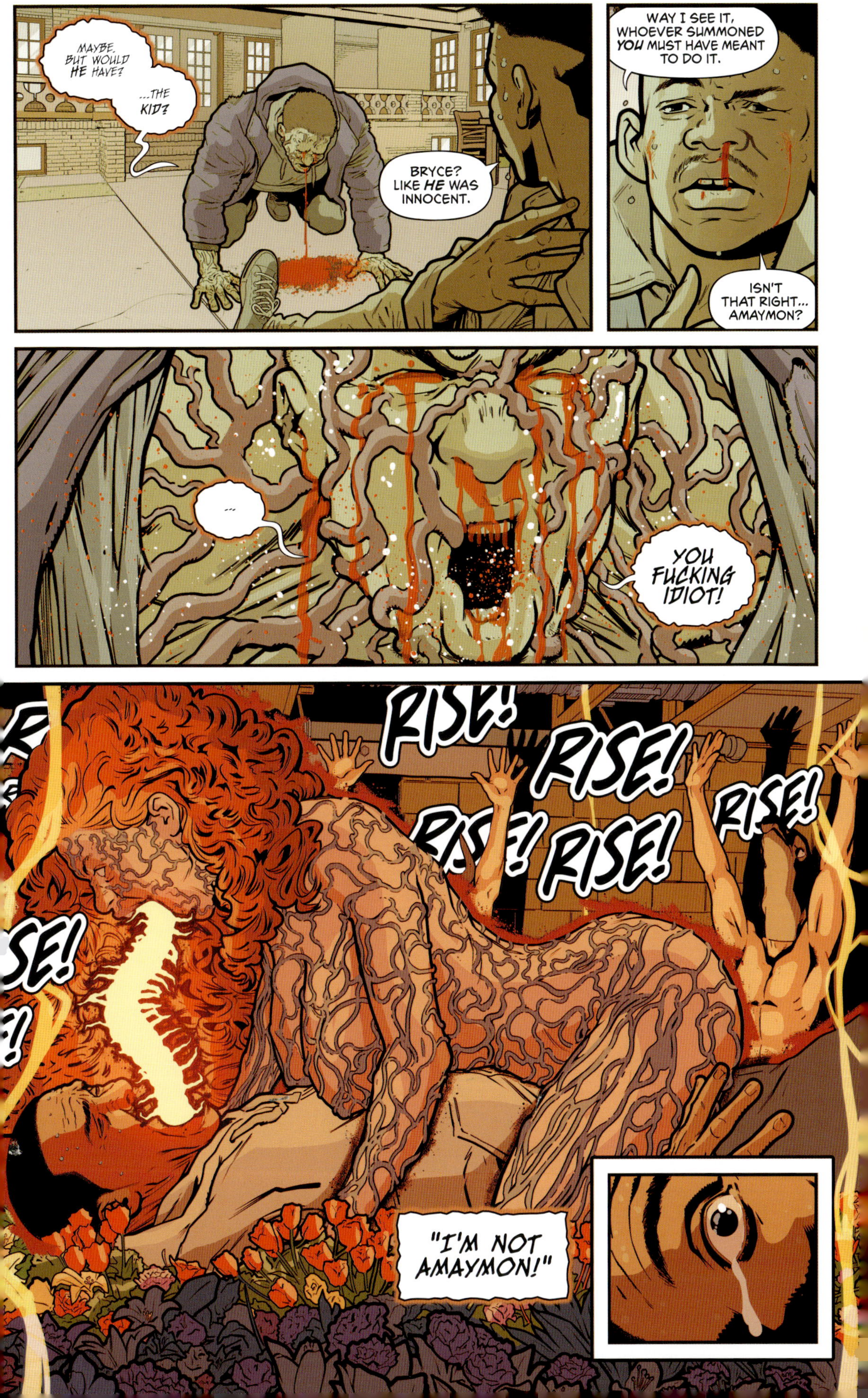
MAYBE. BUT WOULD HE HAVE?
...THE KID?
BRYCE? LIKE HE WAS INNOCENT.
WAY I SEE IT, WHOEVER SUMMONED YOU MUST HAVE MEANT TO DO IT.
ISN'T THAT RIGHT... AMAYMON?
...
YOU FUCKING IDIOT!
RISE!
RISE!
RISE!
RISE!
RISE!
"I'M NOT AMAYMON!"

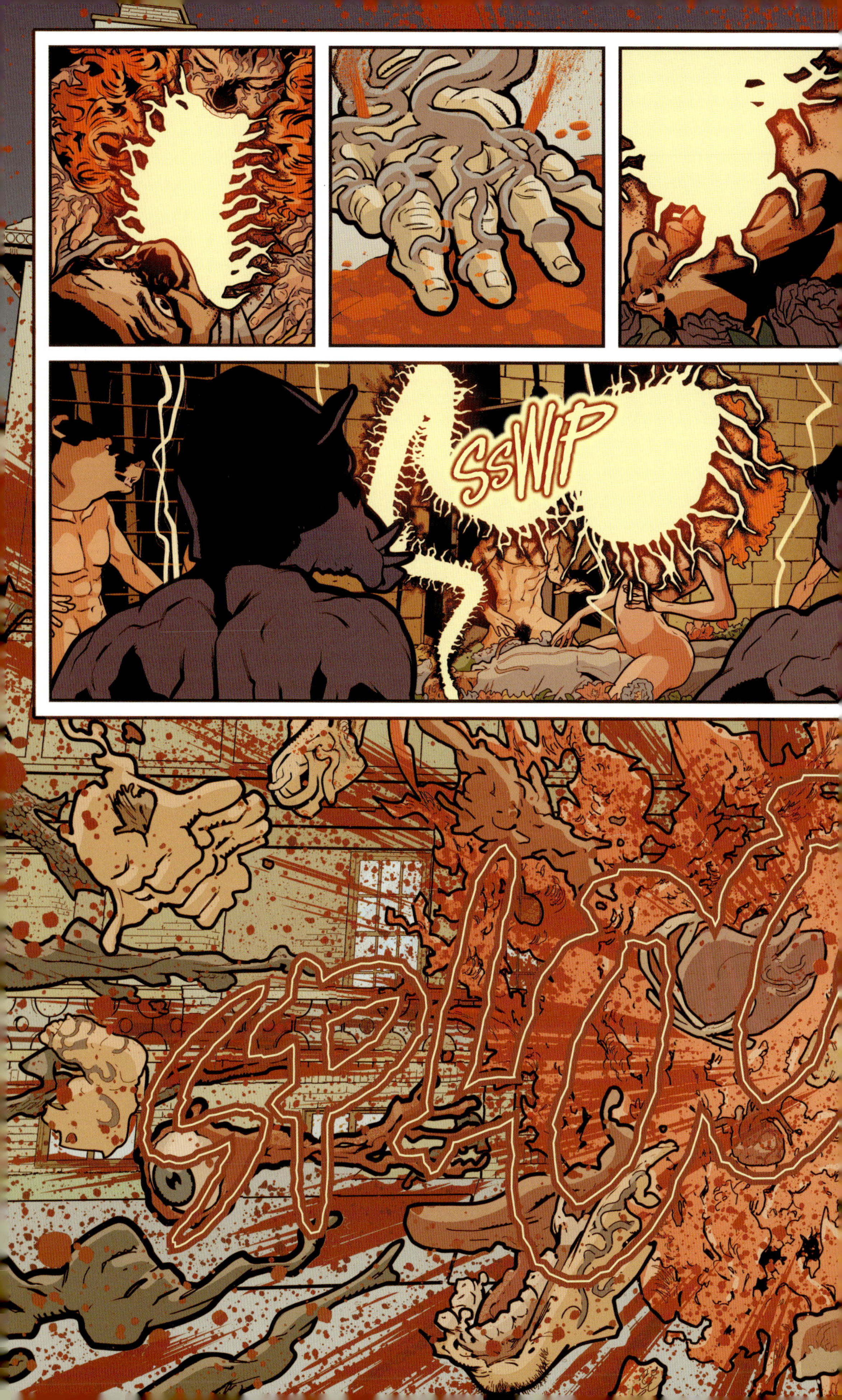
SsWIP

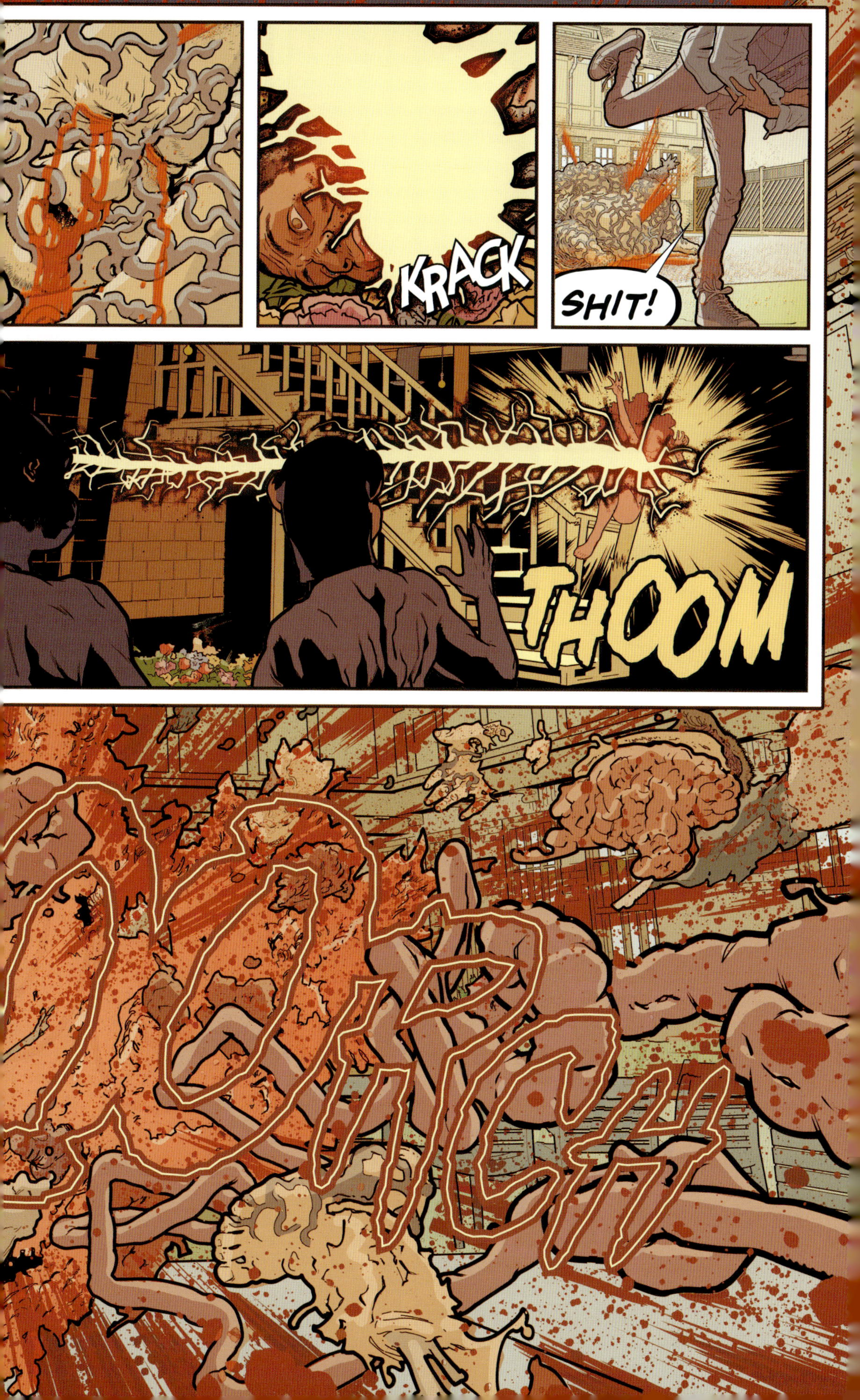
KRACK
SHIT!
THOOM

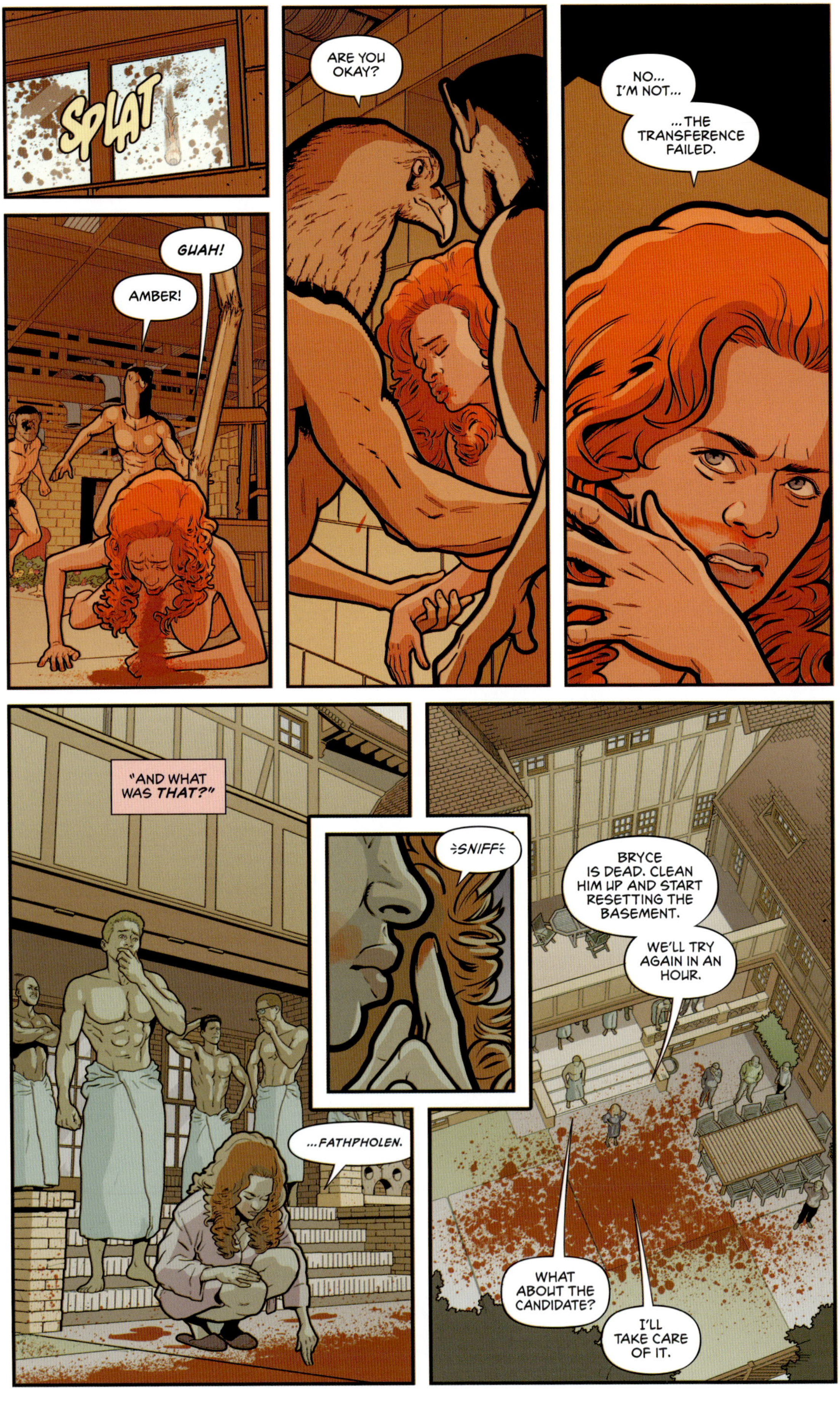
SPLAT
AMBER!
GUAH!
ARE YOU OKAY?
NO... I'M NOT...
...THE TRANSFERENCE FAILED.
"AND WHAT WAS THAT?"
SNIFF
...FATHPHOLEN.
BRYCE IS DEAD. CLEAN HIM UP AND START RESETTING THE BASEMENT.
WE'LL TRY AGAIN IN AN HOUR.
WHAT ABOUT THE CANDIDATE?
I'LL TAKE CARE OF IT.

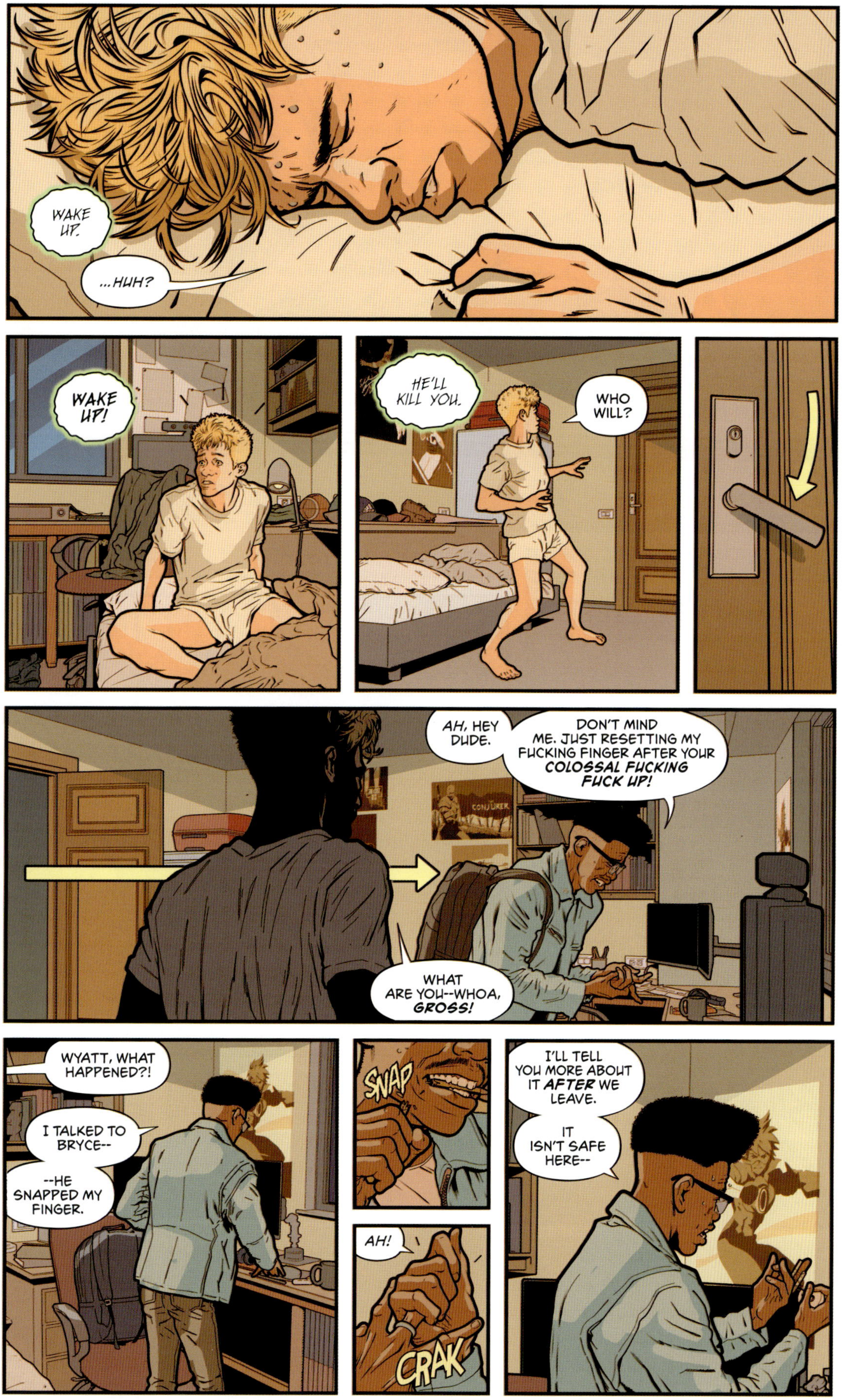
WAKE UP.
...HUH?
WAKE UP!
HE'LL KILL YOU.
WHO WILL?
AH, HEY DUDE.
DON'T MIND ME. JUST RESETTING MY FUCKING FINGER AFTER YOUR COLOSSAL FUCKING FUCK UP!
CONJURER
WHAT ARE YOU--WHOA, GROSS!
WYATT, WHAT HAPPENED?!
I TALKED TO BRYCE--
--HE SNAPPED MY FINGER.
SNAP
AH!
CRAK
I'LL TELL YOU MORE ABOUT IT AFTER WE LEAVE.
IT ISN'T SAFE HERE--

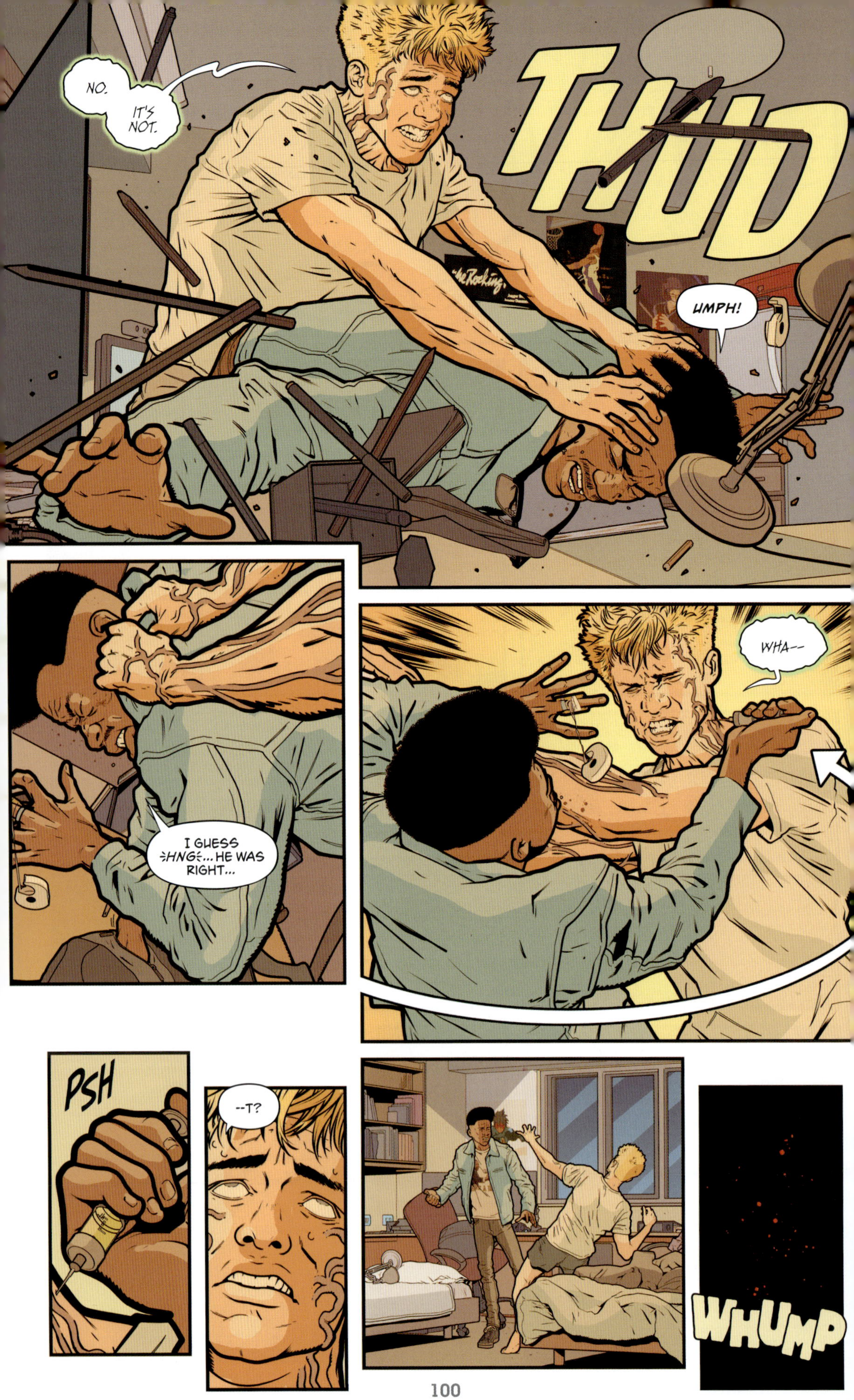
NO.
IT'S NOT.
THUD
UMPH!
I GUESS ⪧HNG⪦... HE WAS RIGHT...
WHA--
PSH
--T?
WHUMP

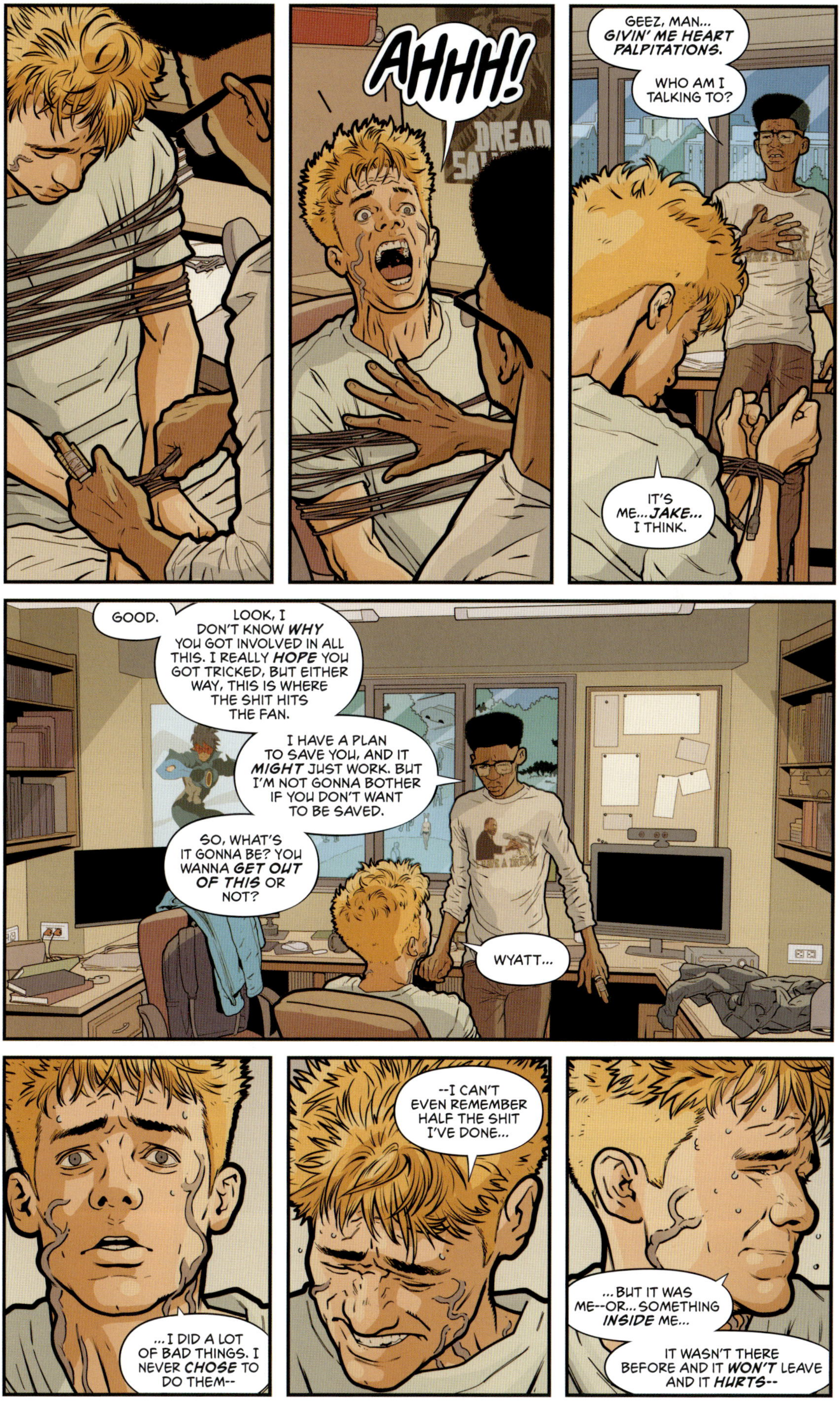

AHHH!
DREAD
GEEZ, MAN... *GIVIN' ME HEART PALPITATIONS.*
WHO AM I TALKING TO?
IT'S ME... *JAKE...* I THINK.
GOOD.
LOOK, I DON'T KNOW *WHY* YOU GOT INVOLVED IN ALL THIS. I REALLY *HOPE* YOU GOT TRICKED, BUT EITHER WAY, THIS IS WHERE THE SHIT HITS THE FAN.
I HAVE A PLAN TO SAVE YOU, AND IT *MIGHT* JUST WORK. BUT I'M NOT GONNA BOTHER IF YOU DON'T WANT TO BE SAVED.
SO, WHAT'S IT GONNA BE? YOU WANNA *GET OUT OF THIS* OR NOT?
WYATT...
...I DID A LOT OF BAD THINGS. I NEVER *CHOSE* TO DO THEM--
--I CAN'T EVEN REMEMBER HALF THE SHIT I'VE DONE...
...BUT IT WAS ME--OR... SOMETHING *INSIDE* ME...
IT WASN'T THERE BEFORE AND IT *WON'T* LEAVE AND IT *HURTS--*

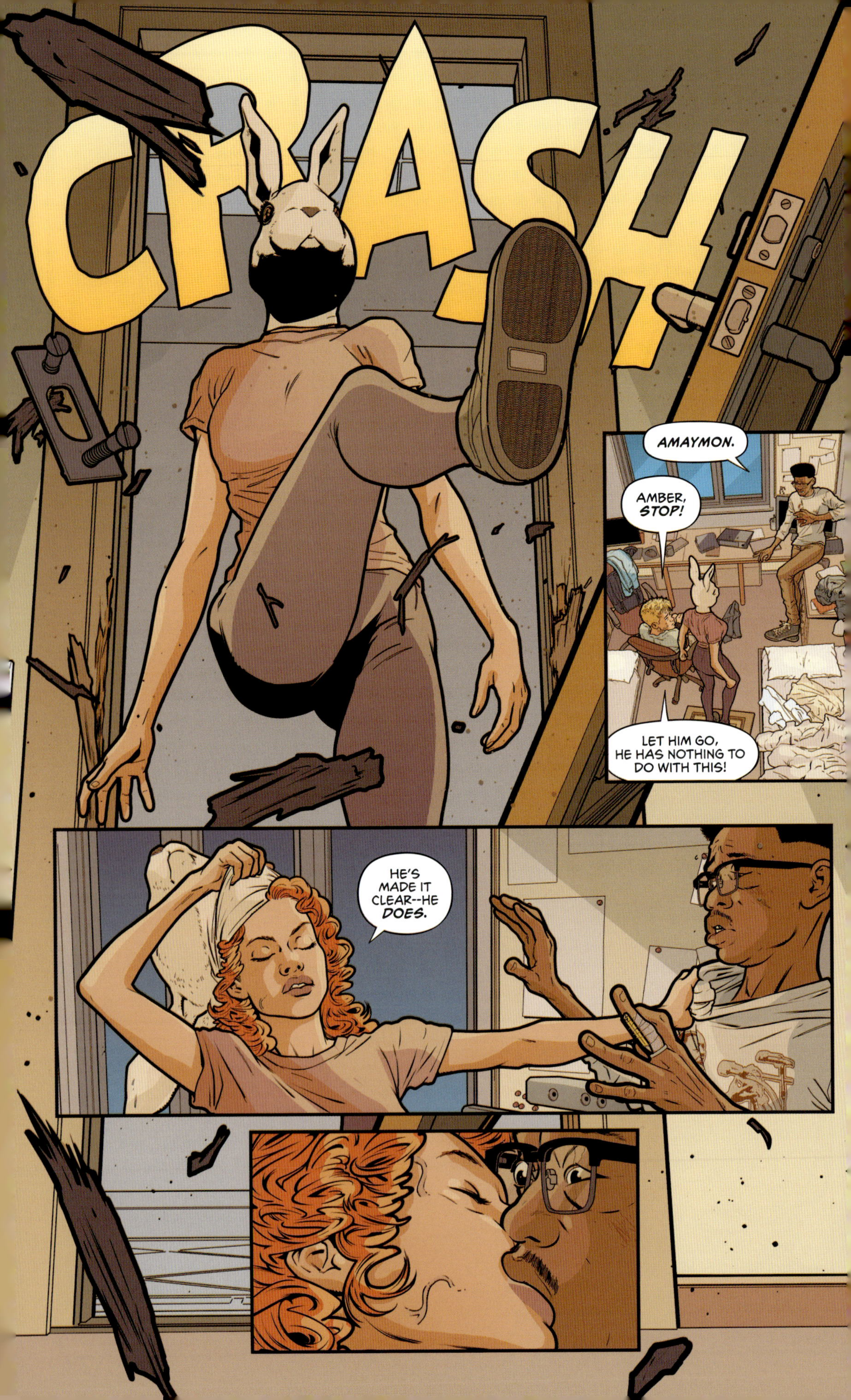
CRASH
AMAYMON.
AMBER, STOP!
LET HIM GO, HE HAS NOTHING TO DO WITH THIS!
HE'S MADE IT CLEAR--HE DOES.

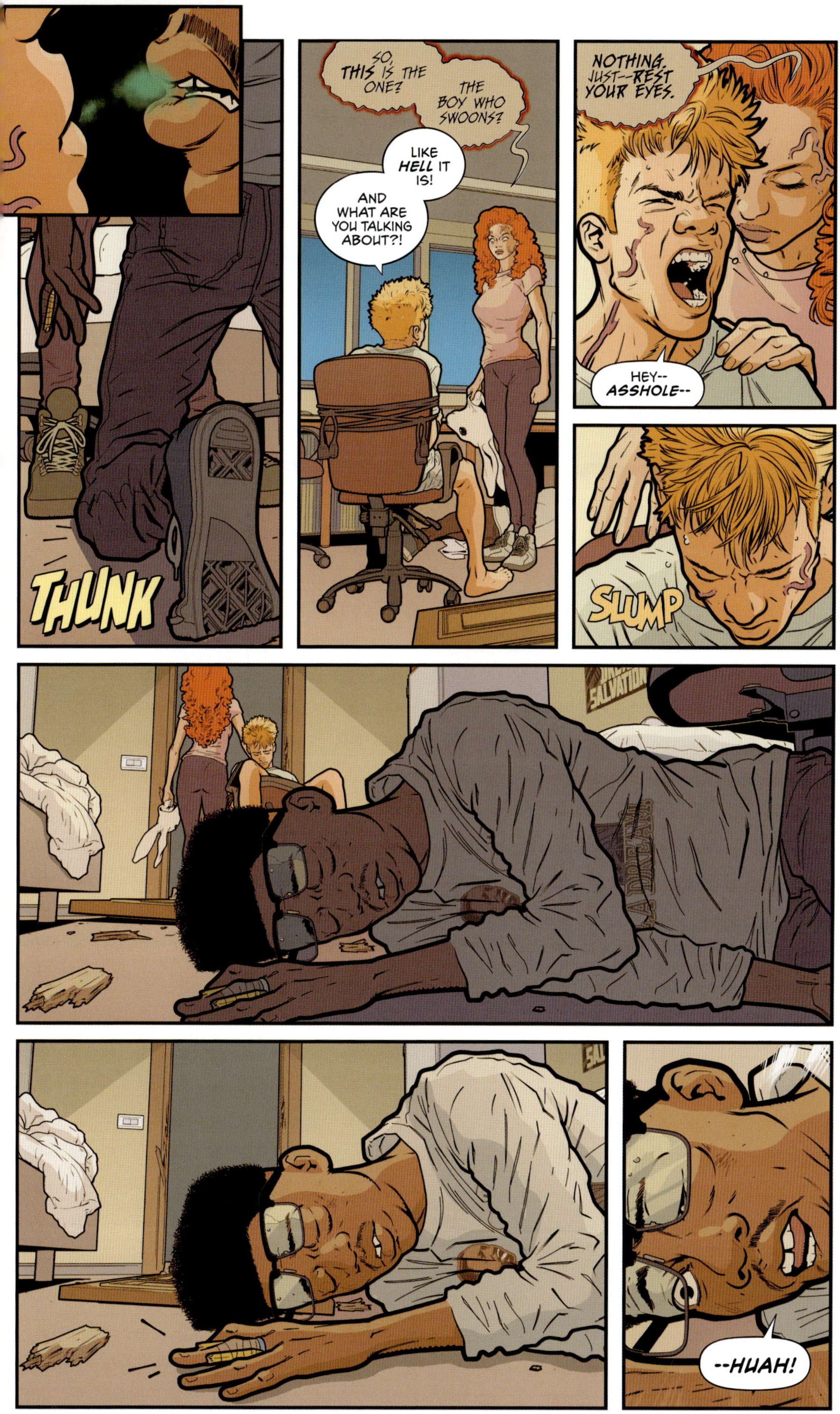
THUNK
SO, THIS IS THE ONE?
THE BOY WHO SWOONS?
LIKE HELL IT IS!
AND WHAT ARE YOU TALKING ABOUT?!
NOTHING. JUST--REST YOUR EYES.
HEY-- ASSHOLE--
SLUMP
SALVATION
--HUAH!

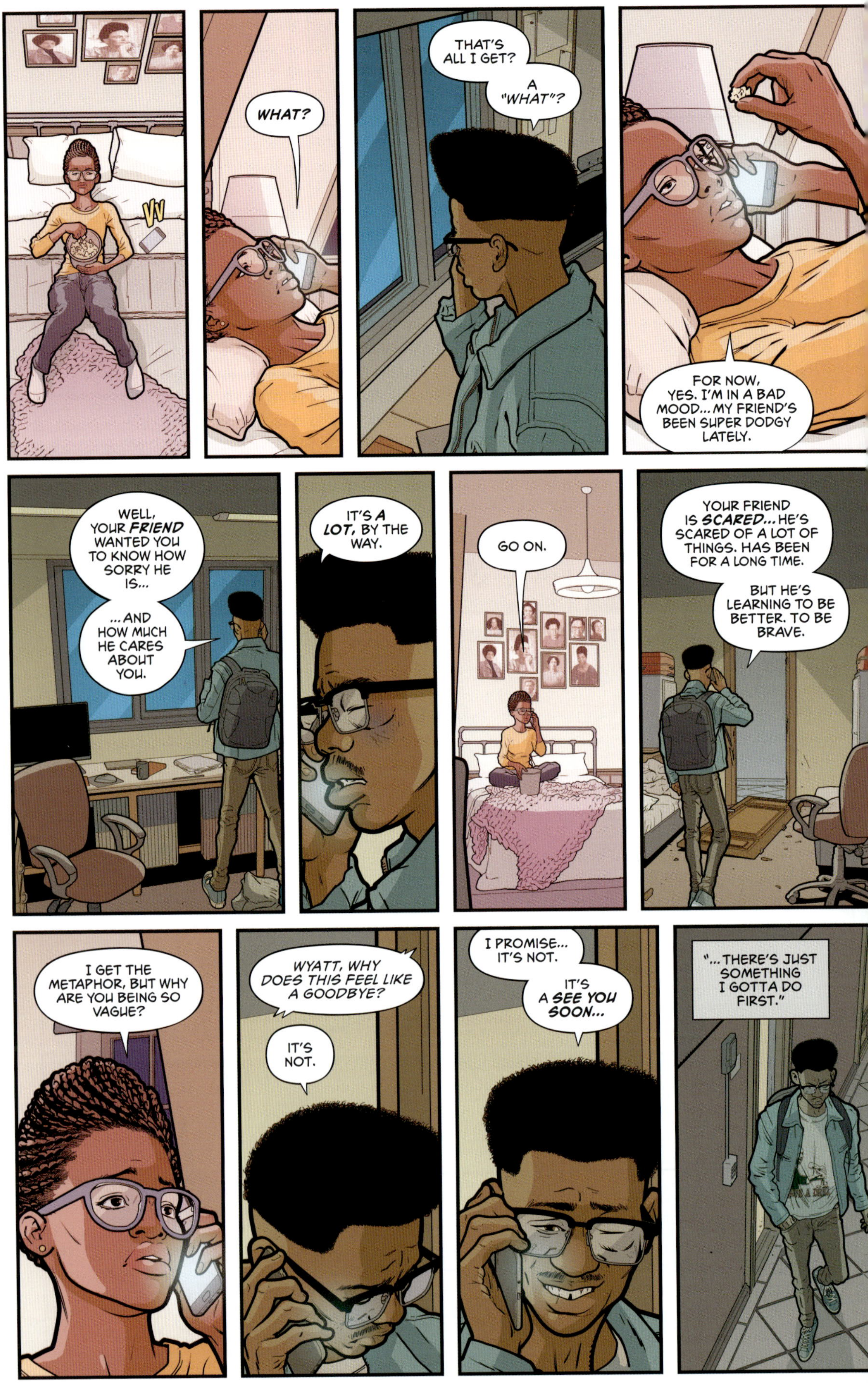
VV
WHAT?
THAT'S ALL I GET?
A "WHAT"?
FOR NOW, YES. I'M IN A BAD MOOD... MY FRIEND'S BEEN SUPER DODGY LATELY.
WELL, YOUR FRIEND WANTED YOU TO KNOW HOW SORRY HE IS...
...AND HOW MUCH HE CARES ABOUT YOU.
IT'S A LOT, BY THE WAY.
GO ON.
YOUR FRIEND IS SCARED... HE'S SCARED OF A LOT OF THINGS. HAS BEEN FOR A LONG TIME.
BUT HE'S LEARNING TO BE BETTER. TO BE BRAVE.
I GET THE METAPHOR, BUT WHY ARE YOU BEING SO VAGUE?
WYATT, WHY DOES THIS FEEL LIKE A GOODBYE?
IT'S NOT.
I PROMISE... IT'S NOT.
IT'S A SEE YOU SOON...
"...THERE'S JUST SOMETHING I GOTTA DO FIRST."

CHAPTER FOUR

GOODBYE.

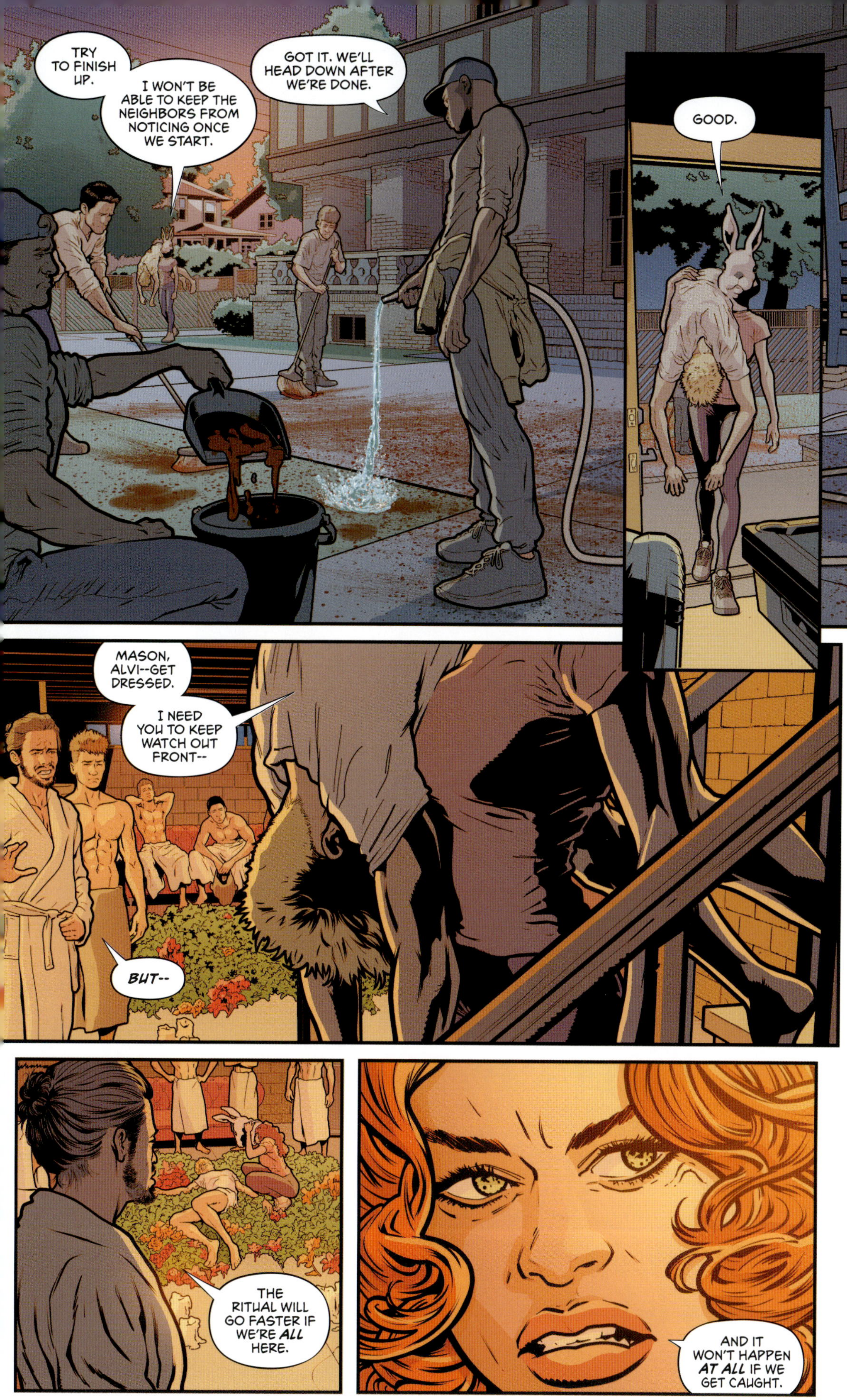
TRY TO FINISH UP.
I WON'T BE ABLE TO KEEP THE NEIGHBORS FROM NOTICING ONCE WE START.
GOT IT. WE'LL HEAD DOWN AFTER WE'RE DONE.
GOOD.
MASON, ALVI--GET DRESSED.
I NEED YOU TO KEEP WATCH OUT FRONT--
BUT--
THE RITUAL WILL GO FASTER IF WE'RE *ALL* HERE.
AND IT WON'T HAPPEN *AT ALL* IF WE GET CAUGHT.

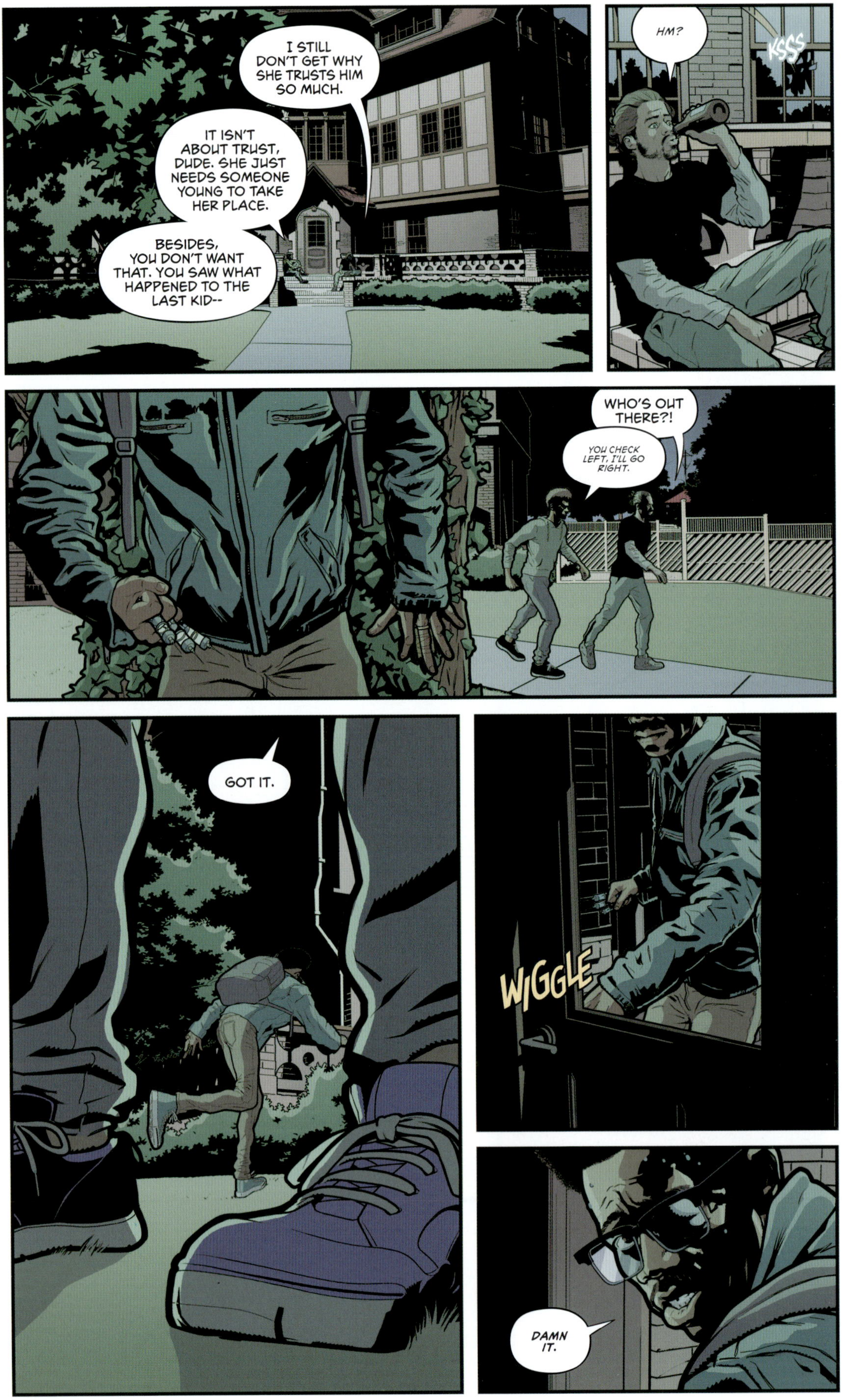
I STILL DON'T GET WHY SHE TRUSTS HIM SO MUCH.
IT ISN'T ABOUT TRUST, DUDE. SHE JUST NEEDS SOMEONE YOUNG TO TAKE HER PLACE.
BESIDES, YOU DON'T WANT THAT. YOU SAW WHAT HAPPENED TO THE LAST KID--
HM?
KSSS
WHO'S OUT THERE?!
YOU CHECK LEFT, I'LL GO RIGHT.
GOT IT.
WIGGLE
DAMN IT.

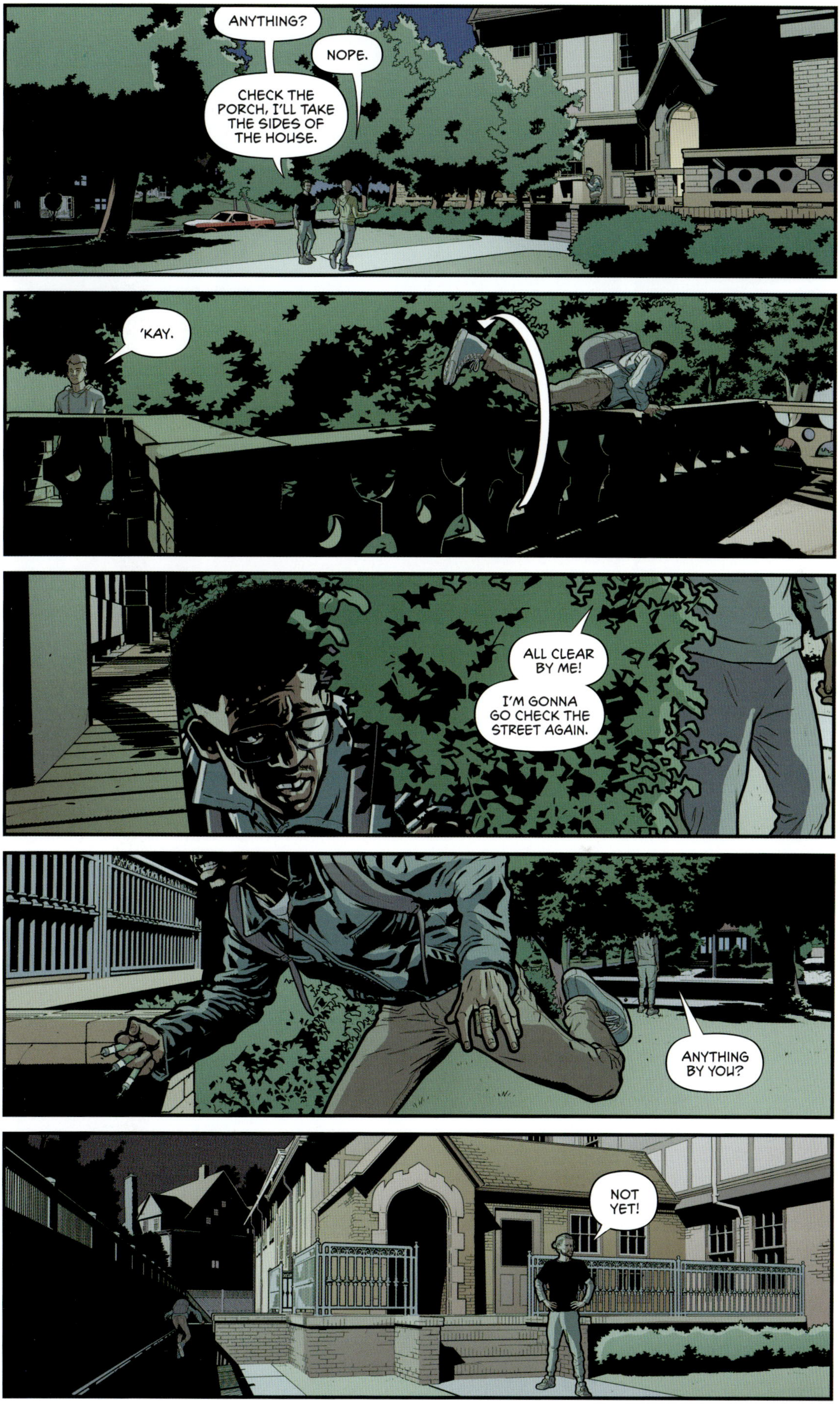
ANYTHING?
NOPE.
CHECK THE PORCH, I'LL TAKE THE SIDES OF THE HOUSE.
'KAY.
ALL CLEAR BY ME!
I'M GONNA GO CHECK THE STREET AGAIN.
ANYTHING BY YOU?
NOT YET!

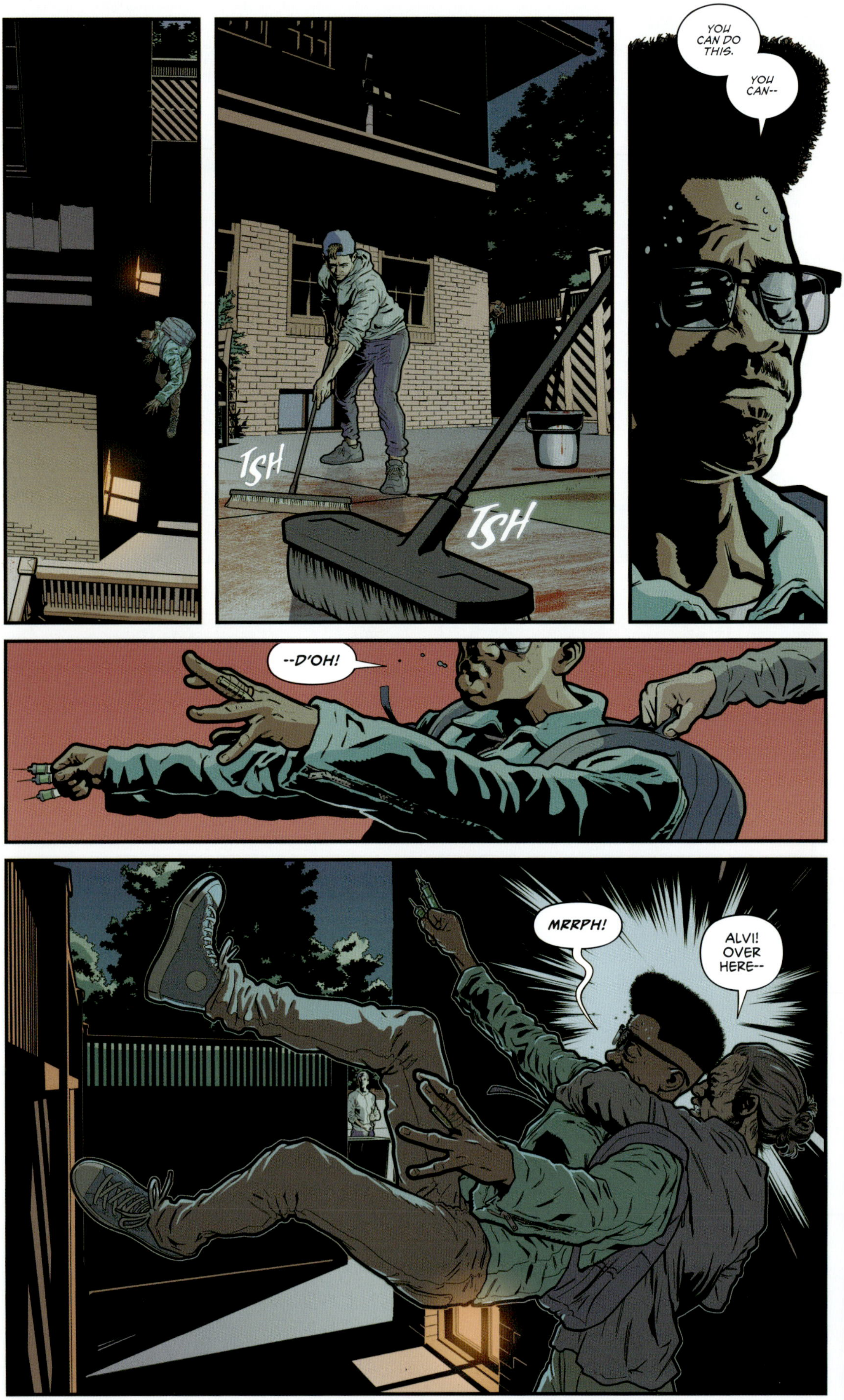

TSH
TSH
YOU CAN DO THIS.
YOU CAN--
--D'OH!
MRRPH!
ALVI! OVER HERE--

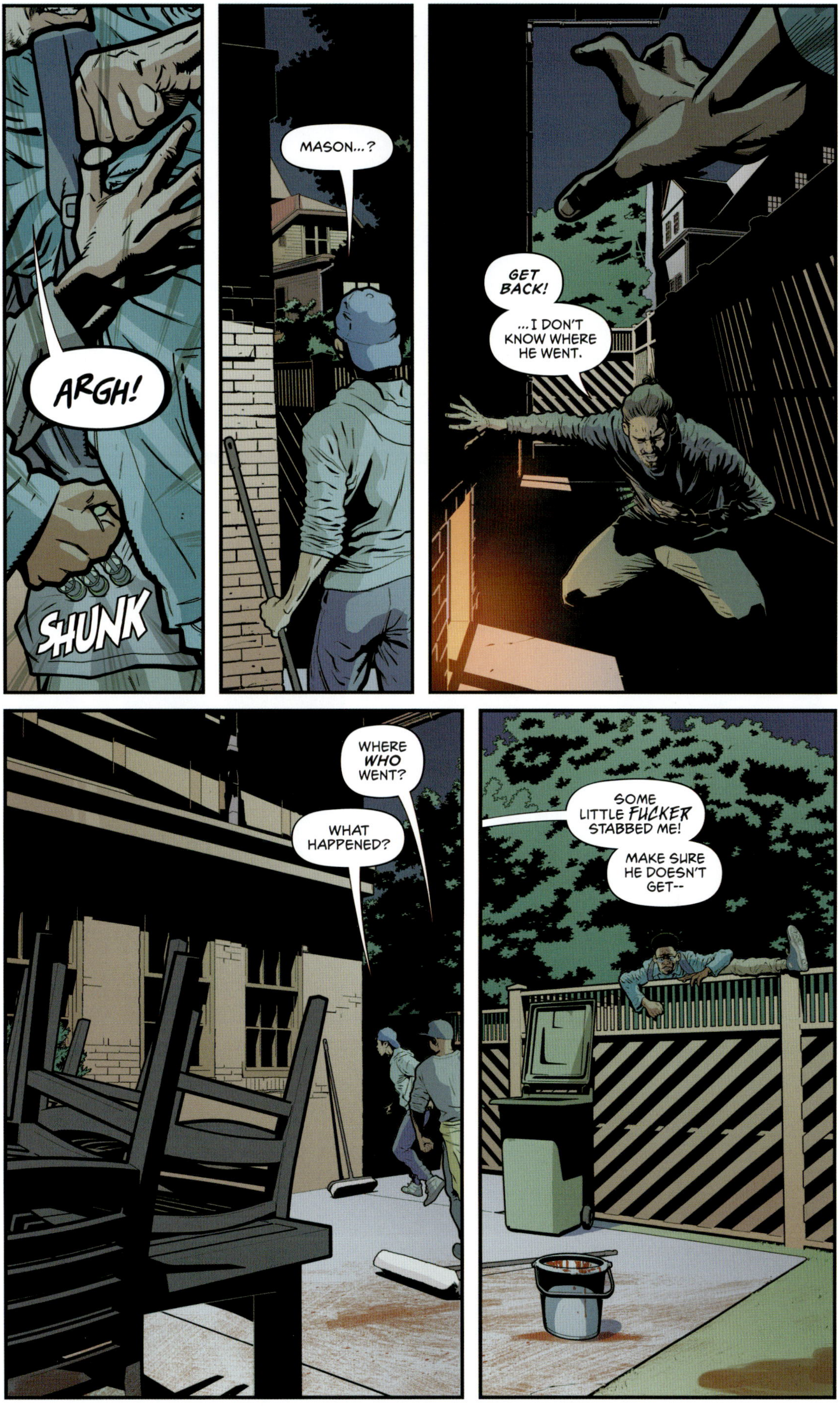
ARGH!
SHUNK
MASON...?
GET BACK!
...I DON'T KNOW WHERE HE WENT.
WHERE WHO WENT?
WHAT HAPPENED?
SOME LITTLE FUCKER STABBED ME!
MAKE SURE HE DOESN'T GET--

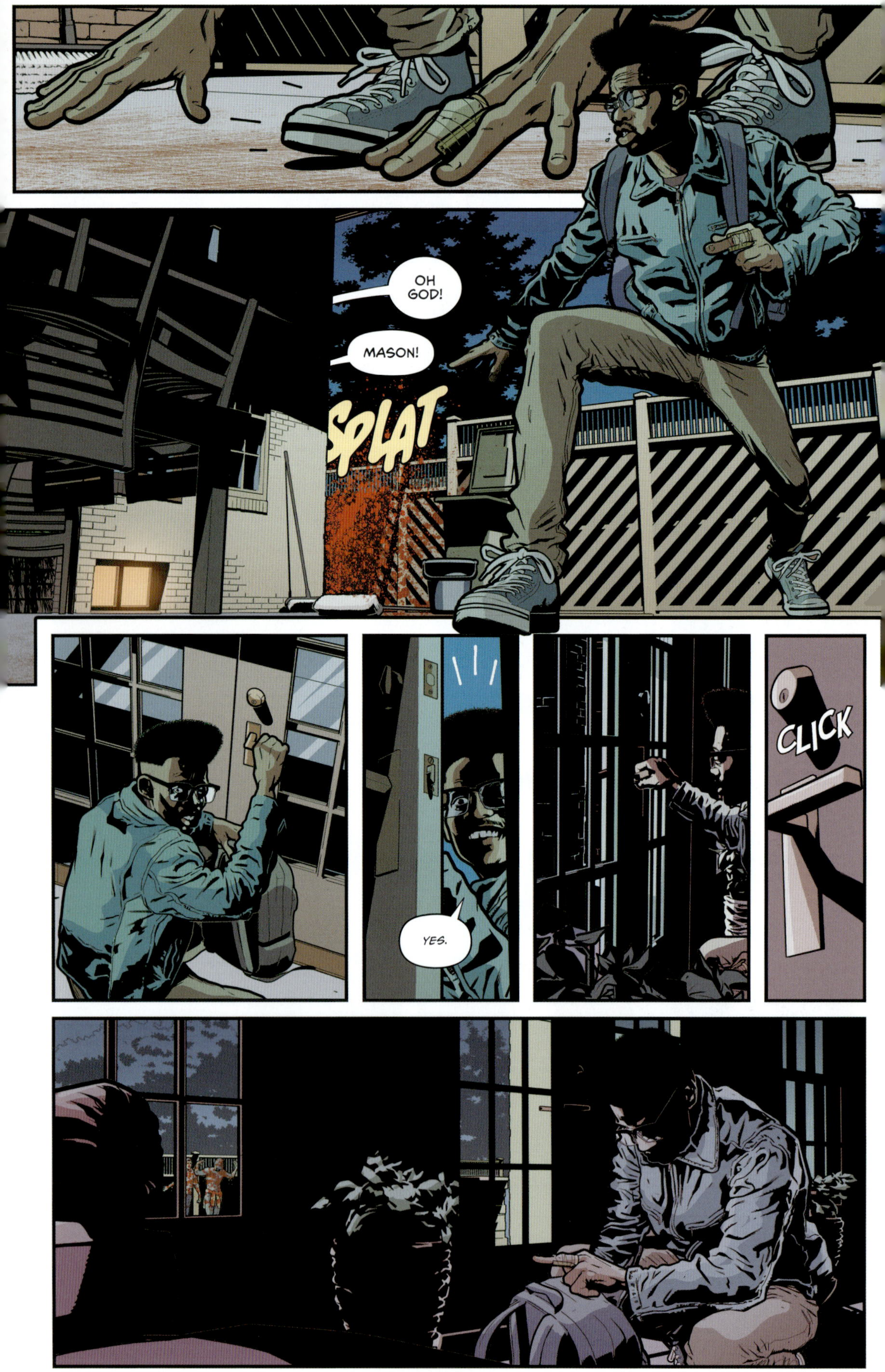
OH GOD!
MASON!
SPLAT
YES.
CLICK

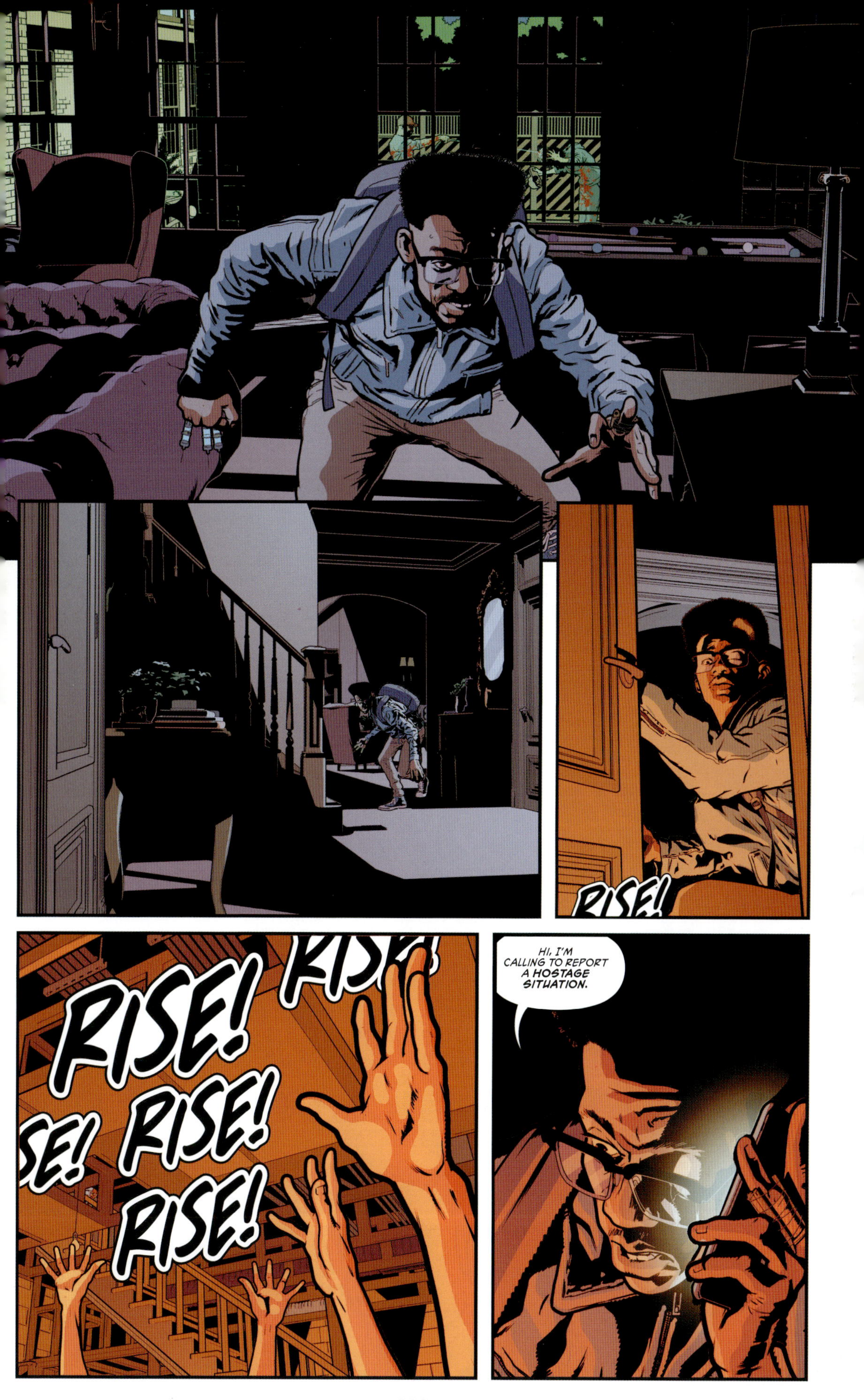
RISE!
RISE!
RISE!
SE! RISE!
RISE!
HI, I'M CALLING TO REPORT A HOSTAGE SITUATION.

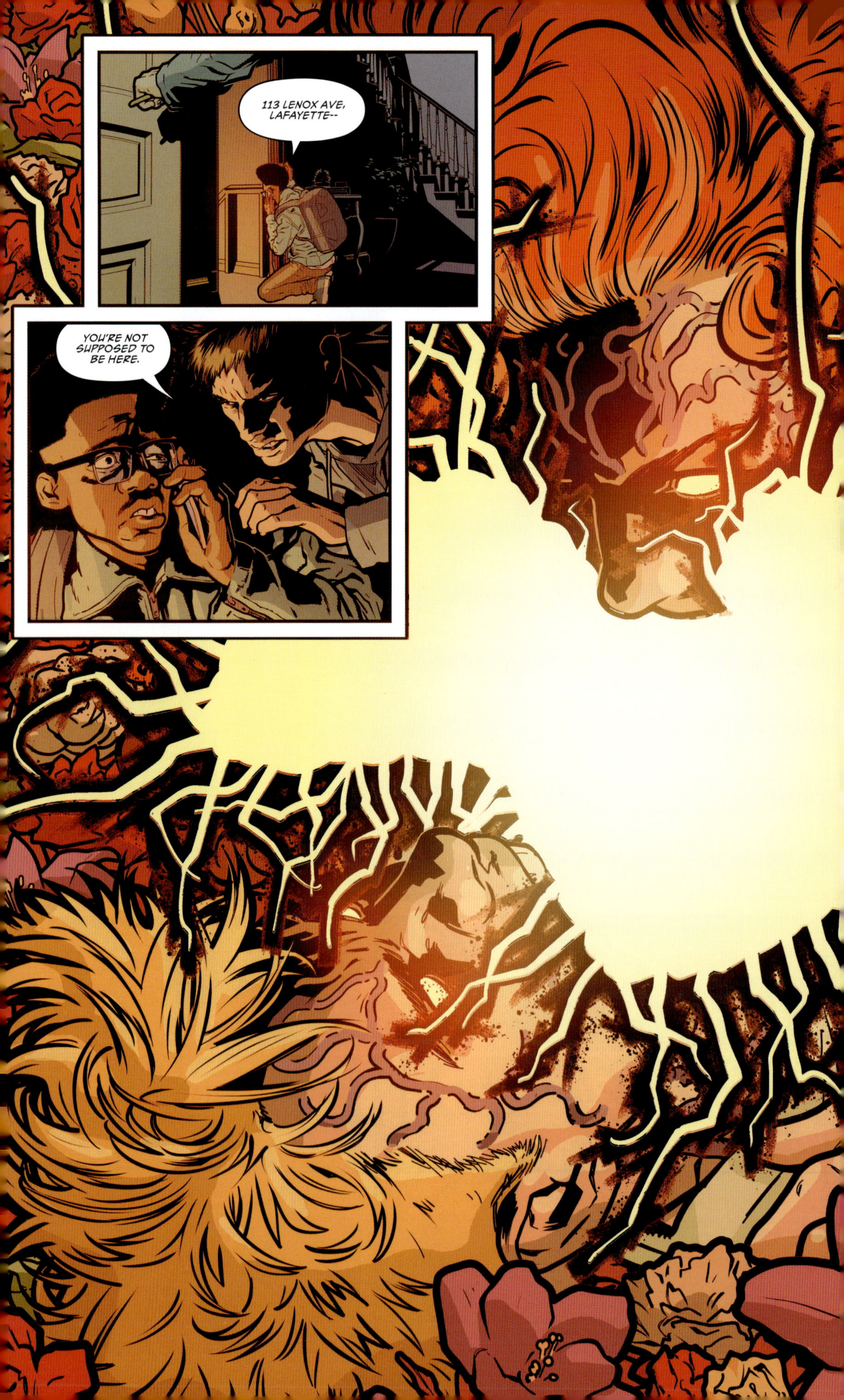
113 LENOX AVE, LAFAYETTE--
YOU'RE NOT SUPPOSED TO BE HERE.

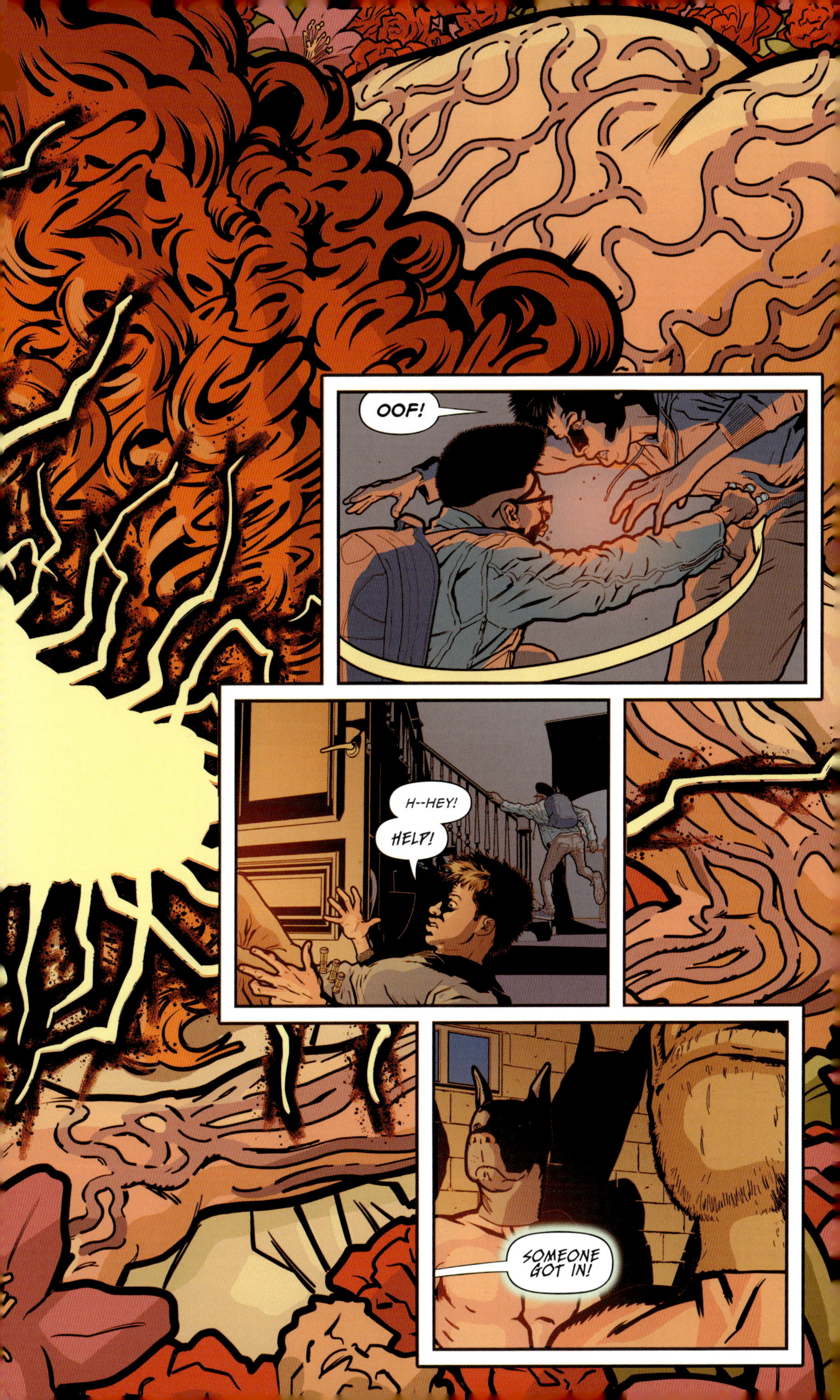
OOF!
H--HEY!
HELP!
SOMEONE GOT IN!

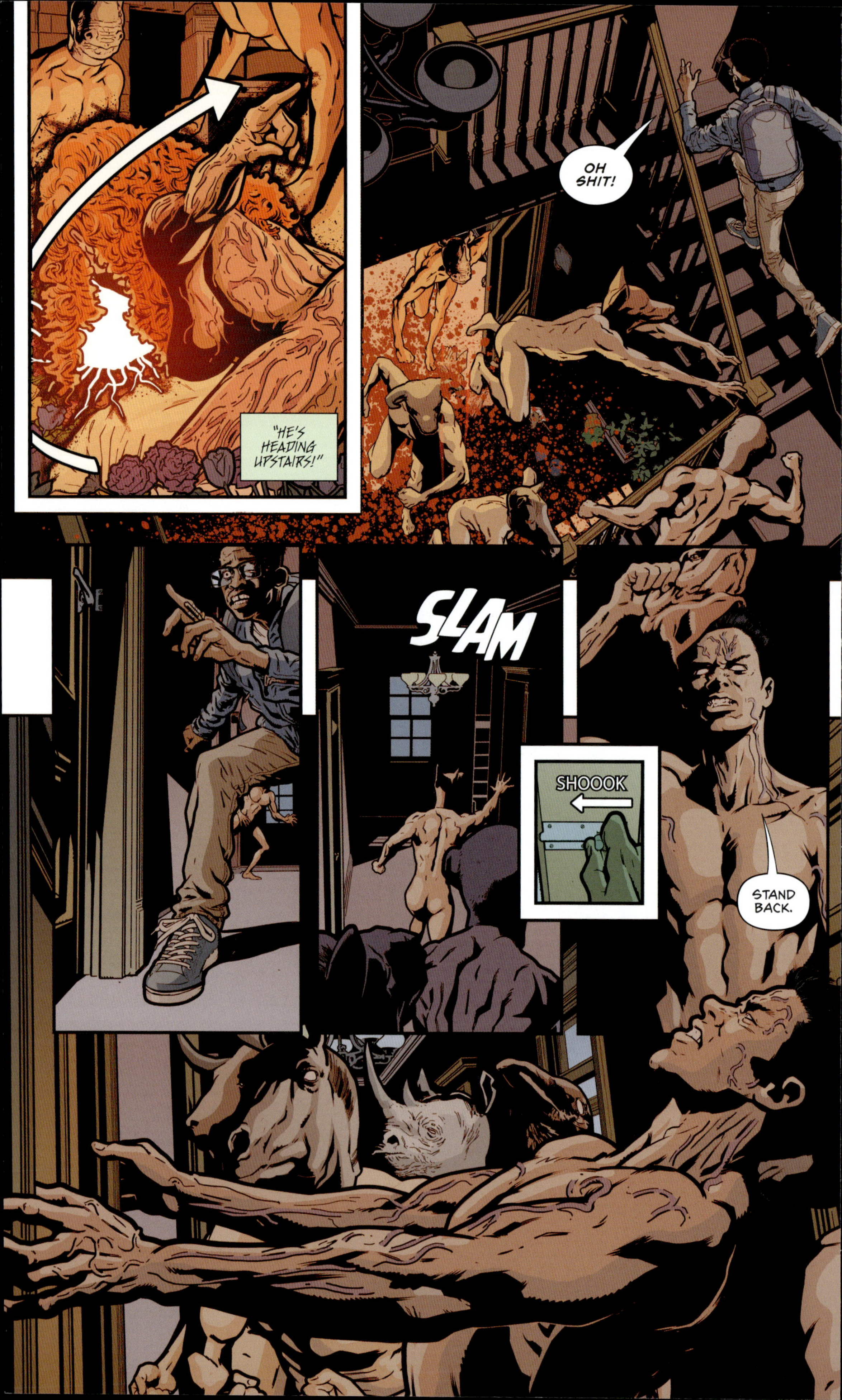
"HE'S HEADING UPSTAIRS!"
OH SHIT!
SLAM
SHOOOK
STAND BACK.

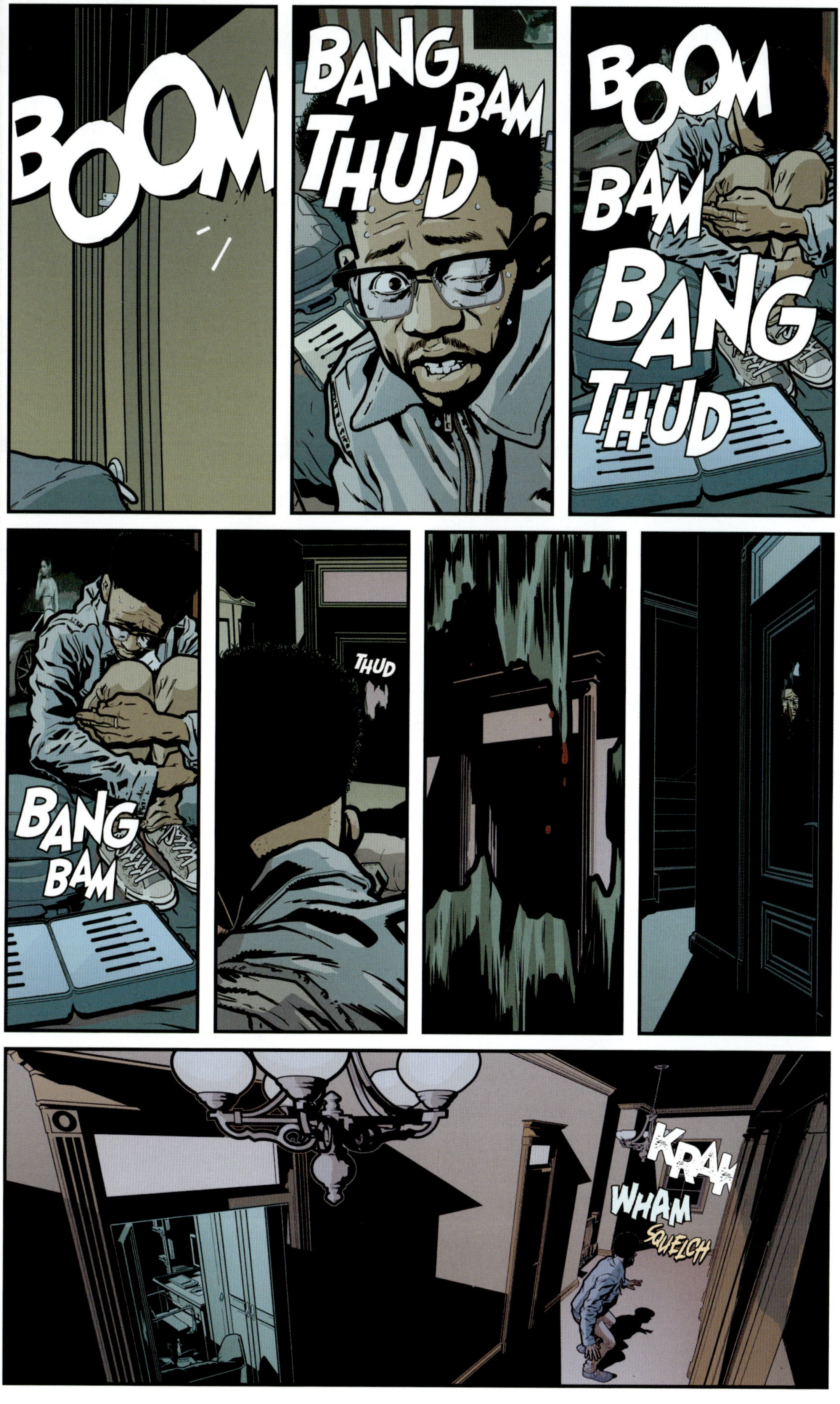
BOOOM
BANG
BAM
THUD
BOOM
BAM
BANG
THUD
BANG
BAM
THUD
KRAK
WHAM
SQUELCH

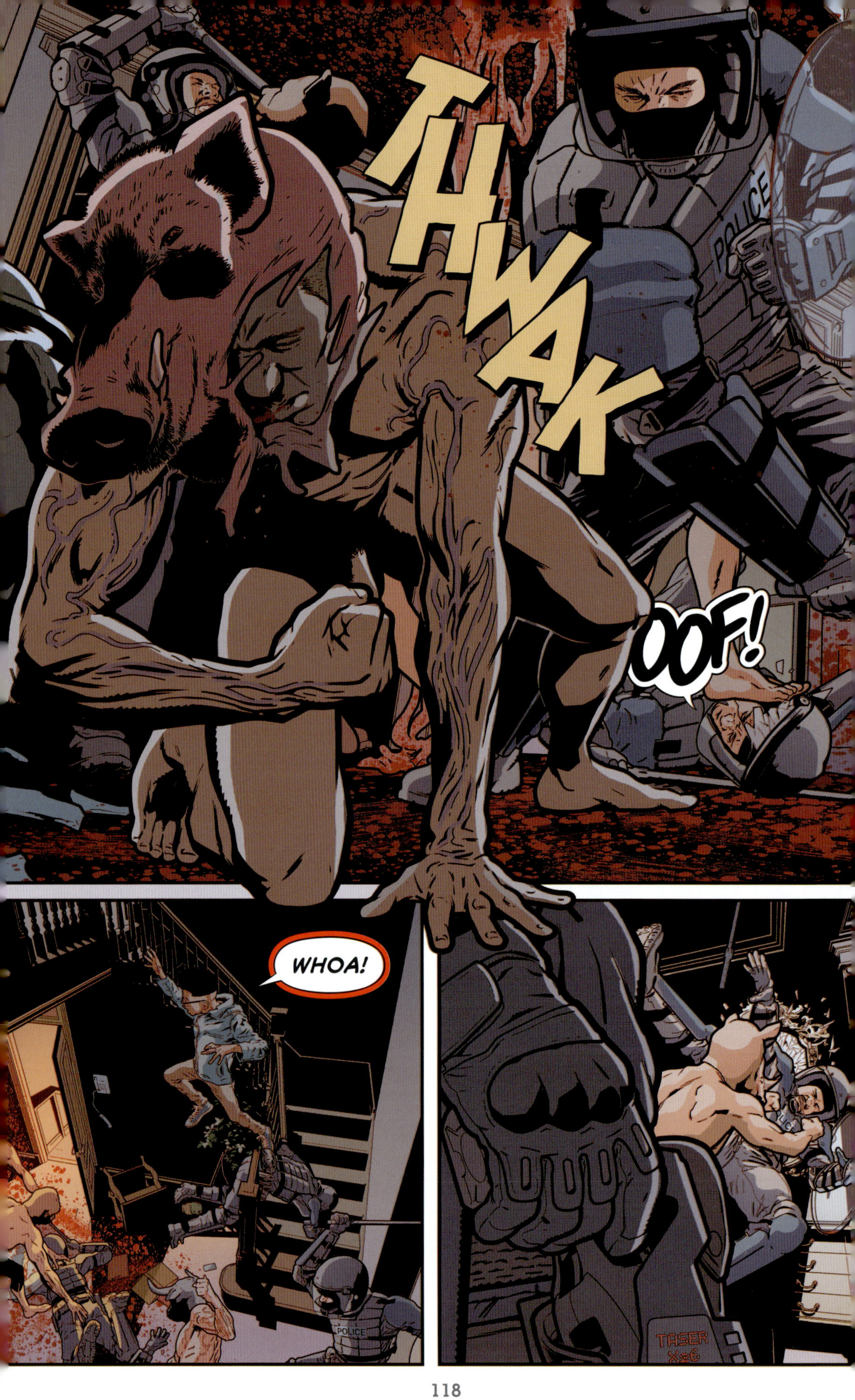
THWAK
OOF!
WHOA!
POLICE
POLICE
TASER
X26

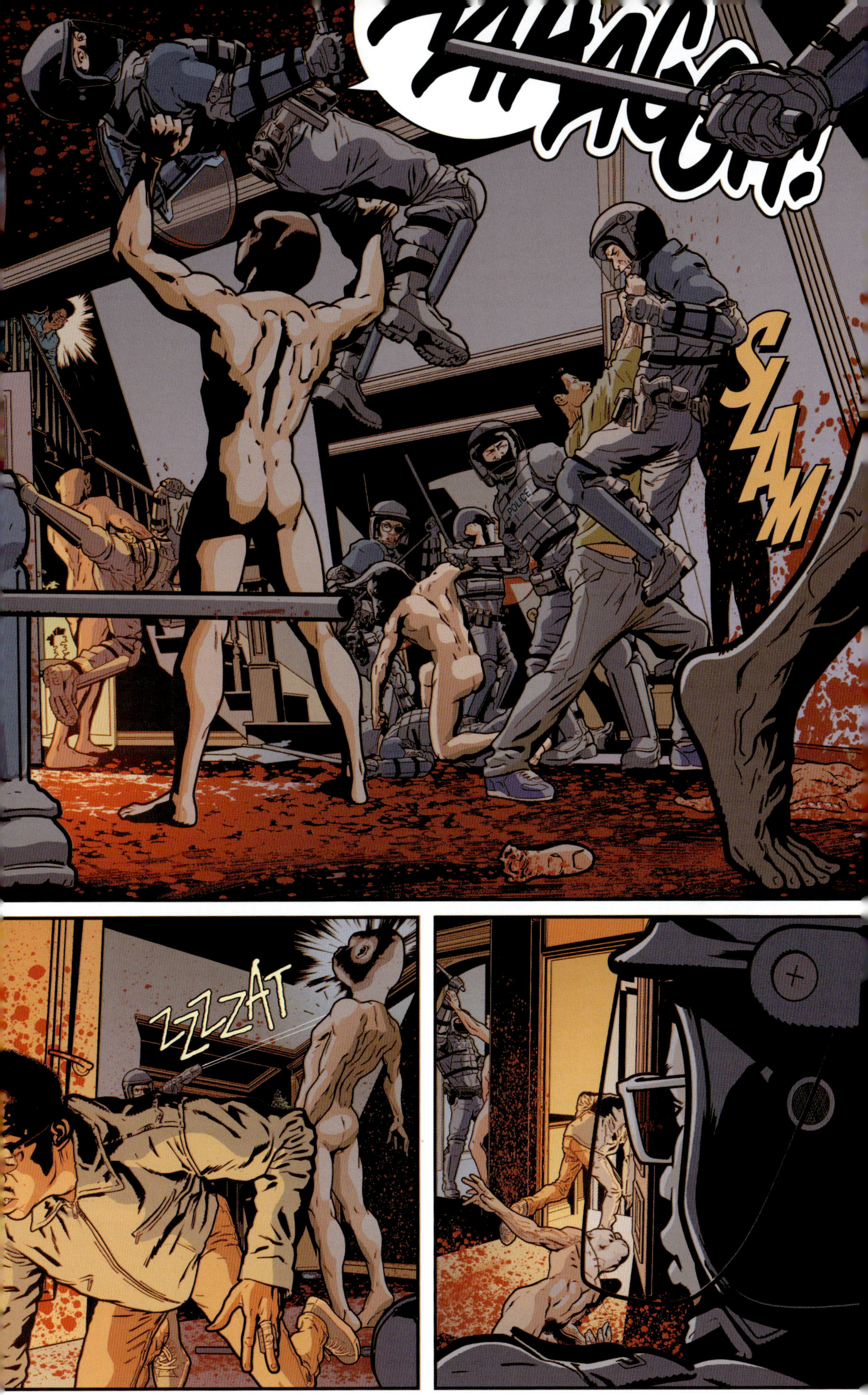
SLAM
POLICE
ZZZZAT

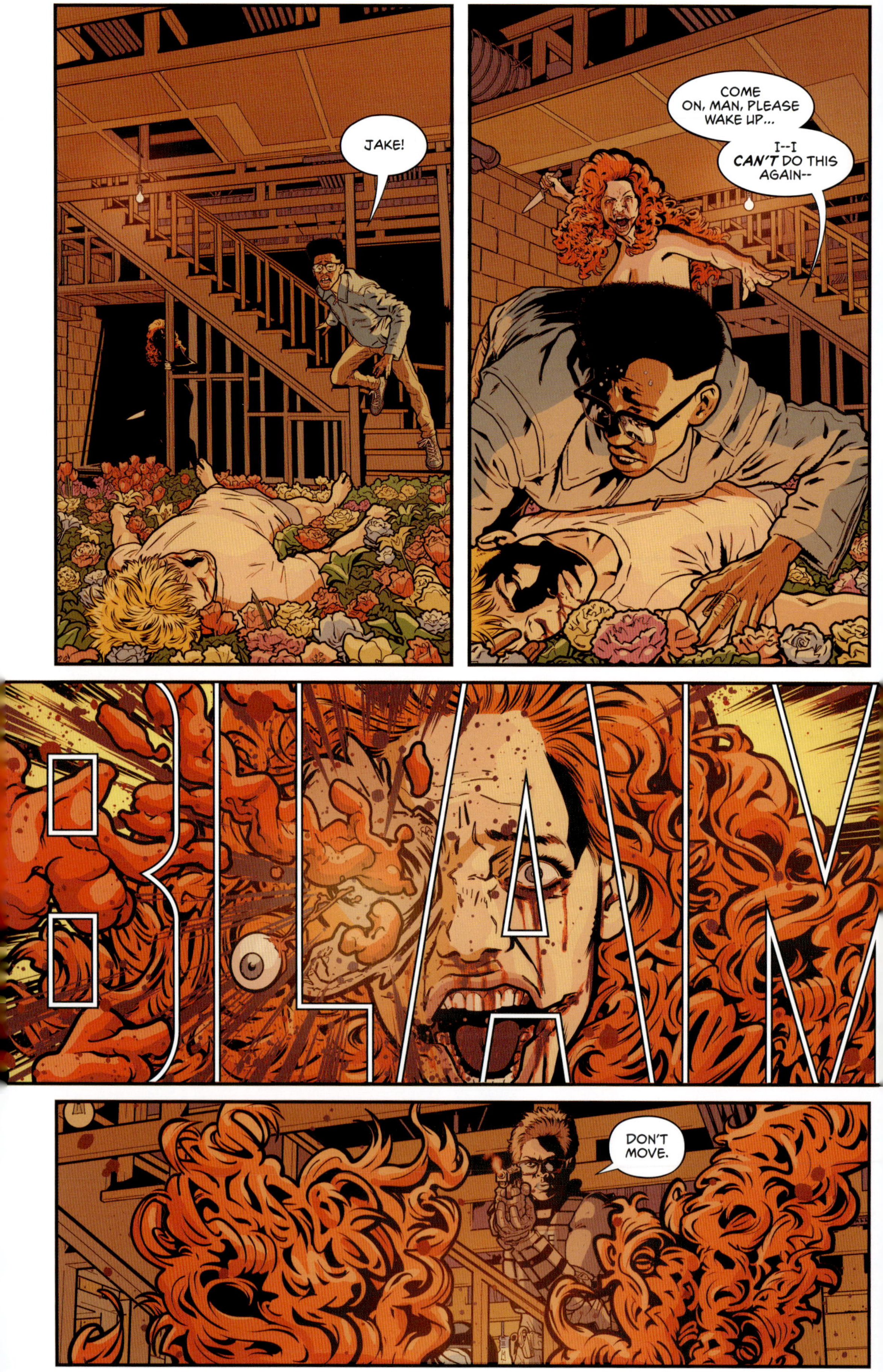
JAKE!
COME ON, MAN, PLEASE WAKE UP...
I--I CAN'T DO THIS AGAIN--
BLAM
DON'T MOVE.

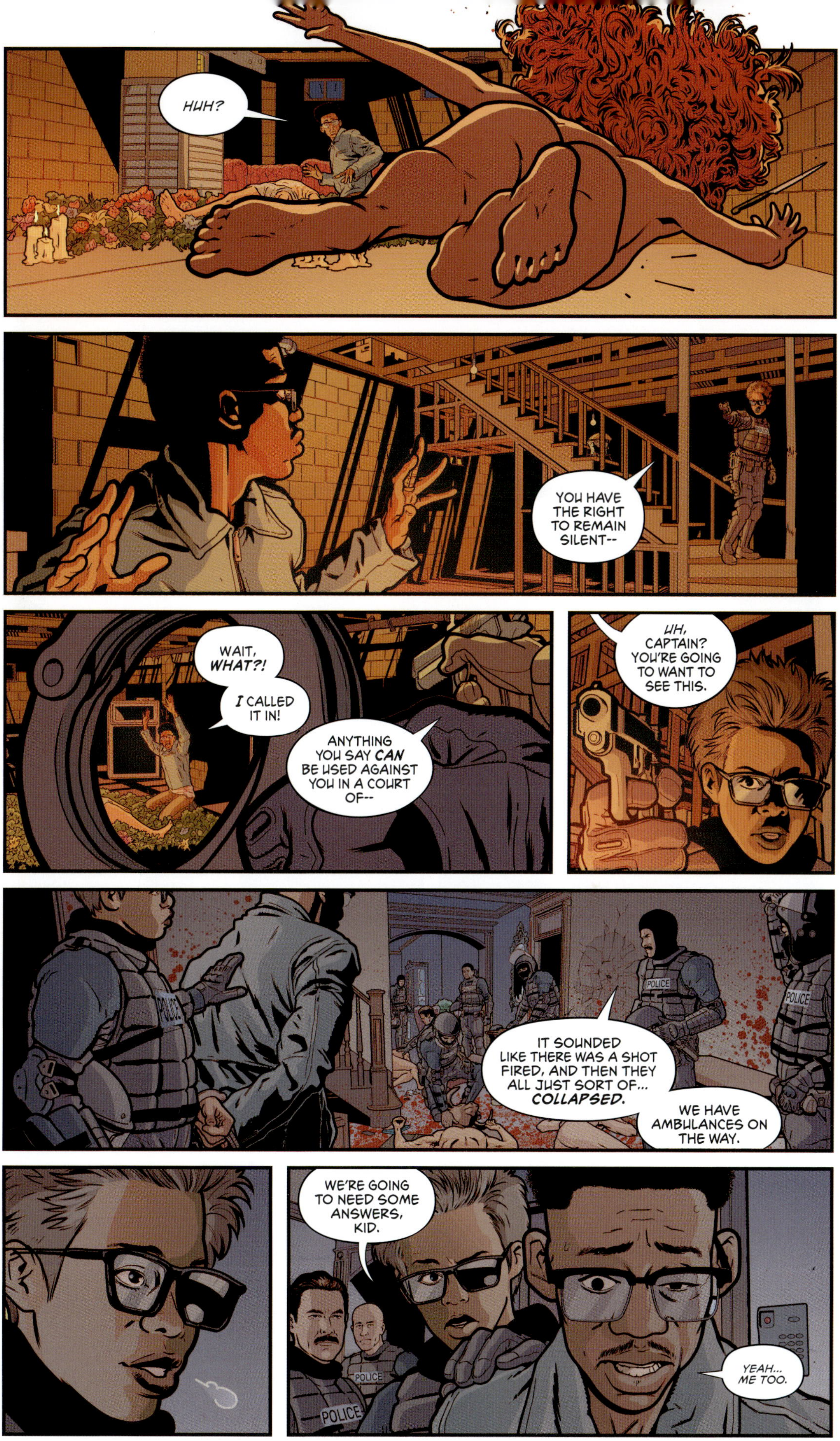
HUH?
YOU HAVE THE RIGHT TO REMAIN SILENT--
WAIT, WHAT?!
I CALLED IT IN!
ANYTHING YOU SAY CAN BE USED AGAINST YOU IN A COURT OF--
UH, CAPTAIN? YOU'RE GOING TO WANT TO SEE THIS.
POLICE
IT SOUNDED LIKE THERE WAS A SHOT FIRED, AND THEN THEY ALL JUST SORT OF... COLLAPSED.
WE HAVE AMBULANCES ON THE WAY.
WE'RE GOING TO NEED SOME ANSWERS, KID.
YEAH... ME TOO.

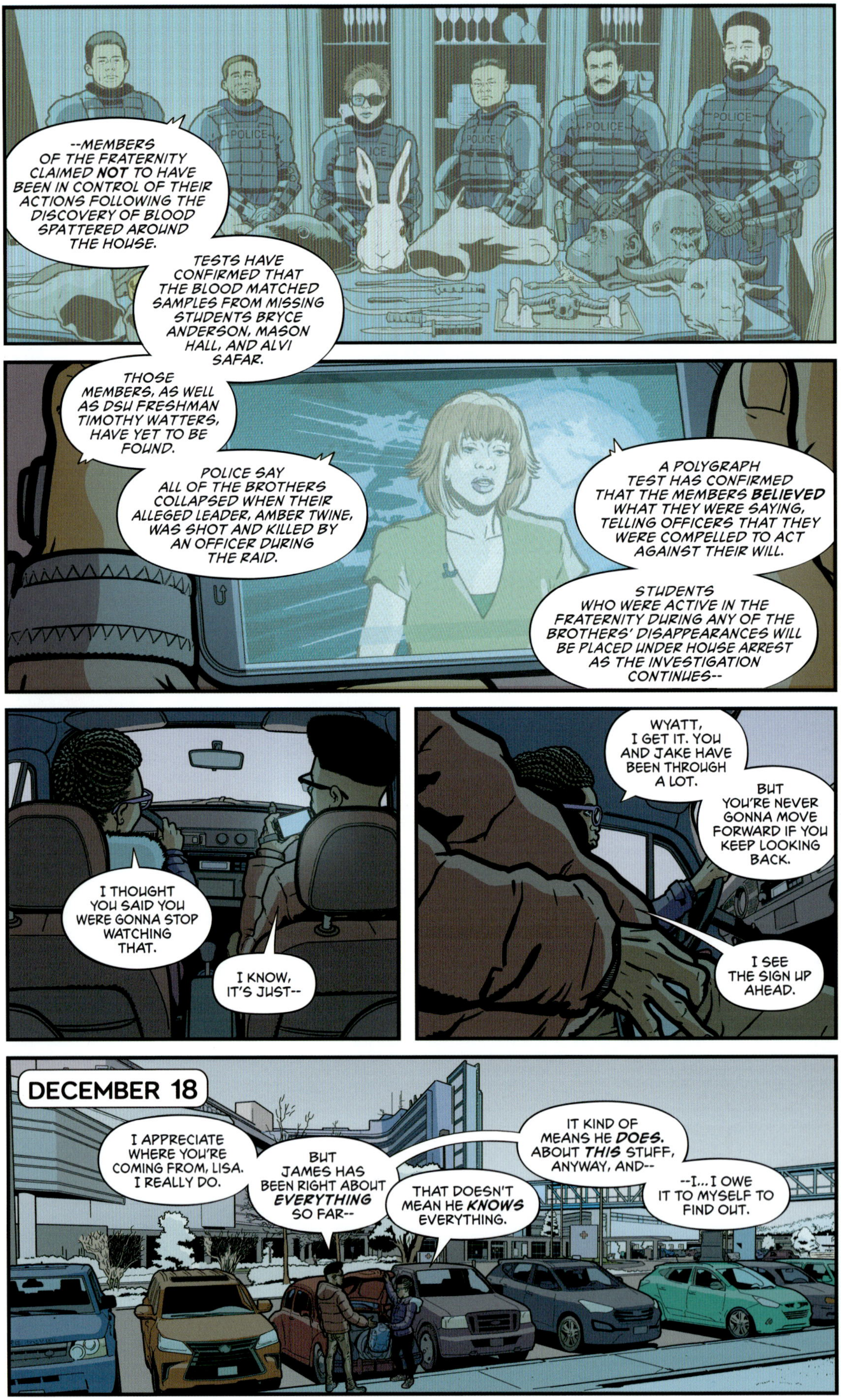
--MEMBERS OF THE FRATERNITY CLAIMED NOT TO HAVE BEEN IN CONTROL OF THEIR ACTIONS FOLLOWING THE DISCOVERY OF BLOOD SPATTERED AROUND THE HOUSE.
TESTS HAVE CONFIRMED THAT THE BLOOD MATCHED SAMPLES FROM MISSING STUDENTS BRYCE ANDERSON, MASON HALL, AND ALVI SAFAR.
POLICE
THOSE MEMBERS, AS WELL AS DSU FRESHMAN TIMOTHY WATTERS, HAVE YET TO BE FOUND.
POLICE SAY ALL OF THE BROTHERS COLLAPSED WHEN THEIR ALLEGED LEADER, AMBER TWINE, WAS SHOT AND KILLED BY AN OFFICER DURING THE RAID.
A POLYGRAPH TEST HAS CONFIRMED THAT THE MEMBERS BELIEVED WHAT THEY WERE SAYING, TELLING OFFICERS THAT THEY WERE COMPELLED TO ACT AGAINST THEIR WILL.
STUDENTS WHO WERE ACTIVE IN THE FRATERNITY DURING ANY OF THE BROTHERS' DISAPPEARANCES WILL BE PLACED UNDER HOUSE ARREST AS THE INVESTIGATION CONTINUES--
I THOUGHT YOU SAID YOU WERE GONNA STOP WATCHING THAT.
I KNOW, IT'S JUST--
WYATT, I GET IT. YOU AND JAKE HAVE BEEN THROUGH A LOT.
BUT YOU'RE NEVER GONNA MOVE FORWARD IF YOU KEEP LOOKING BACK.
I SEE THE SIGN UP AHEAD.
DECEMBER 18
I APPRECIATE WHERE YOU'RE COMING FROM, LISA. I REALLY DO.
BUT JAMES HAS BEEN RIGHT ABOUT EVERYTHING SO FAR--
THAT DOESN'T MEAN HE KNOWS EVERYTHING.
IT KIND OF MEANS HE DOES. ABOUT THIS STUFF, ANYWAY, AND--
--I... I OWE IT TO MYSELF TO FIND OUT.

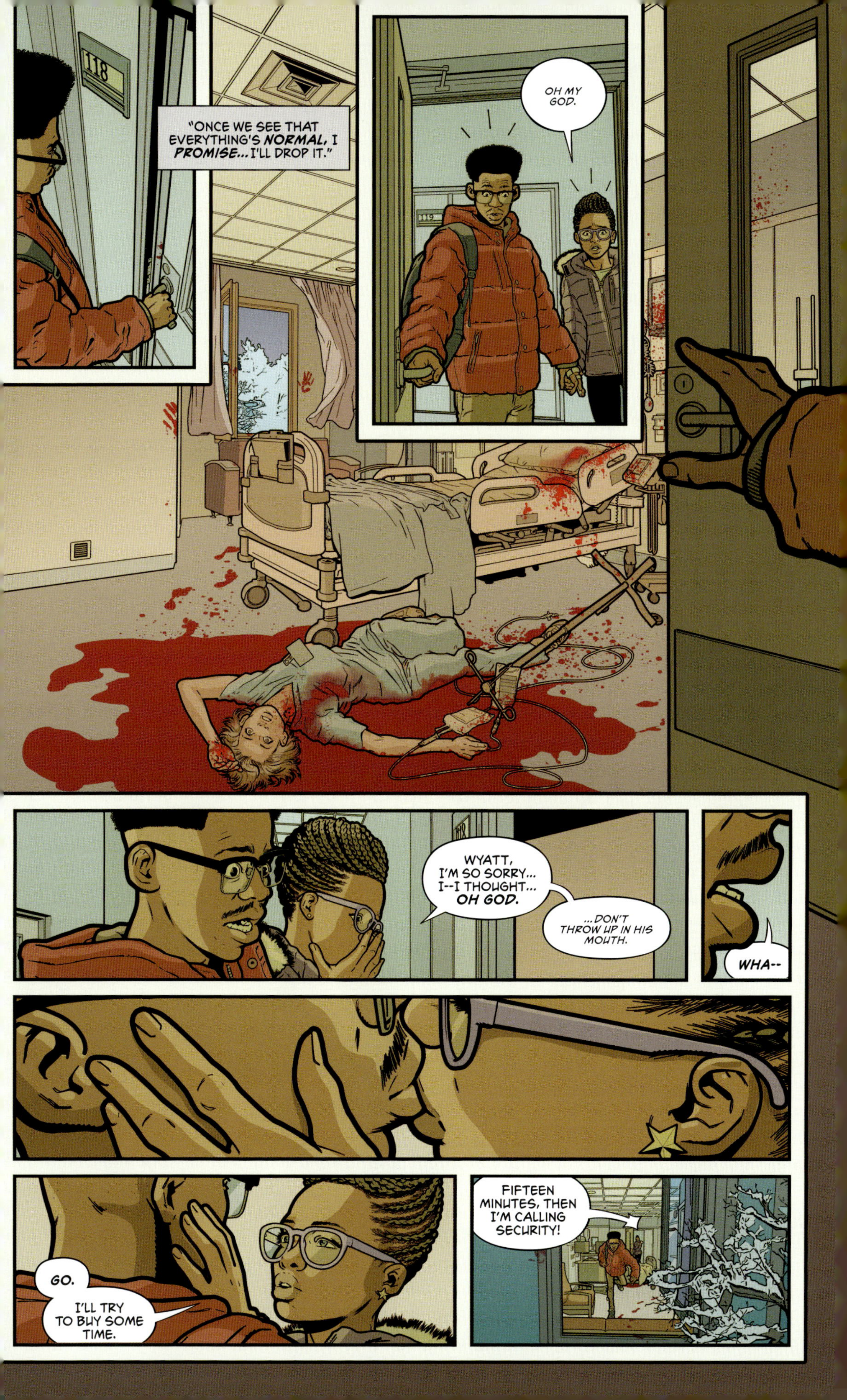
"ONCE WE SEE THAT EVERYTHING'S **NORMAL,** I **PROMISE...** I'LL DROP IT."
OH MY GOD.
WYATT, I'M SO SORRY... I--I THOUGHT... **OH GOD.**
...DON'T THROW UP IN HIS MOUTH.
WHA--
GO.
I'LL TRY TO BUY SOME TIME.
FIFTEEN MINUTES, THEN I'M CALLING SECURITY!

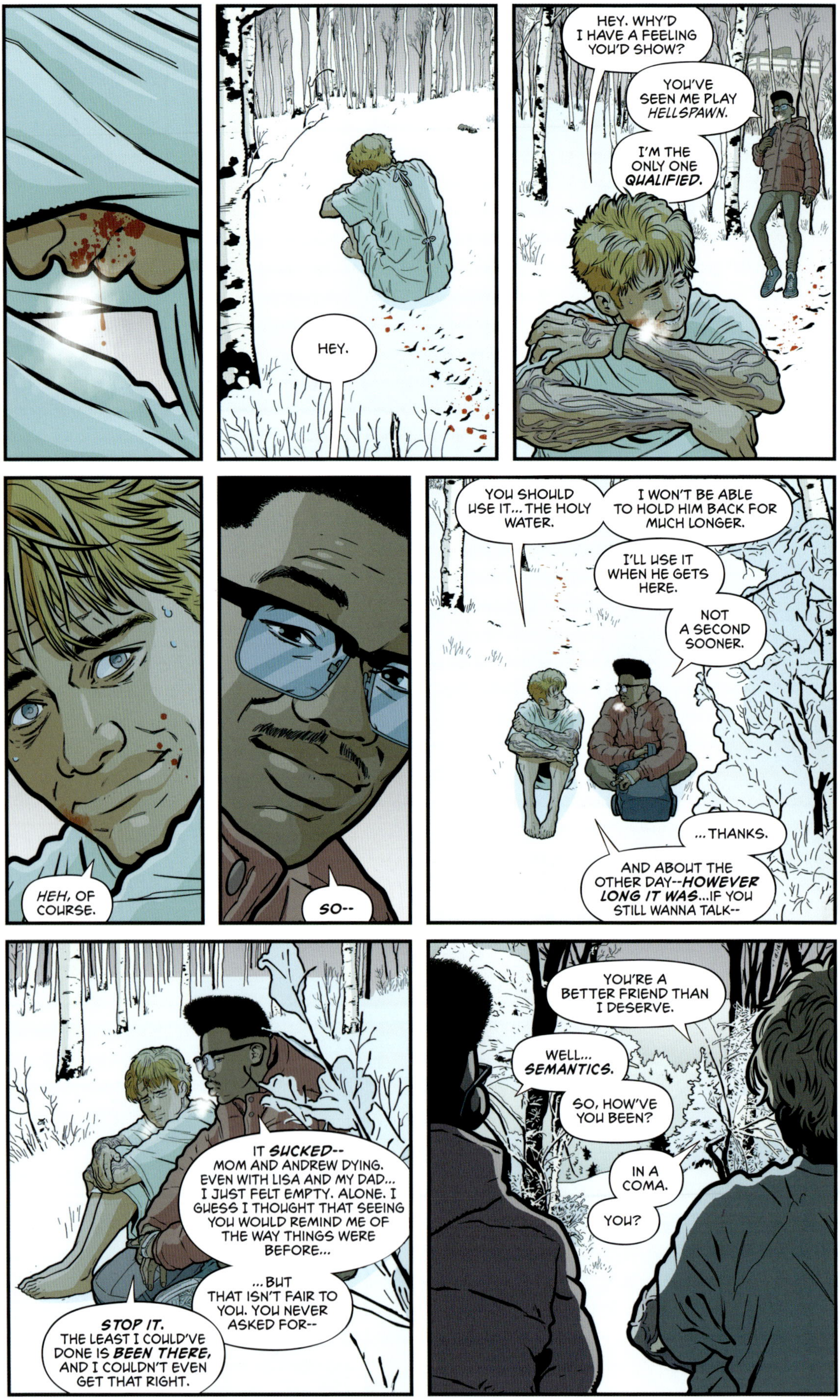

HEY.
HEY. WHY'D I HAVE A FEELING YOU'D SHOW?
YOU'VE SEEN ME PLAY *HELLSPAWN.*
I'M THE ONLY ONE ***QUALIFIED.***
HEH, OF COURSE.
SO--
YOU SHOULD USE IT... THE HOLY WATER.
I WON'T BE ABLE TO HOLD HIM BACK FOR MUCH LONGER.
I'LL USE IT WHEN HE GETS HERE.
NOT A SECOND SOONER.
...THANKS.
AND ABOUT THE OTHER DAY--***HOWEVER LONG IT WAS***...IF YOU STILL WANNA TALK--
IT ***SUCKED***-- MOM AND ANDREW DYING. EVEN WITH LISA AND MY DAD... I JUST FELT EMPTY. ALONE. I GUESS I THOUGHT THAT SEEING YOU WOULD REMIND ME OF THE WAY THINGS WERE BEFORE...
...BUT THAT ISN'T FAIR TO YOU. YOU NEVER ASKED FOR--
STOP IT. THE LEAST I COULD'VE DONE IS ***BEEN THERE,*** AND I COULDN'T EVEN GET THAT RIGHT.
YOU'RE A BETTER FRIEND THAN I DESERVE.
WELL... ***SEMANTICS.***
SO, HOW'VE YOU BEEN?
IN A COMA.
YOU?

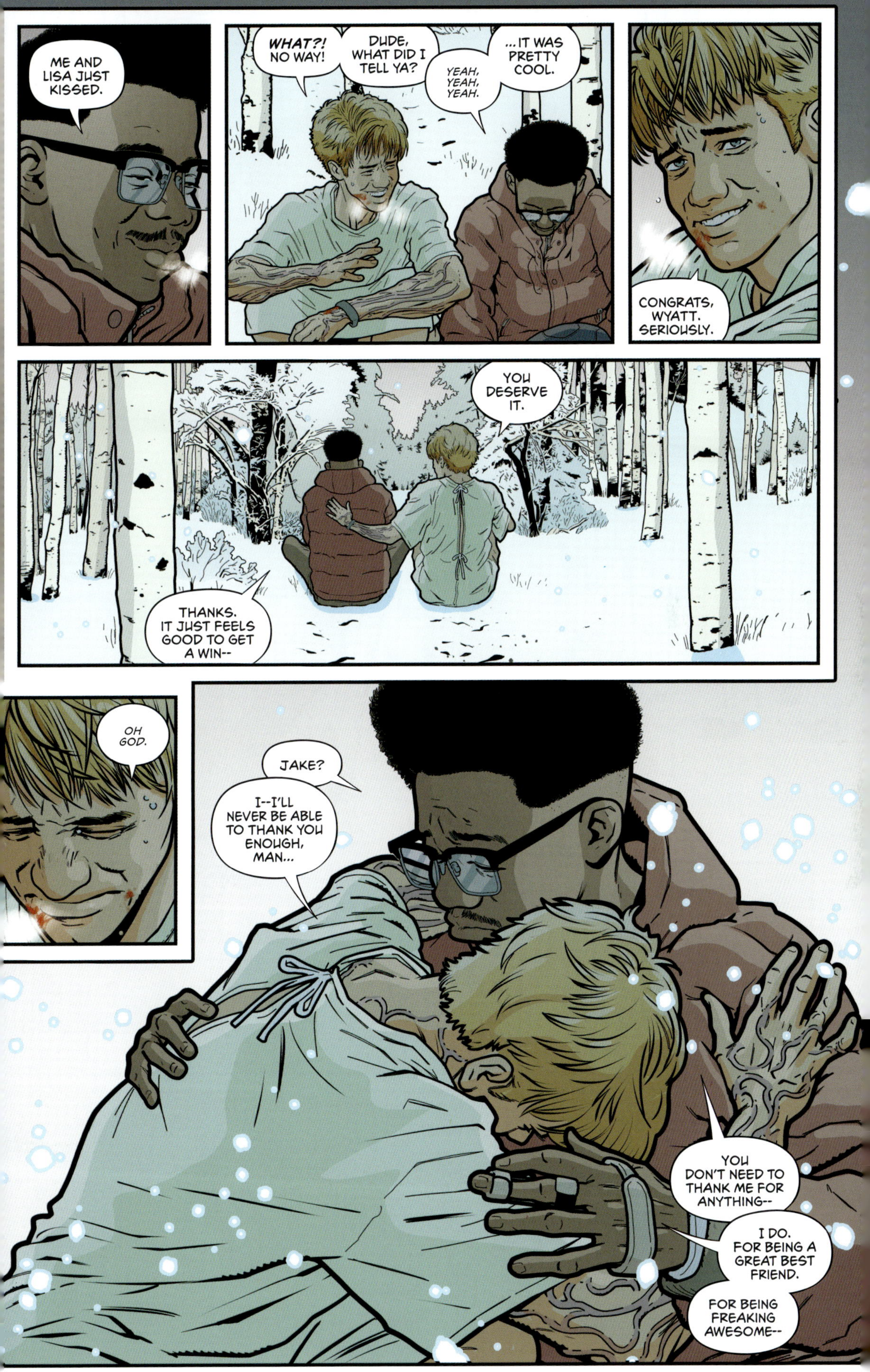

ME AND LISA JUST KISSED.
WHAT?! NO WAY!
DUDE, WHAT DID I TELL YA?
YEAH, YEAH, YEAH.
...IT WAS PRETTY COOL.
CONGRATS, WYATT. SERIOUSLY.
YOU DESERVE IT.
THANKS. IT JUST FEELS GOOD TO GET A WIN--
OH GOD.
JAKE?
I--I'LL NEVER BE ABLE TO THANK YOU ENOUGH, MAN...
YOU DON'T NEED TO THANK ME FOR ANYTHING--
I DO. FOR BEING A GREAT BEST FRIEND.
FOR BEING FREAKING AWESOME--

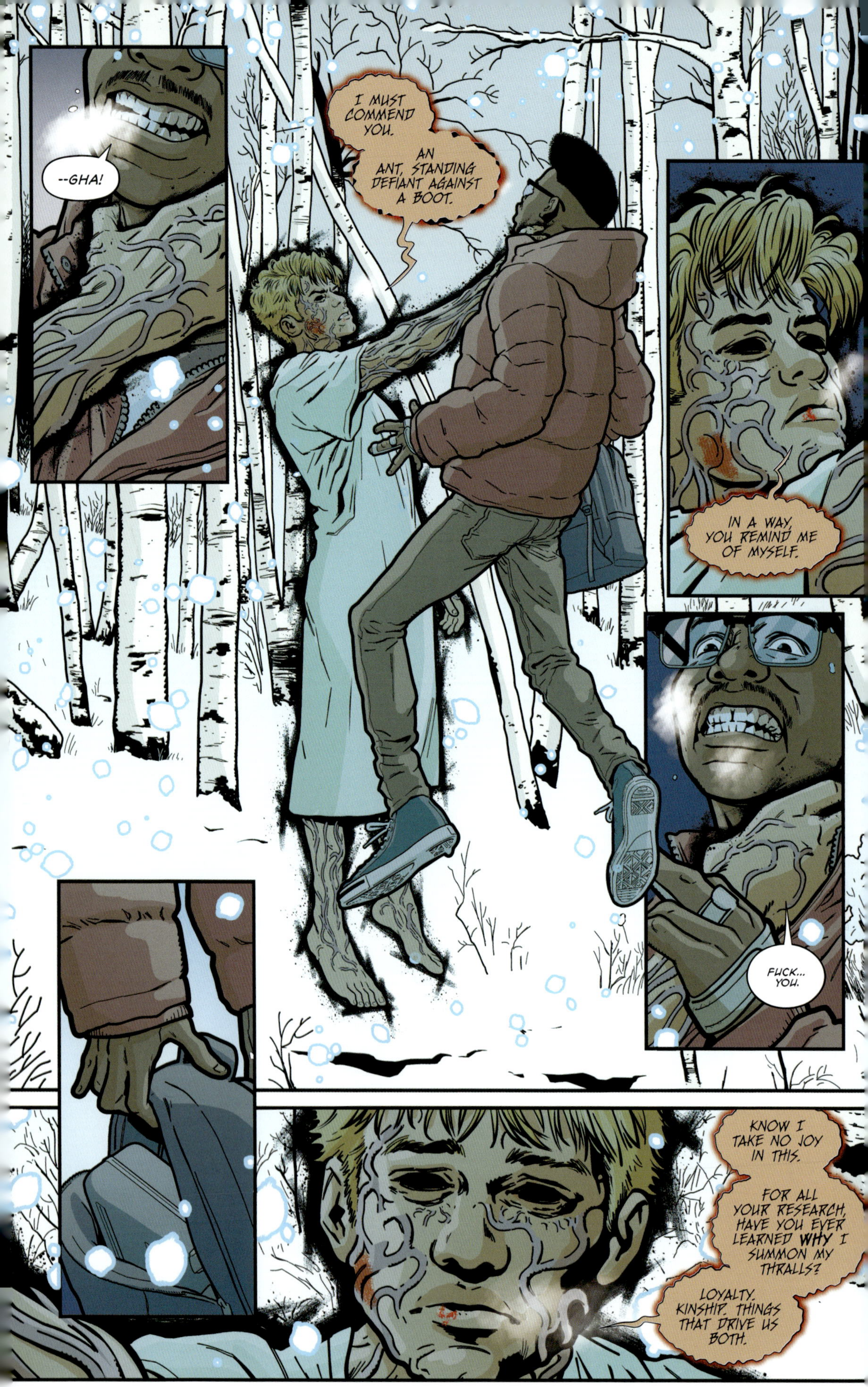
--GHA!
I MUST COMMEND YOU.
AN ANT, STANDING DEFIANT AGAINST A BOOT.
IN A WAY, YOU REMIND ME OF MYSELF.
FUCK... YOU.
KNOW I TAKE NO JOY IN THIS.
FOR ALL YOUR RESEARCH, HAVE YOU EVER LEARNED **WHY** I SUMMON MY THRALLS?
LOYALTY. KINSHIP. THINGS THAT DRIVE US BOTH.

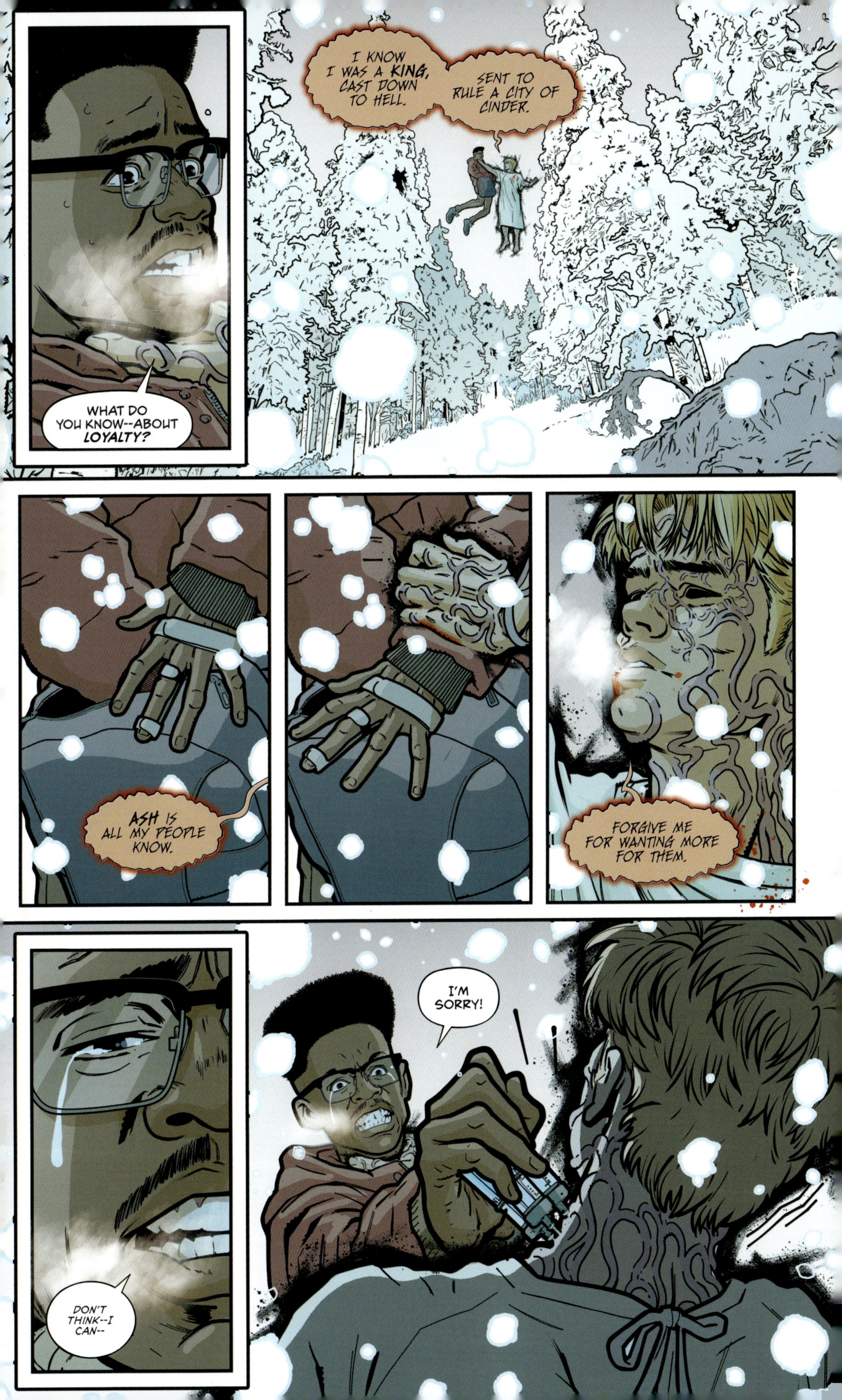
WHAT DO YOU KNOW--ABOUT LOYALTY?
I KNOW I WAS A KING, CAST DOWN TO HELL.
SENT TO RULE A CITY OF CINDER.
ASH IS ALL MY PEOPLE KNOW.
FORGIVE ME FOR WANTING MORE FOR THEM.
DON'T THINK--I CAN--
I'M SORRY!

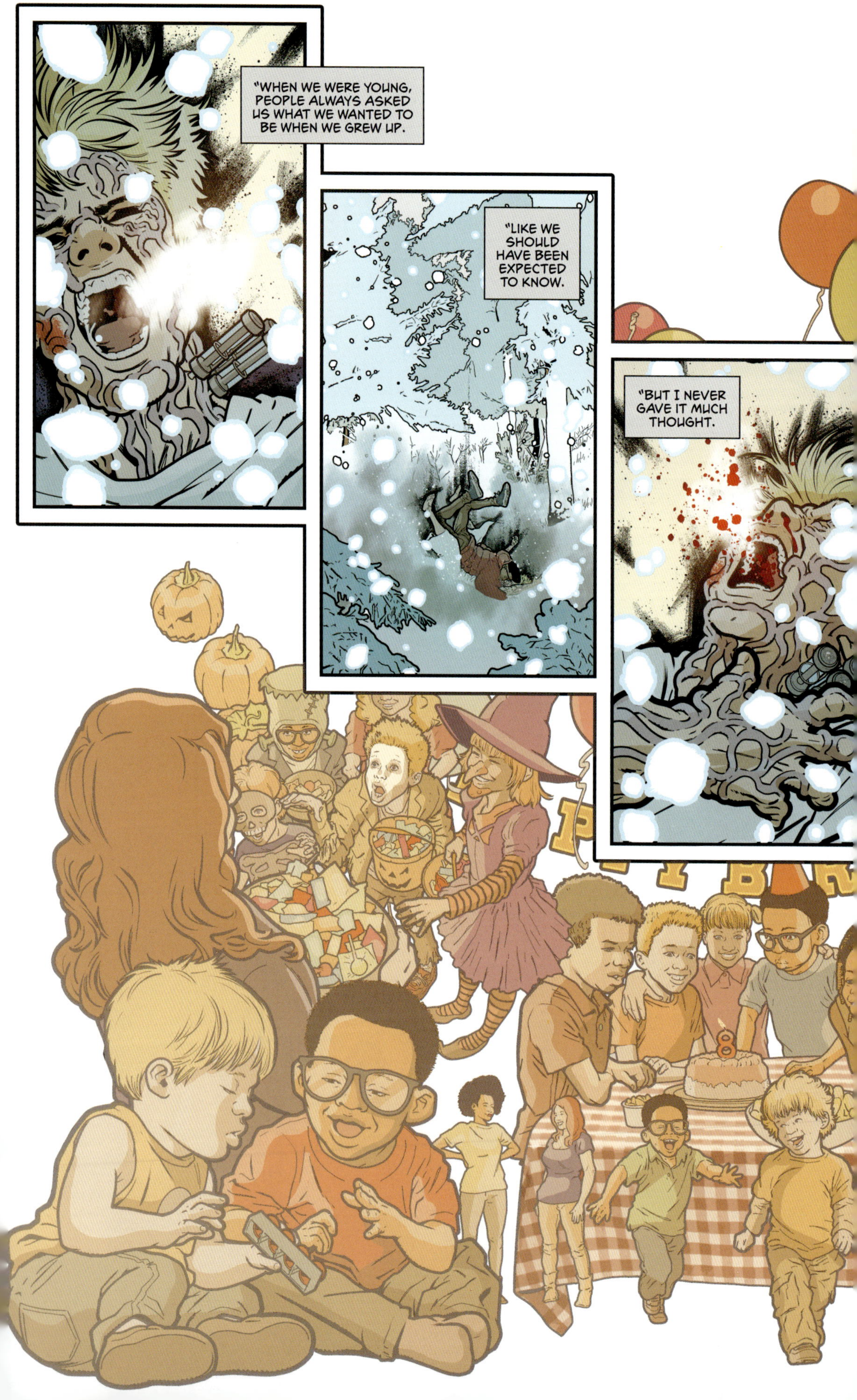
"WHEN WE WERE YOUNG, PEOPLE ALWAYS ASKED US WHAT WE WANTED TO BE WHEN WE GREW UP.
"LIKE WE SHOULD HAVE BEEN EXPECTED TO KNOW.
"BUT I NEVER GAVE IT MUCH THOUGHT.

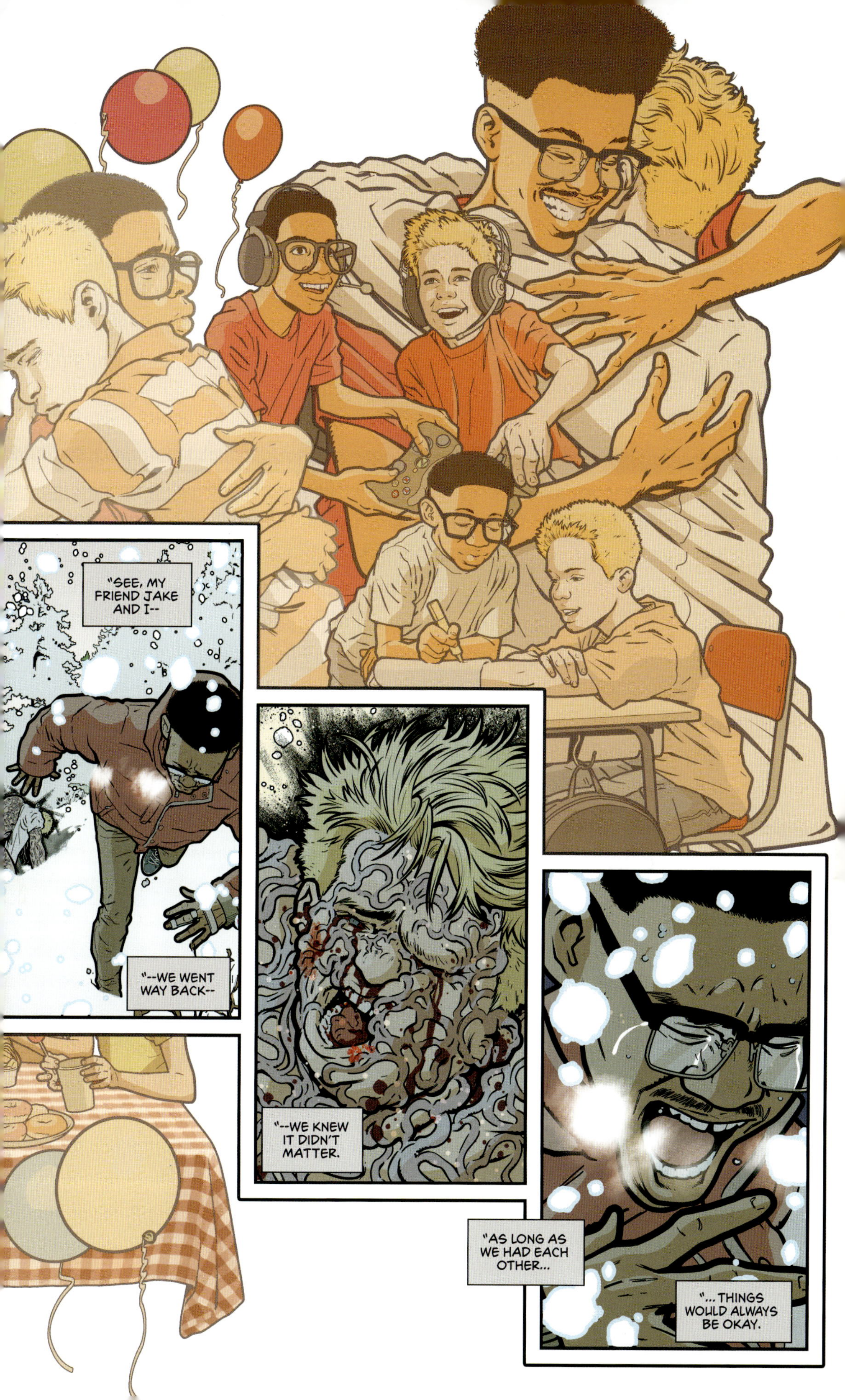
"SEE, MY FRIEND JAKE AND I--
"--WE WENT WAY BACK--
"--WE KNEW IT DIDN'T MATTER.
"AS LONG AS WE HAD EACH OTHER...
"...THINGS WOULD ALWAYS BE OKAY.

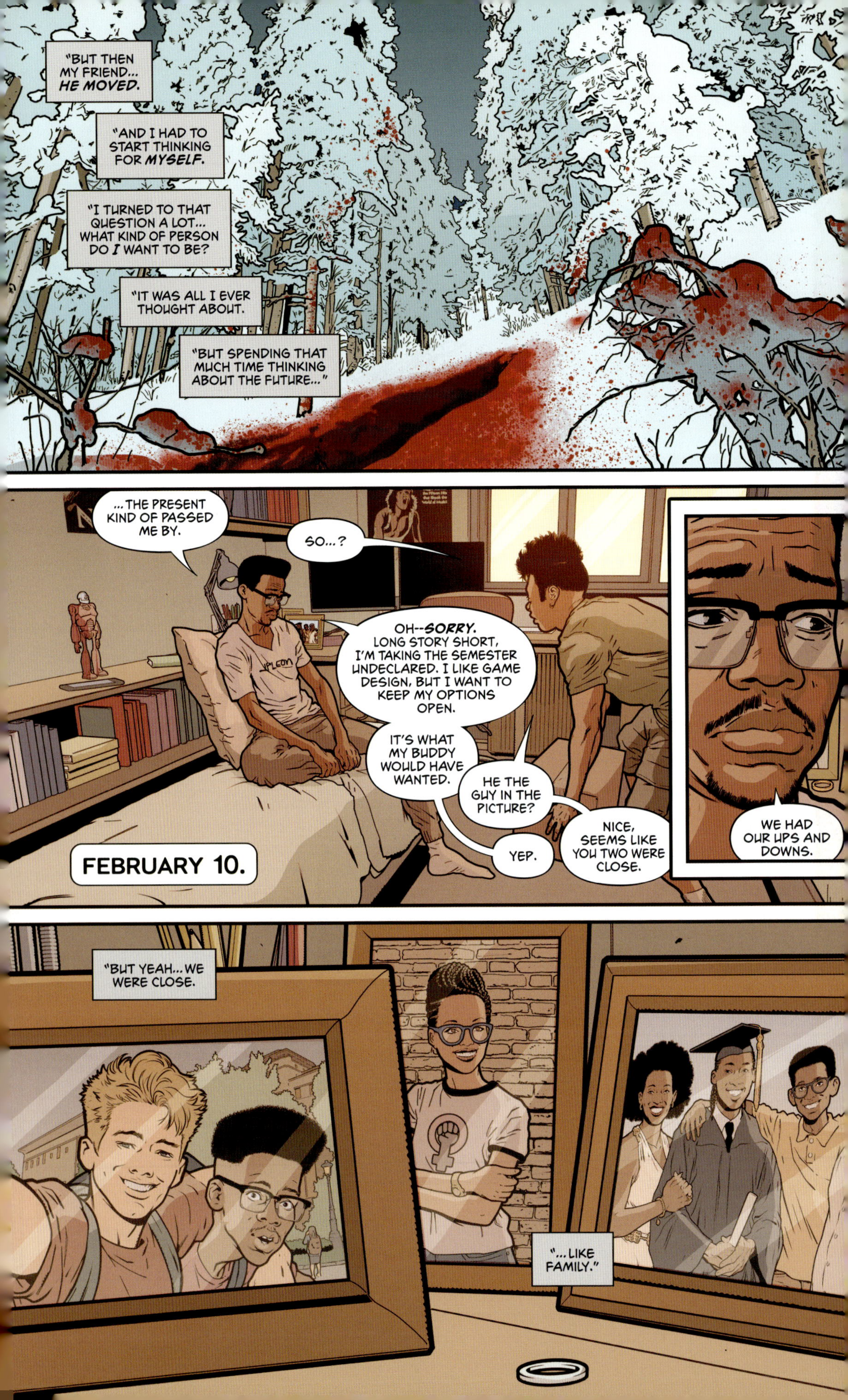
"BUT THEN MY FRIEND... *HE MOVED*.
"AND I HAD TO START THINKING FOR *MYSELF*.
"I TURNED TO THAT QUESTION A LOT... WHAT KIND OF PERSON DO *I* WANT TO BE?
"IT WAS ALL I EVER THOUGHT ABOUT.
"BUT SPENDING THAT MUCH TIME THINKING ABOUT THE FUTURE..."
...THE PRESENT KIND OF PASSED ME BY.
SO...?
OH--*SORRY.* LONG STORY SHORT, I'M TAKING THE SEMESTER UNDECLARED. I LIKE GAME DESIGN, BUT I WANT TO KEEP MY OPTIONS OPEN.
IT'S WHAT MY BUDDY WOULD HAVE WANTED.
HE THE GUY IN THE PICTURE?
YEP.
NICE, SEEMS LIKE YOU TWO WERE CLOSE.
WE HAD OUR UPS AND DOWNS.
FEBRUARY 10.
"BUT YEAH... WE WERE CLOSE.
"...LIKE FAMILY."

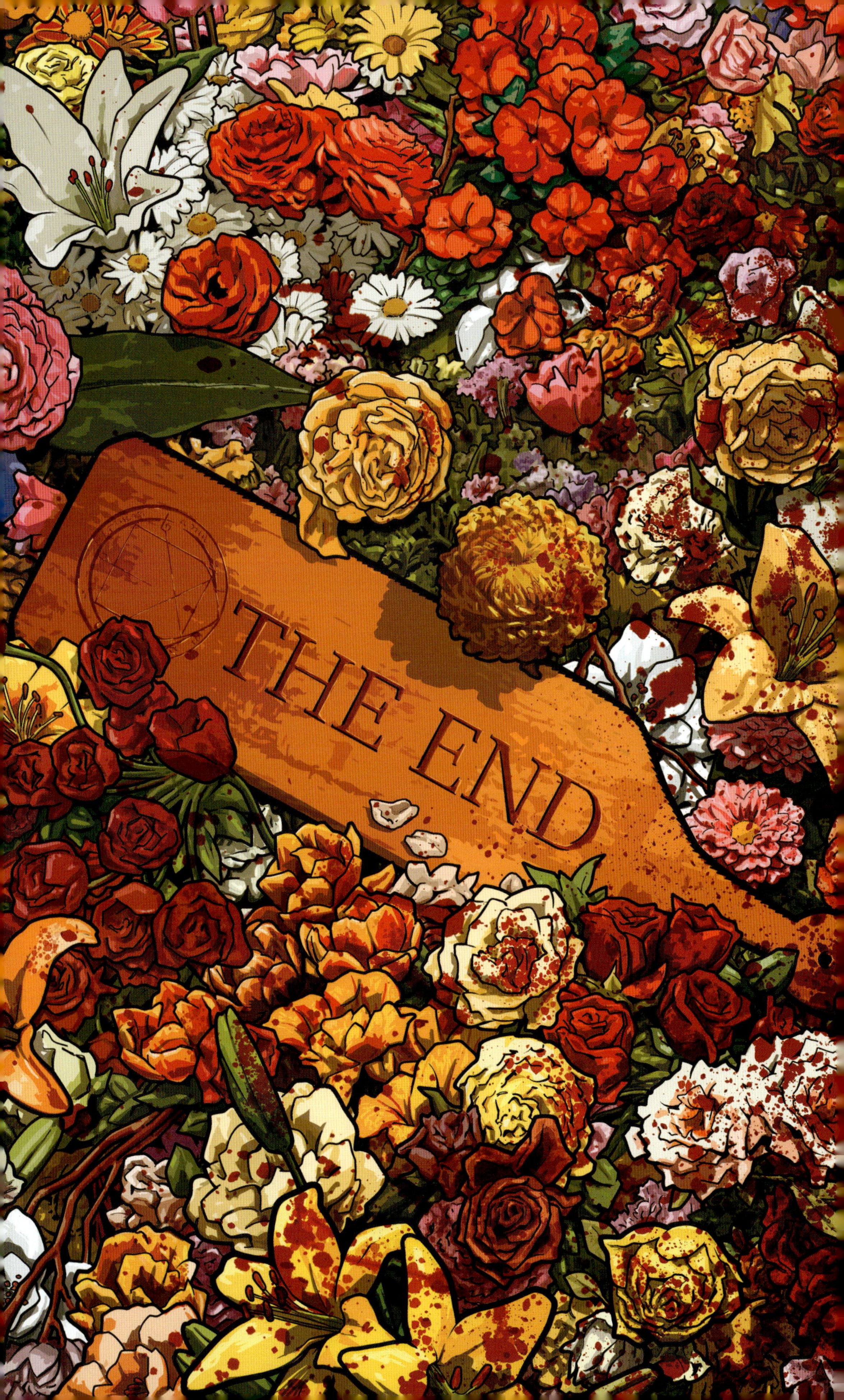
THE END

BUILDING THE FRATERNITY

JON: *Hey everybody, Jon here! Hugo and I can't thank you enough for checking out this weird, creepy little book. For the past year, this story has taken up the better part of our lives. So, we thought it would be fun to peel the curtain back and give a behind-the-scenes look at some of our creative processes, starting with a breakdown of one of our favorite scenes. Take it away, Hugo!*

HUGO: *Thanks, Jon! To start, I visualize the script while I'm reading it, playing out a movie in my head. Once I see it clearly, I put pen to pixels and do the roughs as readable as possible, so we can discuss what works and what can be improved upon.*

Once the layout is greenlit, it's a usual day at the office; Pencils and inks by me, then over to Lee for his magical coloring and DC for some awesome lettering and Sound FX.

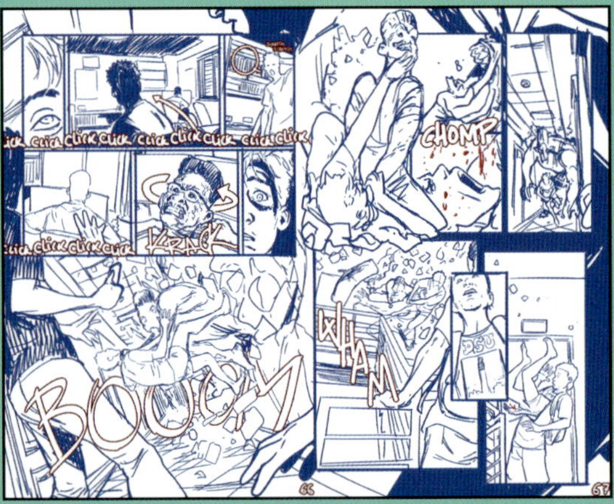
CHOMP
KRACK
WHAM
BOOOM

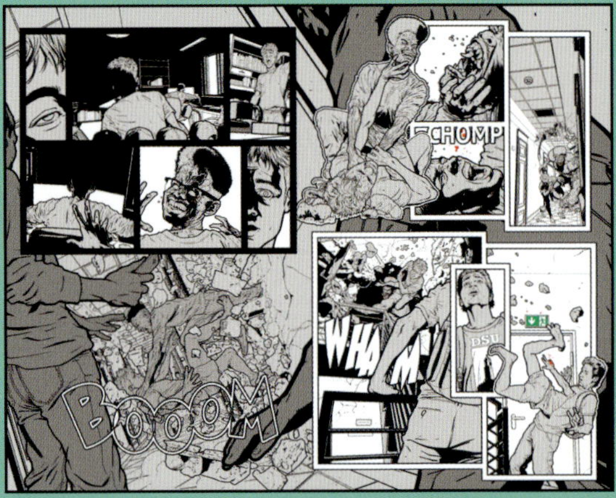
CHOMP
WHAM
BOOOM

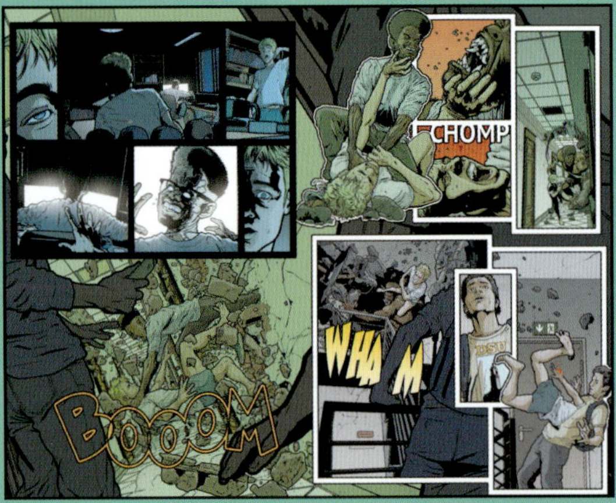
CHOMP
WHAM
BOOOM

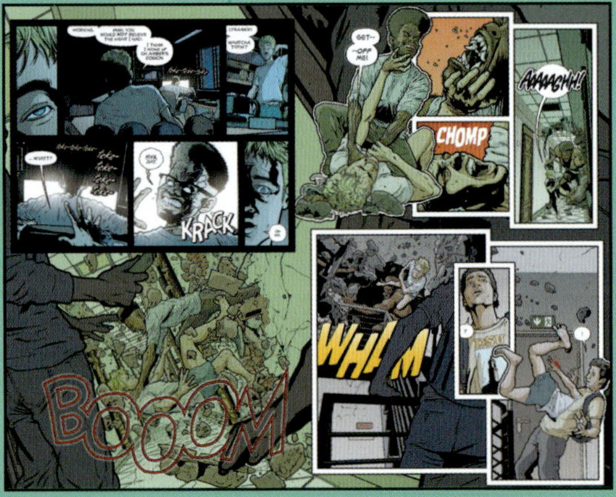
CHOMP
KRACK
WHAM
BOOOM

JON: *Wow, this art stuff is really cool...but the words are cool, too, right? RIGHT?*

HUGO: *Yes, Jon, the words are very cool...*

I was super excited to be able to slip a double homage to two of my favorite horror movies in this scene, The Exorcist *and* An American Werewolf in London*.*

Panel 1: Jake wakes up, rubbing sleep from his eyes.

Panel 2: He turns to see Wyatt's back. Wyatt is hunched over the computer screen, typing furiously.

     Jake: Morning.

     Jake: Man, you would not believe the night I had.

     Jake: I think I woke up on Amber's couch.

SFX: CLICK CLICK CLICK

Panel 3: Jake walks over to Wyatt, curious.

     Jake: *Yaaawn*

Jake: Whatcha typin'?

Panel 4: Jake's POV looking down at Wyatt, whose typing has become faster and even more exaggerated.

     Jake: …Wyatt?

SFX: CLICK CLICK CLICK CLICK CLICK

Panel 5: Wyatt's head turns all the way around, now facing Jake. It should look like there are some broken bones in his neck as a result. His veins are bulging and muscles are flexed.

     Wyatt (Demon): Hiya, Jake.

SFX: KRACK

Panel 6: Small panel showing Jake's fear.

     Jake (Small Text): Oh no.

Panel 7: Large panel. Partially demonized, Wyatt tackles Jake through their dorm room wall into the hallway. It's pretty badass.

SFX: BOOOM

Panel 8: In the dorm building hallway, Demon Wyatt has Jake pinned to the ground. Jake presses an arm up to Demon Wyatt's chin in an attempt to keep him at bay.

     Jake: Get—

     Jake: Off me!

Panel 9: Small panel, tight on Demon Wyatt's mouth. Jake's fingers seem a bit too close to Wyatt's enlarged, jagged teeth.

     SFX: CHOMP

Panel 10: Small panel, tight on Jake shrieking in pain after having his finger bitten off.

     Jake: Aaaaaghh!

Panel 11: Jake breaks free and starts running down the hall as Wyatt evolves into a larger, scarier demon.

Panel 12: Demon Wyatt slams Jake with his arms from behind, sending Jake flying forward.

     SFX: WHAM

Panel 13: A student looks on from down the hall. He's wearing a DSU t-shirt with an image of campus on it.

     Stranger: ?

Panel 14: Jake goes flying into the image as if the t-shirt graphic was an open window.

     Stranger: !

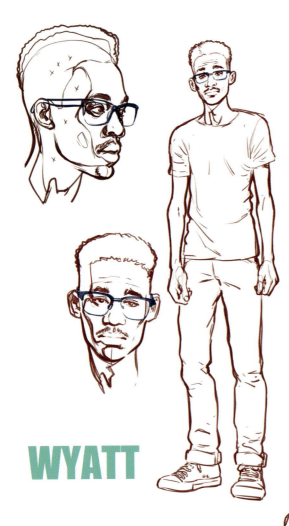

HUGO: *Now for some character designs! Up first is the main man, Wyatt! I remember Jon's descriptions gave me a lot of freedom to develop the looks for these characters. With Wyatt, I tried to mix different elements of some of my favorite '90s sitcom characters. I don't know why, it just kinda felt right. I also knew I wanted to give Wyatt big hair to make him easier to spot on the page. Funnily enough, if you track Wyatt's hair throughout the story, it starts to take on a life of its own!*

WYATT

JON: *One of my favorite things is getting to sit back and see what Hugo comes up with. Gotta say, dude, you killed it with these designs! It always amazes me what you artists can do with so few details. For Wyatt, I knew we needed a homebody; someone who would have a hard time leaving his room for class, let alone to fight an army of demon-possessed frat boys.*

And then, there's Jake. He's more comfortable in his own skin; a bit of Yang to Wyatt's Yin.

JAKE

JON: *For those who don't know, Hugo is kind of a genius. In an earlier draft of the script, Wyatt got all the info he needed on demons from the internet. Then, Hugo floated the idea of assigning that information to an actual character and BOOM—James, the Occultist, was born!*

HUGO: *A genius? ME? I just floated an idea. Then, Jon was able to do the actual creative part and write up one of my favorite characters.*

James was a lot of fun; he has two very distinctive looks for his part in the story. Since we were gonna use him to show the "positive" side of making a deal with a demon, I wanted to emphasize how shabby he looked before signing his soul away (or whatever happens when you get possessed). Now, Antaura has gotten him into shape and they've started a business together. Plus, look at that up-do! Playing with hairstyles is a lot of fun, isn't it?

JON: *It is! Speaking of hair, I loved getting to see Amber's long locks eerily defy gravity during her Amaymon-possession scenes. Talk about a fun character to write! And then there's Bryce. Poor guy, I feel like he always got the short end of the stick. I guess that's what happens when the only description you come up with for a character is "douche."*

SUNGLASSES W RED FRAME
HAWAIIAN SHIRT
TINTED GLASSES (YELLOW? MAGENTA?)
SIGIL TATTOOS ON BACK OF THE HANDS
LITTLE BONES BRACELET
JAMES
JAME'S NECKLACE, IT CAN BE

AMBER

BLONDE
BRYCE

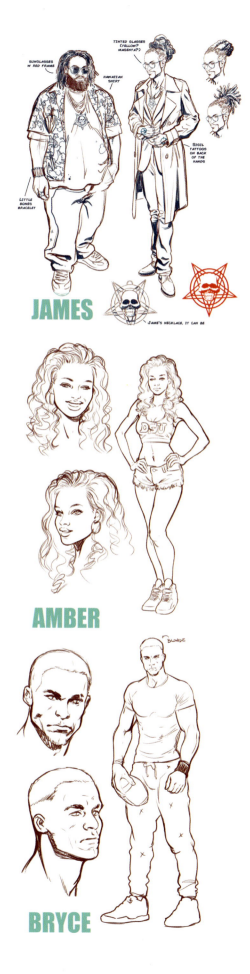

HUGO: *Demon Wyatt, or Dwyatt, is a nightmarish version of our lovable protagonist. I had a clear idea for his facial features, using some Indonesian masks as reference. Developing a look for the body took some more time, though. That's why I tried two different approaches, each scary in their own right. In the end, we went with the bigger, buff one (as you can see in the earlier double-page-spread). What do you think, did we make the right choice?*

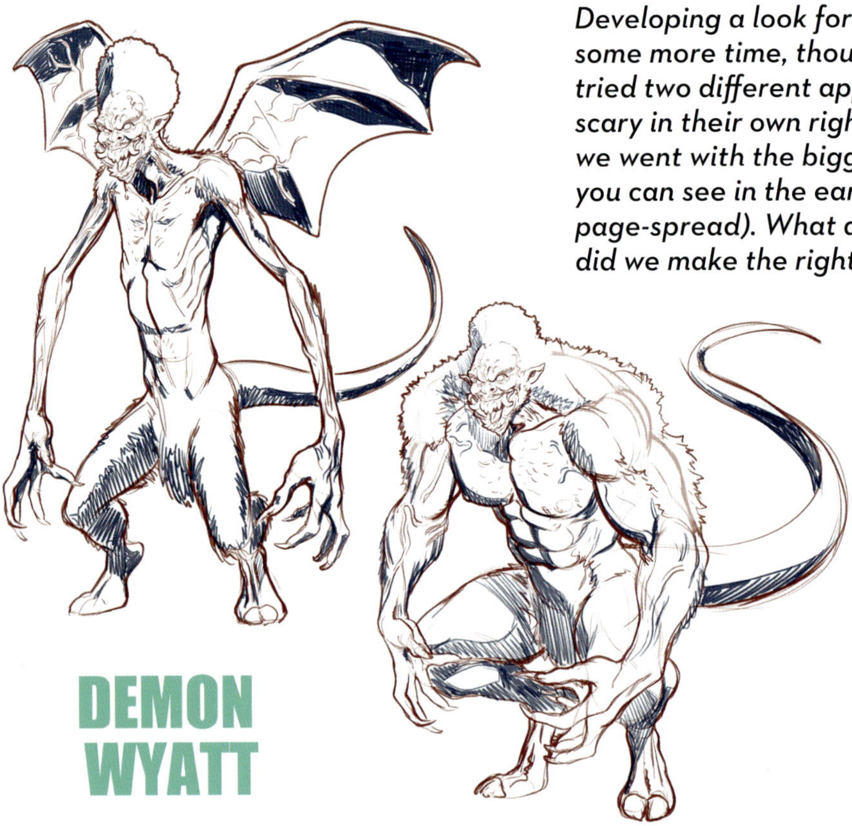

DEMON WYATT

JON: *Fun fact—Captain Miller had a much larger role in the story in an earlier draft of the script. Instead of Wyatt storming the OZN house, Denis was sent there to investigate after Wyatt called the police from the safety of his dorm. Thankfully, our editor reminded us that the main character should probably be there for the book's climactic ending...you win this round, Rob...*

HUGO: *Like most of these characters, Denis was a blast to draw! I really like how her design tells a deeper story than you'd think. Why the eyepatch? Where did the attitude come from? Will we ever know?!*

JON: *I'll never tell... MUAHAHAHA!!!*

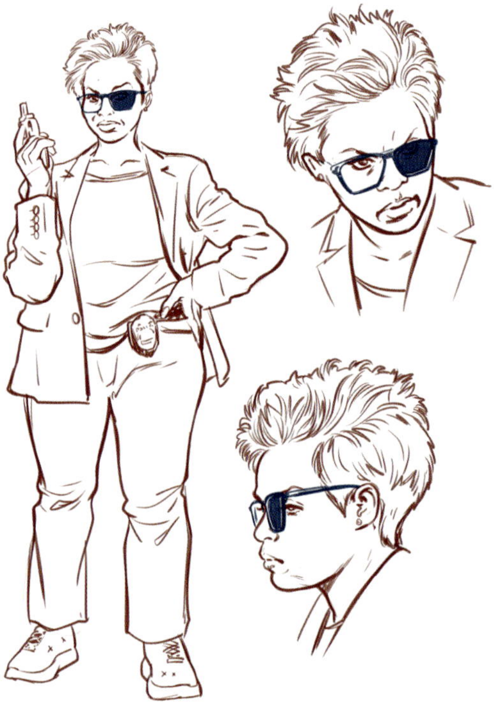

DENIS MILLER